P9-AFC-039

Volume VI

Baby Boomers and the New Conservatism

(1976–1991)

The Twentieth Century

The Progressive Era and the First World War (1900–1918)

The Roaring Twenties and an Unsettled Peace (1919–1929)

The Great Depression and World War II (1930–1945)

Postwar Prosperity and the Cold War (1946–1963)

The Civil Rights Movement and the Vietnam Era (1964–1975)

Baby Boomers and the New Conservatism (1976–1991)

Volume VI

Baby Boomers and the New Conservatism

(1976–1991)

Editorial Consultants
Matthew T. Downey, University of California at Berkeley
Harvey Green, Northeastern University
David M. Katzman, University of Kansas
Ruth Jacknow Markowitz, SUNY College at Oswego
Albert E. Moyer, Virginia Polytechnic Institute

Macmillan Publishing Company
New York
Maxwell Macmillan Canada
Toronto

rporation,
Princeton, N.J.

Project Editor: Richard Bohlander

Associate Project Editor: Michael Gee

Writers: Linda Barrett, Cathie Cush, Galen Guengerich, Lois Markham, Donna Singer

Editors: Risa Cottler, Susan Garver, Amy Lewis, Linda Scher, Betty Shanley, Bonnie Swaim, Frances Wiser

Production Supervisor: Mary Lyn Sodano

Inputting: Cindy Feldner

Interior Design: Maxson Crandall

Cover Design: Mike McIver

Layout: Maxson Crandall, Lisa Evans, Graphic Typesetting Service, Elizabeth Onorato

Photo Research: Cynthia Cappa, Sara Matthews

Maps: Parrot Graphics

Graphs: Virtual Media

Proofreading Management: Amy Davis

Grateful acknowledgment is made for permission to reprint the following previously published material:

From "My Hometown" by Bruce Springsteen. ASCAP. Copyright © 1984 by Bruce Springsteen. Used by permission.

From "Fast Car" by Tracy Chapman. © 1987 by EMI April Music Inc./Purple Rabbit Music. All rights controlled and administered by EMI April Music Inc. All rights reserved. International copyright secured. Used by permission.

From *Bonfire of the Vanities* by Tom Wolfe. Copyright © 1987 by Tom Wolfe. Used by permission.

Photo Credits

Bill Fitz-Patrick/The White House: 32

Courtesy of Honda of America Mfg., Inc.: 74

Courtesy of Sony Corporation: 86

Eli Reed/Magnum Photos: 3 (3rd from left), 62

I. L. Atlan/Sygma: 3 (4th from left), 78

John Greenleigh, Inc./Apple Computer: 71

Langevin/Sygma: 3 (2nd from left), 36

Michigan State University Museum: 21

Mick Hicks/Gamma Liaison: 99 (left)

NASA: 89

National Archives: 14

Official U.S. Coast Guard Photo: 22

Photofest: 92, 93, 95 (both), 101

R. Bossu/Sygma: 80

Reuters/Bettmann: 39, 40, 43, 52, 55, 58 (left), 69, 72, 81, 96, 116, 117

Reuters/Bettmann Newsphotos: 51, 108, 114

Sara Matthews: 76

Trapper/Sygma: 3 (5th from left), 90

UPI/Bettmann: 3 (far left; far right), 10, 18, 25 (both), 27, 28, 42, 44, 46, 48, 50, 58 (right), 60, 70, 73, 83, 84, 88, 98, 99 (right), 104, 107, 110, 111, 112, 115 (bottom)

UPI/Bettmann Newsphotos: 12, 15, 17, 87, 115 (top)

Macmillan Publishing Company
866 Third Avenue
New York, NY 10022

Maxwell Macmillan Canada, Inc.
1200 Eglinton Avenue East, Suite 200
Don Mills, Ontario M3C 3N1

Macmillan Publishing Company is part of the Maxwell Communication Group of Companies

Printed in the United States of America

printing number
1 2 3 4 5 6 7 8 9 10

Library of Congress Cataloging-in-Publication Data

The twentieth century / consultants, Matthew T. Downey . . . [et al.].
p. cm.
Includes index.
Contents: v. 1. The Progressive Era and the First World War (1900–1918)—v. 2. The Roaring Twenties and an Unsettled Peace (1919–1929)—v. 3. The Great Depression and World War II (1930–1945)—v. 4. Postwar Prosperity and the Cold War (1946–1963)—v. 5. The Civil Rights Movement and the Vietnam Era (1964–1975)—v. 6. Baby Boomers and the New Conservatism (1976–1991).
ISBN 0-02-897442-5 (set : alk. paper)
1. History, Modern—20th century. I. Downey, Matthew T.
D421.T88 1992
909.82—dc20 91-40862

Preface

The Twentieth Century is a six-book series covering the major developments of the period, from a primarily American perspective. This is the chronicle of a century unlike any before, one in which the pace of change has accelerated to the point that it is almost overwhelming.

As the century draws to a close, with such major ongoing events as the end of the Cold War and the seeming collapse of communism, it is appropriate to step back from the furious rush forward and examine the significance of the many changes we have seen in what may be the most momentous epoch in the history of the world.

Here, then, is the story of a world transformed by technology: by radio, television, and satellite communications; by automobiles, airplanes, and space travel; by antibiotics, organ transplants, and genetic engineering; by the atomic bomb; by the computer. These are just a few of the advances that have revolutionized the workings of the world and our daily lives.

Here also is the story of a century of history strongly influenced by individuals: Vladimir Lenin and Mao Ze-dong; Franklin Delano Roosevelt, Winston Churchill, and Adolf Hitler; Lech Walesa and Mikhail Gorbachev; Mohandas Gandhi and Martin Luther King Jr.; Theodore Roosevelt, John F. Kennedy, and Ronald Reagan. All have been featured actors in the drama of our times, as conveyed by these pages.

Above all else, it is the story of an American century, one in which a young democratic nation emerged as the world's most powerful force. Through two bitter world wars and an enduring cold war, the dominant influence of the United States on twentieth-century world history and culture is undeniable.

It is the story of the many forces that have transformed the face of our nation from a primarily rural, agricultural society dominated by white people of European heritage to a modern urban, industrialized, and multicultural nation. It is a story of the challenges, successes, and failures that have accompanied these fundamental changes.

Each book of this series focuses on a distinct era of the century. The six titles in the series are:

The Progressive Era and the First World War (1900–1918)

The Roaring Twenties and an Unsettled Peace (1919–1929)

The Great Depression and World War II (1930–1945)

Postwar Prosperity and the Cold War (1946–1963)

The Civil Rights Movement and the Vietnam Era (1964–1975)

Baby Boomers and the New Conservatism (1976–1991)

Each book is divided into six units: The Nation, The World, Business and Economy, Science and Technology, Arts and Entertainment, and Sports and Leisure. The second page of each unit includes a Datafile presenting significant statistical information in both table and graph format. All units include boxed features and sidebars focusing on particular topics of interest.

Additional features of each book include a graphic timeline of events of the period called Glimpses of the Era; a compilation of quotes, headlines, slogans, and literary extracts called Voices of the Era; a glossary of terms; a list of suggested readings; and a complete index.

The series is illustrated with historical photos, as well as original maps, graphs, and tables conveying pertinent statistical data.

Contents

AT A GLANCE

Preface 5
Glimpses of the Era 8
The Nation 10
The World 36
Business and Economy 62
Science and Technology 78
Arts and Entertainment 90
Sports and Leisure 104
Voices of the Era 118
Glossary 122
Selected Readings 124
Index 125
Cumulative Index 129

The Nation 10

A TIME TO HEAL 11

PROMISE AND DISILLUSIONMENT 12
The 1976 Election **12** "The Moral Equivalent of War" **13** Triumph and Despair Abroad **14** America Held Hostage **15** Crisis of Confidence **15**

THE NEW CONSERVATISM 16
The Reagan Revolution **16** A Shot in the Arm **17** Boom Then Bust **19** Into the Nineties **20**

A NEW FACE FOR AMERICA 21
A New Wave of Immigration **22** Growth of the Sun Belt **23** Changes in the Cities **23** The White Backlash **24**

RIGHTS AND RESPECT 25
Black Gains in Political Power **25** Changing Women's Concerns **26** The Graying of America **28** Veterans Speak Out **28** Rights for the Handicapped **29** Gay Rights **29**

THE COLD WAR AND BEYOND 29
The End of Détente **30** Intervention Abroad **30** The Iran-Contra Scandal **31** Summit Success **32**

THE BABY BOOMERS GROW UP 33
The Haves and Have-Nots **33** Issues for the Nineties **35**

Features: Democrats and Republicans Change Face **18** The Supreme Court Shifts to the Right **27** The Use and Abuse of Drugs and Alcohol **34**

The World 36

GLOBAL VILLAGE, GLOBAL CHALLENGES 37
A New World Order **38** Global Economy **38** Global Politics **39** Global Ecosystem **39**

THE COLLAPSE OF COMMUNISM 40
The Soviet Union **41** The End of the Soviet Union **43** Eastern Europe **44** One Germany, Again **45**

PLANNING FOR EUROPE '92 46

TURMOIL IN THE MIDDLE EAST 49
A Time of Change **49** Revolution in Iran **50** Israel and the *Intifada* **51** The Destruction of Lebanon **51** The Persian Gulf War **52**

CONFLICT AND CHANGE IN AFRICA 53
Civil War and Famine **53** New Hope in South Africa **54**

ASIA: LAND OF GIANTS 56
Japan and the Mini-Dragons **56** Southeast Asia **56** Conflict over Democracy in China **57** Religious Conflict in India **58**

DEMOCRACY IN LATIN AMERICA 59
The Debt Crisis **59** Civil Wars and Renewed Democracy **59**

THE CHALLENGES FACING CANADA 61

Features: Mikhail Gorbachev: Leader Without a Country **42** Margaret Thatcher: The "Iron Lady" **48** Nelson Mandela: Antiapartheid Crusader **55** Political Terror in Southeast Asia **57**

Business and Economy 62

THE ECONOMIC ROLLER COASTER 63
The Sluggish Seventies **63** The Changing Role of Government **64** The Rise of Reaganomics **64** Good News and Bad News **65**

COMPANIES EXPERIENCE CHANGES 66
The Game of Business **66** Business Debts Rise **68** The Entrepreneurs **70**

CHALLENGES FACING INDUSTRY 70
Manufacturing Industries **70**
An Information Economy **71** A Global Economy **72**

AMERICA'S TRANSPORTATION PROBLEMS 73
The Automobile Industry **73**
The Airline Industry **74** Future Transportation Needs **75**

THE CHANGING JOB MARKET 75

Features: Crisis in the Savings and Loan Industry **67** Vast Fortunes Are Made on Wall Street **69** Lee Iacocca: A Success Story **73** Consumer Power in the American Marketplace **76**

Science and Technology 78

A PLANET AT RISK? 79
Ozone Depletion **79** The Greenhouse Effect **80** Acid Rain **80** Waste Disposal **81**

TECHNICAL GAINS AND HUMAN LOSSES 82
AIDS **82** Cancer **83** Critical Issues **84**

THE PC REVOLUTION 85
Personal Computers **85** Computers Everywhere **85**

LOOKING FOR ANSWERS TO FUNDAMENTAL QUESTIONS 86
Exploring the Mysteries of Space and Matter **86** Biotechnology Research **87**

TRIUMPHS AND TRAGEDY IN SPACE 88
The Shuttle Program **88** Space Probes **89**

Feature: An Era of Environmental Disasters **81**

Arts and Entertainment 90

TV VIEWERS GET MORE CHOICES 91
The Rise of Cable Television **91** Mass Entertainment Reflects Times **92**

CHANGES IN THE MOVIE INDUSTRY 94
The Epics Come of Age **94** Movies with Mass Appeal **95** Black and Foreign Films **96**

MADONNA, MICHAEL, AND MORE 97
Stars on the Scene **97** Using Music for Political Activism **98**

INSTANT NEWS GOES INTERNATIONAL 99
The World of News **99** The Magazine Business **100**

THE BUSINESS OF BROADWAY 101

CELEBRITY AND CENSORSHIP 102

SOMETHING TO READ FOR EVERYONE 102
Books Reflect the Times **102**

Features: Spike Lee: Filmmaker with an Attitude **96** The Salman Rushdie Affair **103**

Sports and Leisure 104

SPORTS IN THE ERA 105
The Fitness Boom **105** The Business of Sports **106**

PROBLEMS AFFECT THE OLYMPIC GAMES 106
The Olympics and Politics **106**
Olympic Issues **107** Olympic Stars **107**

CHANGES IN BASEBALL 108
The Free-Agency Dispute **108**
Superstar Players **109**

BASKETBALL'S POPULARITY GROWS 110

FOOTBALL ENCOUNTERS CHALLENGES 111

MONEY DOMINATES MANY COLLEGE SPORTS 112
College Sports Remain Popular **113**

OTHER SPORTS ENJOY SUCCESS 113
Tennis **113** Boxing **114**
Golf **115** Yachting **116**
Bicycle Racing **116**

AMERICANS PURSUE FUN WITH INTENSITY 116
High-Tech Consumer Products **116**
Other Forms of Entertainment **117**
Fashion Trends **117**

Features: The Pete Rose Fiasco **110** Athletes and Drug Use **112** Martina Navratilova Dominates Women's Tennis **114** The Great Gretzky: A Hockey Superstar **115**

GLIMPSES OF THE ERA

1976

- Feb. 12 FDA bans production of red dye no. 2 after studies link it with cancer
- Apr. 22 Barbara Walters is first woman to anchor network television news program
- July 20 *Viking I* lands on Mars
- July 21–24 During American Legion convention in Philadelphia, 29 die of mysterious disease
- Sept. 9 Mao Ze-dong dies

1977

- Jan. 20 Jimmy Carter becomes 39th president
- Mar. 27 582 passengers and crew die when two Boeing jumbo jets collide on runway on Canary Islands
- Apr. 29 Alex Haley wins special Pulitzer Prize for *Roots*
- May 30 TransAlaska Pipeline System completed
- Aug. 12 Space shuttle *Enterprise* makes first test flight

1978

- Mar. 24 After 16-week strike, 165,000 miners approve wage increase
- July 26 Louise Brown, world's first test-tube baby, born in England
- Nov. 18 More than 900 followers of Jim Jones commit suicide in Guyana

1979

- Mar. 28 Accident occurs at nuclear reactor on Three Mile Island, near Harrisburg, Pennsylvania
- Nov. 1 Federal government announces bailout of Chrysler Corporation
- Nov. 3 90 people, including 63 Americans, taken hostage at American embassy in Tehran, Iran
- Dec. 27 Soviet Union invades Afghanistan

1980

- Apr. 12 U.S. Olympic Committee votes not to attend Moscow summer Olympics in response to Soviet Union's 1979 invasion of Afghanistan
- Apr. 24 8 Americans killed and 5 wounded in attempt to rescue American hostages in Iran
- May 18 Mount Saint Helens erupts in Washington State
- June 16 Supreme Court rules that living organisms may be patented
- Aug. 24 Labor unrest in Poland leads to strike of 200,000 workers

1981

- Jan. 20 Ronald Reagan becomes 40th president. 52 American hostages released in Iran
- Mar. 30 President Reagan shot and wounded in assassination attempt
- May 13 Turkish student shoots and injures Pope John Paul II
- Sept. 25 Sandra Day O'Connor becomes first woman Supreme Court justice
- Oct. 6 Egyptian president Anwar Sadat assassinated
- Dec. 13 Martial law imposed in Poland

1982

- Apr. 2 Argentina seizes Falkland Islands and begins conflict with Great Britain
- June 30 Equal Rights Amendment defeated
- Sept. 15 *USA Today* begins publication
- Oct. 5 264,000 bottles of Tylenol recalled after 7 people die from cyanide-laced capsules
- Dec. 2 Barney Clark becomes first recipient of artificial heart

1983

- Mar. 2 Final episode of *M*A*S*H* has largest television audience to date
- Sept. 1 269 die when Korean Air Lines Boeing 747 is shot down by Soviet missile
- Oct. 23 241 U.S. Marines in Lebanon killed in terrorist attack
- Oct. 25 U.S. invades Grenada

GLIMPSES OF THE ERA

1984

May 7	Soviets announce boycott of Los Angeles summer Olympics
Oct. 31	Prime Minister Indira Gandhi of India killed by Sikh bodyguards
Nov. 6	Ronald Reagan wins second presidential term
Dec. 3	Poisonous gas leak in Bhopal, India, kills 2,500 people

1985

Mar. 11	Mikhail Gorbachev elected president of Soviet Union
May 25	Cyclone and tidal wave kill 10,000 people in Bangladesh
July 13	Live Aid concerts raise $95 million for African famine relief
Sept. 19	Earthquake in Mexico kills 25,000 people
Oct. 7	Palestinian terrorists hijack Italian cruise ship *Achille Lauro*

1986

Jan. 28	Space shuttle *Challenger* explodes, killing 7 crew members
Apr. 16	U.S. bombs Libya in retaliation for terrorist attacks
Apr. 26	Explosion at Chernobyl nuclear plant in Soviet Union exposes population to radiation
May 1	1.5 million black workers go on strike in South Africa
Nov. 3	Iran-Contra scandal revealed

1987

Jan. 20	Anglican church envoy Terry Waite kidnapped in Lebanon
Feb. 21	Pop artist Andy Warhol dies
Oct. 19	Stock market plunges 508 points
Oct. 23	Senate rejects nomination of Robert Bork to Supreme Court

1988

Feb. 5	General Manuel Noriega indicted in Miami on drug-smuggling charges
May 15	Soviet Union begins to withdraw troops from Afghanistan
Dec. 1	Pakistan's Benazir Bhutto becomes first woman prime minister of Muslim state
Dec. 7	Earthquake in Armenia kills 55,000
Dec. 21	Air crash over Lockerbie, Scotland, kills 270

1989

Jan. 20	George Bush becomes 41st president
Mar. 24	*Exxon Valdez* runs aground in Gulf of Alaska, spilling 240,000 barrels of oil
May 17	1 million students occupy Beijing's Tiananmen Square in prodemocracy demonstrations
June 3	Iran's Ayatollah Ruhollah Khomeini dies
Oct. 17	Earthquake hits San Francisco Bay area, minutes before third game of World Series, causing over 60 deaths
Dec. 20	U.S. invades Panama

1990

Feb. 11	Nelson Mandela freed after 27 years in prison in South Africa
Aug. 2	Iraq invades Kuwait
Oct. 2	Senate confirms David Souter as associate justice of Supreme Court
Oct. 3	East Germany and West Germany reunified

1991

Jan. 16	Persian Gulf War begins
Aug. 19–21	Attempted coup in Soviet Union
Oct. 22	Senate confirms Clarence Thomas as associate justice of Supreme Court
Dec. 28	Soviet Union dissolved

THE NATION

Reeling from the multiple conflicts of the 1960s and early 1970s—Vietnam, racial violence, Watergate, the generation gap—the American people launched a new era in 1976 by celebrating a more distant past. The 200-year anniversary of the Declaration of Independence that year commemorated a happier America—or at least ideals more pleasant than recent reality.

But the Bicentennial was not the only party in this era. The nation also celebrated the 200-year anniversary of the Constitution, the 100-year anniversary of the Statue of Liberty, and the 500-year anniversary of the historic voyage of Christopher Columbus.

The festivals staged to mark these occasions aimed to create a sense of unity and common purpose. But other factors were at play. The gender and ethnic identity awakened in the 1960s revealed the rich diversity of American society, but some felt that this emphasized Americans' differences rather than their common bonds. An economic boom created a growing distance between "haves" and "have-nots" that became worse when recession struck in the late 1980s. The politics of special-interest groups forced politicians to choose constantly between alienating one potential voter or another. The result was often governmental inaction.

Two conservative Republican presidents (above) led the nation for most of this era. The feel-good administration of Ronald Reagan helped break the national mood of despair and guilt. In its place, Reagan instilled a can-do attitude, but what could be done had to fit the conservative agenda. George Bush's administration was built on foreign-policy successes—some that were planned and some that happened by chance. These presidents celebrated the past, but serious challenges for the future lurked underneath.

AT A GLANCE

- **A Time to Heal**
- **Promise and Disillusionment**
- **The New Conservatism**
- **A New Face for America**
- **Rights and Respect**
- **The Cold War and Beyond**
- **The Baby Boomers Grow Up**

DATAFILE

U.S. population	1970	1980	1990
Total (in millions)	203.3	226.5	248.7
Urban	73.5%	73.4%	75.2
Rural	26.5%	26.6%	24.8
White	87.5%	85.5%	80.3%
Black	11.1%	11.7%	12.1%
Other	1.4%	2.8%	7.6%

Social data	1976	1989
Birthrate (live births per 1,000 pop.)	14.6	16.2
Mortality rate (per 1,000 pop.)	8.8	8.7
Murder rate (per 100,000 pop.)	8.8	8.7
Persons ages 5–17 in school (per 100 pop.)	87.6	88.8

Voter turnout

Year	Turnout	Year	Turnout
1976	59.2%	1984	59.9%
1980	59.2%	1988	57.4%

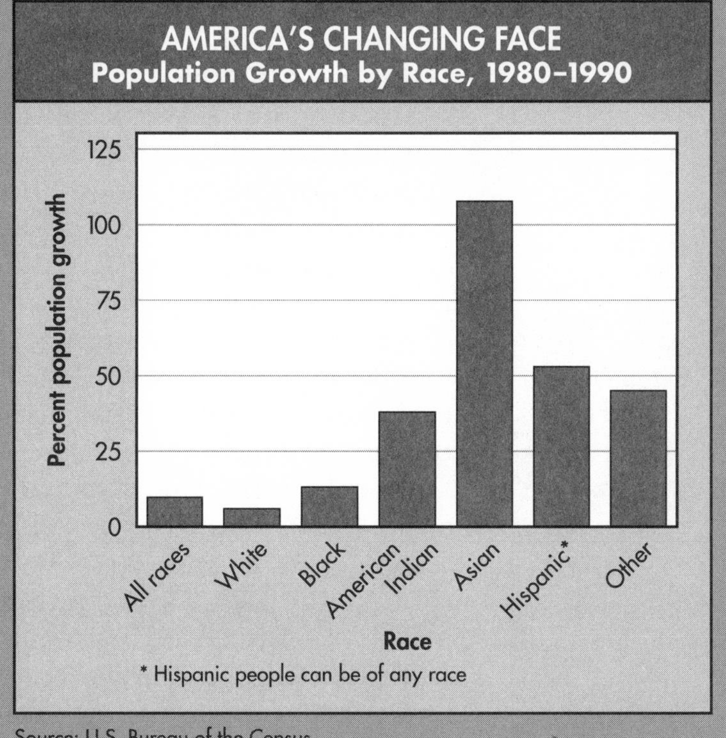

Source: U.S. Bureau of the Census.

A TIME TO HEAL

The Vietnam War and the Watergate scandal left most Americans with a bitter taste in their mouths. People viewed the government—especially the presidency—with distrust. Because Congress had conducted thorough and vigorous investigations into the Watergate scandal, that branch of government appeared to be the most reliable. People began to look to Congress, instead of to the president, for leadership.

Congressional investigators learned that the Central Intelligence Agency (CIA) had used illegal break-ins and wiretaps to spy on American citizens under both Presidents Johnson and Nixon. The FBI, too, had been used by Nixon to harm political enemies. Appalled by these clear violations of civil rights, one senator remarked, "We are not a wicked country, and we cannot abide a wicked government."

Hearing the constant news of abuses of power, many Americans believed that the power of the presidency had grown out of control. Congress sensed this concern—and saw a chance to enhance its own political power against the presidency. It passed a number of laws that reduced the power of the executive branch to act without congressional agreement. The Senate created a committee to watch the actions of the CIA. Another law, an ethics bill, tried to control the business dealings of government officials.

Despite the doubts raised by Vietnam and Watergate, Americans celebrated the nation's Bicentennial in a big way. Throughout 1976, millions of people turned out for parades, picnics, fireworks displays, historical reenactments, rodeos, and concerts celebrating the nation's birthday.

The festivities reached a climax on July 4. In San Antonio, Texas, people staged a beautiful balloon race. In New York City, graceful sailing ships from 34 countries glided into the harbor. In Philadelphia, President Gerald Ford rang the Liberty Bell. Across the nation, Americans looked back in pride. But hard times were still to come.

▼ America celebrated the 100-year anniversary of the Statue of Liberty on July 4, 1986. Millions in New York saw the event in person from streets, skyscrapers, and boats, and millions more watched the festivities on television. Originally a gift from France to symbolize the promise of democracy, the statue has also come to represent America's immigrant heritage.

PROMISE AND DISILLUSIONMENT

In 1974 *People* magazine quoted James Earl "Jimmy" Carter, the governor of Georgia: "The longer [Nixon] stays in office, the better it is for the Democrats and the worse it is for the country and for Republicans." In the next two years Carter seized the chance and ran for the presidency. When he began his campaign, Carter was greeted by the question "Jimmy who?" When he finished, he was being called "Mr. President."

The 1976 Election

In a vigorous campaign Carter stressed economic issues and the need for a higher moral tone in government. Understanding Americans' disgust with abuse of power and scandal, Carter stressed that he was an outsider. He pledged to restore people's confidence in government and to heal the nation's wounds. He said the government should work effectively but honestly. "Why not the best?" he asked, focusing on his record as a naval academy graduate and nuclear engineer. "I will never lie to you," he told the nation. He promised to establish a "government as good as the American people."

Armed with these reassurances—and acting out a brilliant campaign strategy—Carter swept through the 1976 Democratic primaries. Disheartened and disillusioned by the struggling economy and the Watergate scandals, for which they blamed the Republican administration, Democrats united behind the peanut farmer from Georgia. Even an old political hand like Chicago's mayor Richard Daley rallied to Carter. "This man's . . . got something we need more of," Daley said. "He's got a religious tone in what he says, and maybe we should have a little more religion in the entire community. The man talks about true values. Why shouldn't we be sold on him?"

Carter's opponent was President Gerald Ford. Ford, a congressman from Michigan, had been appointed by Nixon to replace Vice President Spiro Agnew when Agnew resigned over charges of corruption. With Nixon's departure from the White House, Ford assumed the presidency—the first president to serve without being elected to the executive branch. A likable man, Ford nevertheless had to live down his pardon of Nixon and **inflation** that could not be controlled. These factors were too much for him to overcome. Voter turnout was poor, and the election was close. But Carter won.

Carter's first act as president was to stroll down Pennsylvania Avenue hand in hand with his wife, Rosalynn, en route to the White House from his swearing-in at the Capitol. Nixon and most other modern presidents had ridden in limousines. After the anger and conflict of the Johnson and Nixon years, the gesture was welcome. Other healing touches followed. Carter wore blue jeans and wool cardigan sweaters, he conducted fireside chats like Franklin Roosevelt, and he held a national radio call-in program, inviting ordinary citizens to ask him questions. The changes were refreshing—surely, people thought, this new president would not trample on citizens' rights. Critics said that these steps were all for show.

"The Moral Equivalent of War"

Throughout most of the 1970s America suffered from what was called "stagflation"—slow economic growth (stagnation) with rapidly rising prices (inflation). Prime causes of this difficulty were the cost of energy and the country's reliance on foreign oil. Soon after becoming president, Carter launched a campaign to battle the nation's shortage of oil and other energy sources. Energy was a major problem, he said; the steps to be taken were "the moral equivalent of war."

He urged Americans to cut their use of imported oil by turning to other sources of fuel. As a result, the use of nuclear energy increased in the late 1970s. This increase, however, alarmed many, who questioned its safety. Some people responded to Carter's call to conserve energy by driving less or lowering thermostats at home or office. Others saw the "energy crisis" as an idea generated by business in order to raise profits.

Carter saw the problem as real, however, and tried to take steps to increase the flow of domestic oil. He urged **deregulation** of the oil industry and managed to remove government controls over oil prices. The plan was to let oil prices rise so that oil companies could earn more. With their higher earnings, they would drill for more oil. With more American oil flowing, the country's need for foreign oil would be reduced. Any excess profits that

SOUTHERNER IN THE WHITE HOUSE

Jimmy Carter's election as president marked the first time that a resident of the Deep South had reached that position since Andrew Johnson during the Reconstruction era. It symbolized the growing importance of the South in U.S. politics.

FBI STING NABS MEMBERS OF CONGRESS

Congress's image was tarnished as a result of an FBI investigation that lasted from 1978 to 1980. From the FBI's findings, seven members of Congress and several state and local officials were convicted of bribery and related charges. The scandal was called "Abscam"—short for "Abdul scam," after one of two imaginary Arab sheikhs used by the FBI to trick the officials into accepting bribes. The sheikhs supposedly wanted such favors as help in gaining entry into the country and in building casinos. The corruption charges were difficult to deny—the FBI videotaped the officials taking money.

CARTER PARDONS DRAFT RESISTERS

In his first year in office, President Carter took a step to try to put the pain and conflict of the Vietnam War into the past. He offered a complete amnesty—or freedom from prosecution—to all those who had avoided the draft during that war. Many young men had fled to Canada to prevent their induction into the Army because they opposed the war. Carter's action allowed these men to come back to the United States without fear of being arrested.

the oil companies earned would be taxed by the government.

The plan may have been sound, but Carter's overall energy policy failed. Reliance on foreign oil was not reduced. Plans for more nuclear reactors were tied up in courts by environmentalists who opposed that form of power. Use of wind or sun power never became widespread.

And the economy did not improve. Under Carter, interest rates reached an all-time high. By making borrowing expensive, these rates held down consumer spending and construction work. Unemployment and inflation remained high, too.

Triumph and Despair Abroad

Another important goal for the Carter administration was to restore America's confidence in the nation's foreign policy. Aware that people wanted no more Vietnams, the president promised a moral leadership in the world. He saw human rights as the basis of his foreign policy. He championed other nations' right to free elections, freedom of religion, freedom to travel, and free speech. He denied foreign aid to countries that mistreated citizens for political reasons, whether they were allies of the United States or not.

Following the policies of Nixon and Ford, Carter worked toward arms reductions and continued **détente** with the Soviets. Nevertheless, U.S.-Soviet relations worsened. Carter openly supported Soviet citizens who disagreed with their government, which angered Soviet leaders. He also took a strong stand against the Soviet invasion of Afghanistan by refusing to let American athletes participate in the 1980 Moscow Olympics. This decision irritated Soviet leaders.

Carter did have some diplomatic successes, however. He established formal relations with the People's Republic of China. He built better relations with nations of Africa and Latin America. A landmark of this policy was a treaty that transferred control of the Panama Canal to Panama. Signed in September 1977, the treaty tried to undo decades of U.S. imperialism in Latin America.

Carter's major diplomatic success, however, was the Camp David Accords. In September 1978 Carter invited Egyptian president Anwar Sadat and Israeli prime minister Menachem Begin to the presidential retreat in Camp David, Maryland. There Carter skillfully maneuvered these two leaders of countries with histories of bitter hatred to reach a peace agreement. Israel agreed to return the Sinai

▼ President Carter looks on as Israeli prime minister Menachem Begin (left) and Egyptian president Anwar Sadat shake hands at Camp David.

peninsula, which it had occupied, to Egypt. Sadat and Begin won the 1978 Nobel Peace Prize.

America Held Hostage

This success—indeed, Carter's entire presidency—was overshadowed by a foreign-policy fiasco that began in November 1979. Soon after the overthrow of the shah of Iran, Iranian citizens seized the American embassy in Teheran and captured U.S. citizens as hostages.

Carter tried quiet diplomacy to free the hostages, but the new leader of Iran, the Ayatollah Ruhollah Khomeini, refused to release them. Iranians were angry at years of U.S. support for the shah, whom they saw as an oppressive ruler. In April 1980, Carter ordered a military rescue mission, but the plan failed, and the president had to admit its failure in a national TV address. This failure added to a feeling that America had become powerless and that the U.S. military had lost its ability to fight. The hostage crisis proved to be the death of the Carter presidency. The hostages were finally released, but not until Carter was replaced by Ronald Reagan. They were freed a few hours after Reagan took the oath of office.

Crisis of Confidence

Throughout the Carter presidency, the national feeling seemed to be defeatist. People saw many problems, and many limits, but they did not see any solutions.

The environment looked like a disaster. Industrial growth in years past produced headlines about environmental problems now. Cancer and early death afflicted the people in a New York community called Love Canal, which had been built on a toxic-waste dump.

The energy crisis was not being solved. Oil spills made petroleum a messy energy source. Meanwhile, an accident at the Three Mile Island nuclear reactor in central Pennsylvania further alarmed people about the safety of all nuclear plants.

The economy foundered. Joblessness was up, but so were prices and interest rates. Jobs were being lost to foreign competition, and the U.S. auto and steel industries were seriously ailing.

Carter attempted to rally the country behind him with a televised speech in which he suggested that a "crisis of confidence" had overcome Americans. But many people saw the crisis not as the nation's, but as Carter's. What had once been his strengths were now perceived as faults. His humanity was seen as weakness, his openness as vulnerability.

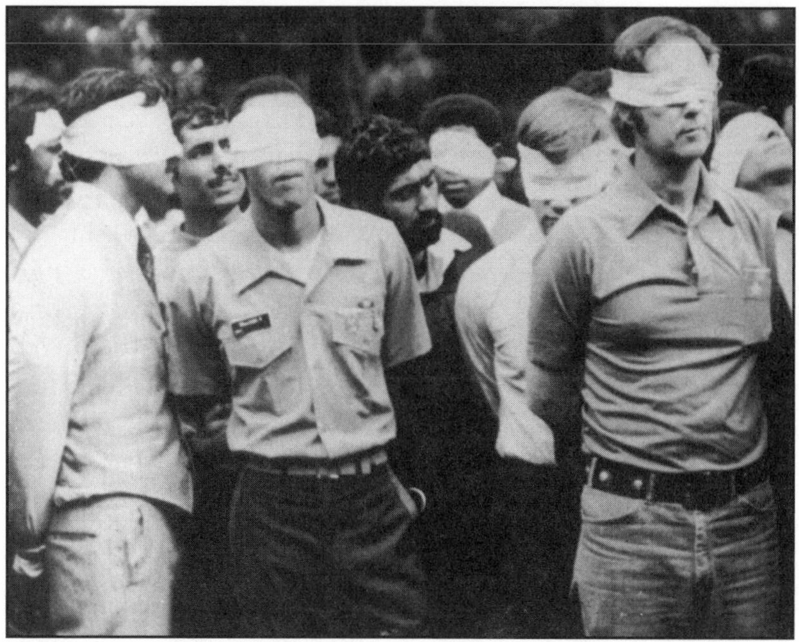

▲ On the first day of their long and terrifying ordeal, the American hostages were paraded blindfolded before the Iranian people. The Iranian hostage crisis stayed at the forefront of public attention from November 1979 until January 1981. For 444 days, the news was filled with stories about the hostages, the prospects for their return, and U.S. relations with Iran.

THE NEW CONSERVATISM

To challenge the faltering Carter, the Republicans nominated Ronald Reagan, former actor, television show host, and governor of California. Many people scoffed at Reagan's background, but "the Great Communicator," as he was called, used a friendly, honest, upbeat speaking style to convince voters that he could turn America toward a more promising, more confident direction.

Reagan himself questioned his own qualifications. "My God, what am I doing in politics? The things I've done so far are far away from this," he wondered once. But then he added, "A substantial part of the political thing is acting and role-playing, and I know how to do that." In 1980, after a landslide election victory, Reagan got a chance to play the biggest role of his life.

The Reagan Revolution

Reagan reached the White House on more than his acting skill. Frustration with what people saw as decades of decline had led to anger over the role of government, the state of the economy, and the slackening of national morality. Reagan turned that anger into hope—hope for change.

Ever since the New Deal era, Congress and the White House had helped the federal government **bureaucracy** grow. For the past two decades, many people had come to question the liberal idea that government should provide social welfare services. Signaling the country's new mood, in 1978 the people of California passed a **referendum** called Proposition 13. This measure reduced property taxes, the major source of funds for local government. It also limited the money that the state could spend on social programs.

Coupled with this growing mistrust of the **welfare state,** many people were calling for less government involvement in the economy. Clearly something needed to be done—the economy had suffered more than a decade of inflation, slow economic growth, and increasing foreign competition. Business leaders pointed to government regulation of everything from prices to hiring practices to pollution control. All of these rules, they said, made it harder to compete and more costly to do business. President Carter had heard these concerns and had taken some steps to deregulate business, yet businesses wanted more action.

Support for the swing toward conservatism also came from evangelical Christians. This movement of religious rebirth had many things in common with the political conservatives, and the two became closely allied. They both opposed drugs, pornography, abortion, and homosexual rights. Preachers with television ministries, like Jerry Falwell, influenced millions of viewers and voters. As a leading voice in the movement, Falwell founded the Moral Majority, which became a powerful political group.

Reagan responded to these concerns. He promised sharp cuts in government spending, especially in social welfare programs. He vowed to end what he saw as the neglect

"HONEY, I FORGOT TO DUCK"

In Ronald Reagan's first year in office, he was shot by John W. Hinckley Jr. The bullet entered one of the president's lungs, but quick surgery and his strong constitution brought him through. People were heartened by Reagan's joking comment to his wife: "Honey, I forgot to duck."

Press Secretary James Brady was seriously wounded in the head in the assault. Years later Brady began to push for a handgun control law. In the face of a powerful progun lobby, Reagan refused to endorse the bill while president. However, he announced his support for it after he retired.

SAN FRANCISCO BANS HANDGUNS

In 1982 San Francisco, California, banned the sale and possession of handguns. The first of its kind in the country, the law gave pistol owners 90 days to dispose of their weapons. California voters rejected a similar statewide measure that same year.

The San Francisco law was passed despite a heated challenge from the National Rifle Association (NRA). The group, which opposes all gun-control measures, hired former cowboy actor Roy Rogers to promote its views. Supporters of the law countered with statistics about how many people in the United States since 1963 had been killed by gunfire (400,000), wounded by gunshots (1.7 million), and robbed at gunpoint (2.7 million).

of national defense by increasing defense spending. He planned to cut taxes to stimulate business growth, which he would also aid by deregulating. He vowed to close down government agencies and cut back on government jobs. Carter had promised to make the government as good as the American people. Reagan said he would get the government off Americans' backs.

With this political agenda, Reagan appealed to a wide range of voters. He continued the Republican hold on western states. He cemented the alliance that Nixon had begun to forge between Republicans and blue-collar workers and members of old ethnic groups of the North. He even won in the South, despite regional pride in Carter. Here, too, Reagan continued a trend begun with Nixon. With this broad support, Reagan was swept into the White House by a landslide.

A Shot in the Arm

Soon after the election the Reagan team put into practice its theories on how to fix the country's crippled economy. Reagan's advisers based their policy on a theory called **supply-side economics**. The theory put an emphasis on stimulating the means of production—or supply side—as opposed to policy since the New Deal, which emphasized consumption, or the demand side. The theory held that by cutting income taxes, the government would make more money available for saving and investment. People—and businesses—would invest this money, which would create new businesses and new jobs. This increased economic activity would then provide added tax revenue to the government—making up for the money lost by cutting taxes in the first place. In the end, everyone wins: businesses enjoy profits, workers get more jobs, and government maintains its tax revenue. It sounded great.

The White House began a vigorous program of government spending cuts. The goal was to balance the budget and lower inflation. These cuts mostly affected the social programs that had been building since the New Deal of the 1930s. Hit hard were such programs as aid to cities, food stamps, welfare, and school lunches. To cut taxes, Reagan pushed the Economic Recovery Tax Act through Congress.

Reagan also pursued his policy of deregulation. He relaxed government regulation of such industries as banking and finance. To ease environmental regulations, Reagan appointed officials who favored economic development over environmental protection. Most businesses welcomed the new policies,

▲ Antiabortion protesters gather in front of the Supreme Court to mark an anniversary of the *Roe v. Wade* decision that legalized abortion. The debate over abortion rights moved into the heart of American politics in the 1980s.

DEATHS

Hubert H. Humphrey, politician, 1978

William O. Douglas, Supreme Court justice, 1980

Sam Ervin, politician, 1985

William Casey, CIA director, 1987

Abbie Hoffman, activist, 1989

Democrats and Republicans Change Face

▲ Jesse Jackson greets supporters during the 1988 campaign.

In the 1970s and 1980s the shape of the two political parties was changing. At the heart of these changes was the breakup of the New Deal coalition, which had been built during the presidency of Franklin Delano Roosevelt. He had forged a linkage of northern urban ethnics, liberals, farmers, union members, southern whites, and blacks. The coalition lasted for decades. It was the civil rights movement and the Vietnam War that started breaking it up.

With Democratic support for civil rights for blacks in the 1950s and 1960s, white southern Democrats began to split with the party. But the political skill and increased government spending of Lyndon Johnson held the party together.

As liberal Democrats became more vocal in their opposition to the Vietnam War, white southern Democrats—who by and large supported it—had another reason to leave the party. And leave they did, voting for Alabama governor George Wallace's third-party campaign in 1968. Wallace also gained support from northern urban ethnics. These voters, too, supported the war, and they were concerned about such issues as school busing and affirmative action.

Richard Nixon began to court those two groups. He appealed to them as the "silent majority," and he tried (but failed) to appoint conservative southerners to the Supreme Court. His actions paid off in 1972, when he swept the South and won large numbers of votes from the northern urban ethnics.

The elections of Reagan and then Bush confirmed these changes. Both of these Republican candidates received many votes in the South, which was splitting along racial lines: white men voted Republican, and black men and women voted Democratic. Both candidates also won votes from urban ethnics and union members.

As some of their old support dried up, the Democrats looked in new directions. They staged big voter-registration drives among blacks and Hispanics.

The Democrats also looked for more minority candidates. The one with the most spectacular success was Jesse Jackson. A Baptist minister, Jackson had been active in the 1960s civil rights movement with Martin Luther King Jr. In 1984 he made a strong bid for the Democratic presidential nomination. His 1988 campaign for that nomination was even stronger.

Women were increasingly becoming Democratic voters. In general, Democrats supported "women's issues," such as abortion, subsidized child care, and paid maternity leave. Republicans, on the other hand, opposed abortion, resisted government spending on child care, and saw paid maternity leave as a problem for their supporters from business. A "gender gap" arose. Men tended to vote Republican and women Democratic.

In 1984 Geraldine Ferraro was nominated as the Democratic candidate for vice president—the first woman candidate for either of the top two national offices nominated by a major party. Her choice was a symbol of the growing force that women had in the Democratic party—and their new status in the nation as a whole.

but environmentalists rallied forces against them.

By the end of Reagan's first term, inflation had begun to slow, and interest rates came under control. But these gains came only with the recession of 1981 to 1983. And even after the recession had ended, unemployment remained high, especially among black men. Agriculture was suffering, and family farms failed every day. The increase in defense spending coupled with lower government revenues due to the tax cuts had created a huge **deficit** in the federal budget.

Boom Then Bust

"America is back and standing tall," Reagan announced at the start of his 1984 presidential campaign. The recession was ending: the tax cuts had stimulated the economy, and demand was growing again. The deregulation of the financial industry led to intense activity in the money markets. Money managers made millions of dollars on Wall Street by buying and selling bonds—or companies. People watched these deals with interest; they were even more fascinated by the lifestyles of these new millionaires.

The Baby Boom generation of the post–World War II period was coming of age. With a high proportion of the group having college educations, these people became the new white-collar workers. They came to be known as "young urban professionals," or "Yuppies," and their increased spending seemed to be a sign of economic health. Often living in two-income families, the Yuppies helped create a boom in service industries. Restaurants, resorts, and health spas all enjoyed growth.

While some got rich in the probusiness climate of the Reagan years, the poor got much poorer. They were squeezed by four factors. First, many new jobs—almost 3 million a year—had been created by the end of Reagan's second term, but most were in low-paying service industries. Second, the unemployment rate had not gone lower than 6 percent, and many were without work. Third, the poor were hit by the effects of many years of inflation. Although prices were no longer rising as rapidly, they had leveled off much higher than they had been before. Fourth, federal cutbacks in social welfare spending put the burden for these programs on states and cities. But neither could maintain the level of

NEW WORDS

Yuppie
Star Wars (SDI)
refusenik
skinhead
DINK (Double Income No Kids)

▼ Part of the 1980s boom is reflected in the sharp rise in the number of Americans earning a half-million dollars or more a year.

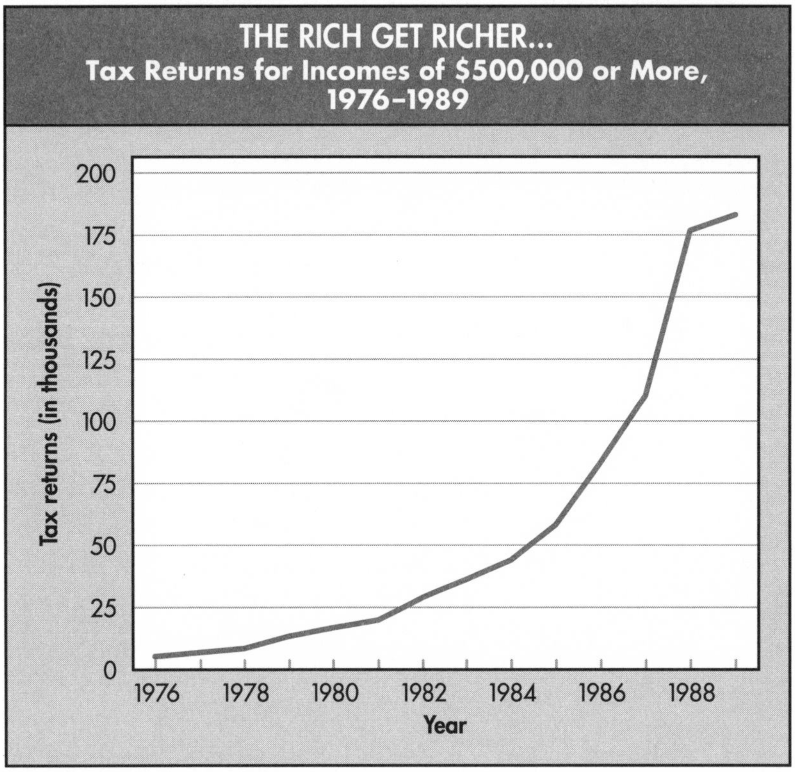
THE RICH GET RICHER...
Tax Returns for Incomes of $500,000 or More, 1976–1989
Tax returns (in thousands)
0
25
50
75
100
125
150
175
200
1976
1978
1980
1982
1984
1986
1988
Year

Source: Internal Revenue Service.

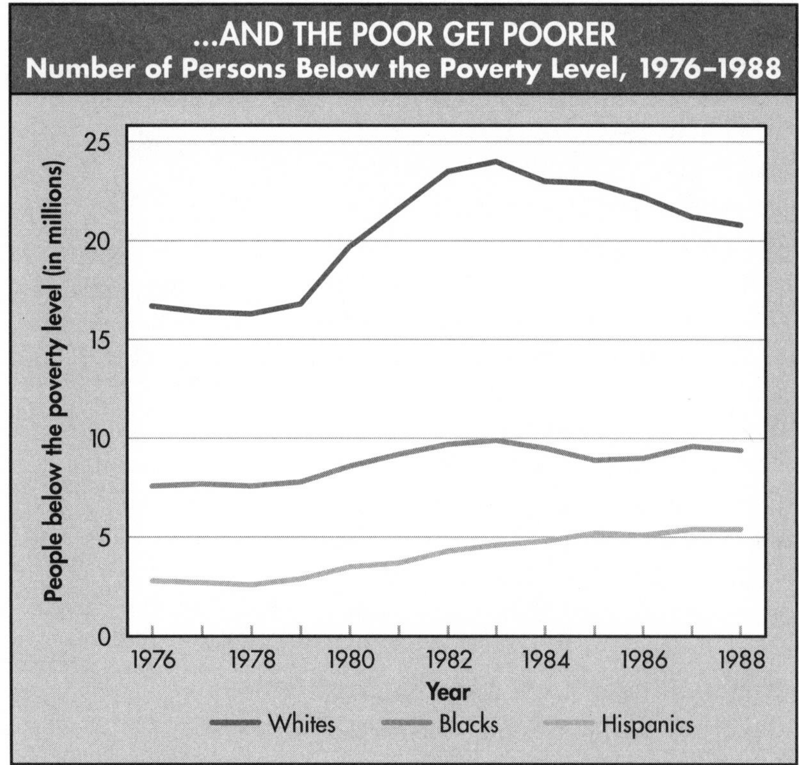

Source: U.S. Bureau of the Census.

▲ The deep recession of the early 1980s dropped millions more Americans below the poverty line. Although the economic boom that followed halted the increase, there were still more than 30 million Americans—about 12 percent of the nation—living in poverty in 1988.

spending that Washington had managed for years. The result was reduced aid to the poor.

By 1986 the federal budget deficit was more than $200 billion, the highest in history. Across the nation borrowing was heavy. The government borrowed to finance its interest payments. Businesses borrowed to fund new **mergers**—or to pay off the debt for past mergers. This tower of credit was built on a shaky foundation of low personal savings, however. Then on October 19, 1987, the stock market came tumbling down. The market fell 508 points on that "Black Monday," the single largest drop in history. The market soon recovered, but the crash was an unsettling sign that something was wrong with the economy.

Reagan had other bad news in 1987. News of the Iran-Contra scandal broke out—and the scandal came to roost in the White House (see "The Cold War and Beyond"). Details of meetings revealed through this scandal and in other news stories seemed to paint a picture of the president as confused and not in control. But although some of the evidence in the case was damaging to his administration, Reagan in the end survived. Called "the Teflon president" because nothing bad seemed to stick to him, Reagan left the White House still widely popular.

Into the Nineties

To succeed Reagan as president, the Republicans chose his vice president, George Bush. The 1988 election pitted Bush against Massachusetts governor Michael Dukakis. The campaign was a negative one, as each candidate played to voters' emotions by presenting the other candidate in a bad light. In an aggressive campaign, Bush portrayed Dukakis and the Democrats as being soft on crime. His ads used the example of Willie Horton, a black inmate who committed rape and murder while on a weekend leave from a Massachusetts prison. Although the Democrats called these ads unfair and even racist, the chords Bush's campaign struck helped usher him into the White House.

Voters felt that things were going well. The country seemed prosperous, and it was at peace. Inflation was low, and unemployment—although high for some groups—was down from the near-10 percent level of the early 1980s. The budget deficit was growing, but voters liked Bush's pledge of no new taxes. He won a decisive victory, taking 40 of 50 states.

In President Bush's first term, the economy reappeared as a problem. Attempts to rein in the budget deficit were hampered by conflicting demands from Republican Bush and the Democrat-led Congress. The recession of the early 1990s made many Americans uneasy about their future.

Bush took some steps on other issues. He attacked the growing problem of drug use with a publicity campaign and programs to beef up drug-law enforcement. He focused attention on the problems of the schools, staging an education **summit** with the nation's governors. But he maintained the Republican position, which called for state and local funding of these programs. He refused to increase federal spending significantly.

President Bush seemed to spend more time and energy on foreign policy. He ordered troops into Panama in December 1990 to help establish an elected government—and to seize Panamanian dictator Manuel Noriega, accused of drug trafficking in the United States. He negotiated major arms-reduction agreements with Soviet president Mikhail Gorbachev (see "The Cold War and Beyond"). He led an international **coalition** against Iraq's **annexation** of Kuwait in 1990 and 1991, committing half a million U.S. troops in the process (see The World). He used all the leverage he could muster to get Arabs and Israelis to agree to come to peace conferences in Madrid and Washington, D.C. to try to settle the long-standing conflicts of the Middle East.

A NEW FACE FOR AMERICA

The face and landscape of America changed throughout this era. Large numbers of Asians and Latin Americans immigrated to the country. Americans faced new challenges as they lived and worked side-by-side with people from different ethnic and cultural backgrounds. This adjustment was sometimes difficult, painful, or even dangerous.

There was also a great deal of movement in this period. Everyone, it seemed—both **immigrants** and those already in the country—was on the move. Some migrated to the cities; others left them. Many industries—and many people—left the northeastern states to go south and west. The American family

ELLIS ISLAND

The restored buildings of Ellis Island in New York Bay were opened as a museum of immigration in September 1990. Ellis Island opened as an immigration station in 1892, and it handled more than half of the immigrants entering the United States during the peak years of immigration. Between 1892 and 1924 more than 16 million people passed through Ellis Island. Mass immigration ended in 1924, and the station was fully closed in 1954.

A New Way of Life for the Hmong

Since 1980 about 100,000 Hmong immigrants from Laos have settled in the United States. The Hmong were mountain-dwelling farmers who had remained largely untouched by Western culture. Their traditions and customs made it more difficult for them than for some other ethnic groups to adapt to American life.

Some Hmong men in the United States have been stricken by a strange disease. Called Sudden Unexplained Death Syndrome (SUDS), it occurs in other groups as well but seems to strike the Hmong the most. In this condition seemingly healthy men die in their sleep or become unconscious and die. Doctors believe that the disease reflects the difficulty of adjusting to a new culture, but they cannot be sure. Because Hmong religious beliefs prohibit autopsies, doctors cannot learn the exact cause of SUDS.

▲ During the 1970s and 1980s many Haitians fled the desperate poverty of their country for the United States. In 1980 a wave of Cuban and Haitian "boat people" created a dilemma for U.S. immigration officials. Although most of the Cubans were admitted as political refugees, the majority of Haitian economic refugees were turned back. Most of those who stayed lived for years in immigration detention centers.

saw significant changes as a result of all this movement—and because of the changing economy.

A New Wave of Immigration

The Immigration Act of 1965 and a policy that opened the doors to Asian refugees in the late 1970s brought tens of thousands of Asians into American cities. Immigration increased for people from Africa and Latin America as well. In the 1970s and 1980s Asian and Latin American immigrants vastly outnumbered those from Europe. People poured in from Korea, China, Japan, India, Mexico, Central America, and the Caribbean.

Refugees came from Southeast Asia and Latin America seeking political freedom and economic opportunity. The "boat people" fled Communist rule in Vietnam, Cambodia, and Laos. These immigrants benefited when a law was passed in November 1978 that allowed 47,000 Indochinese to settle in the United States. Cuba's Fidel Castro sent nearly a hundred thousand noncommunist Cubans, including hundreds of criminals, to the United States in 1980. Haitians continued to flee their troubled country, as did people from the nations of Central America that were touched by civil war.

The increased immigration raised many concerns—just as increased immigration from Southern and Eastern Europe had done earlier in the century. Some Americans feared losing their jobs to immigrants willing to work for lower wages. In areas with large numbers of Spanish-speaking immigrants, controversy raged over **bilingual education.** Supporters argued that non–English-speaking children would learn better if the schools taught them in their native language. Opponents said that those children would need to learn English in order to succeed in the United States.

New immigrants in the cities faced conflict with one another and with the people who already lived there. The immigrants themselves faced problems of adaptation, bigotry, low-paying work, and poverty. Conflicts between Hispanics and blacks in Miami and between Koreans and blacks in New York City are just two examples of the kind of tension between groups that frequently flared into violence.

In the American Southwest, many immigrants continued to toil as migrant farm workers, planting and harvesting crops, although their numbers were diminishing. A large proportion of these workers were illegal aliens, or people who had come from another country without following the formal procedures. Because they had no legal status, these workers were beyond the reach of government social programs. Without any hope of government support, they could be treated harshly by employers.

In 1985 Congress passed the Immigration Control and Reform Act. It attempted to solve the problem of illegal aliens with two steps. First, it outlawed the hiring of illegal aliens. Second, it granted amnesty to any illegal aliens already in the country. By registering with the government, they could become legal residents of the United States.

Growth of the Sun Belt

Despite many changes in population, the nation's metropolitan areas continued to grow. Growth was particularly great in the cities and the suburbs of the Sun Belt—the South and the Southwest. Examples are Atlanta; the Texas cities of Houston, Dallas, Fort Worth, and San Antonio; the Tampa Bay area and Miami; and Phoenix and Tucson, Arizona. California, too, continued to attract more and more new residents.

Retirees and others moved from northern suburbs to southern suburbs. Factories and workers also moved south. The North was hit hard by the recession of the 1970s and by the decline in the auto and steel industries. Some areas of the Northeast—especially the coastal cities from Washington to Boston—revived by developing jobs in service industries. Banking and finance, communications, health care, and the computer industry became major employers in these areas.

The movement to the Sun Belt had profound social and political effects. The number of representatives that a state has in the Congress is based on that state's population. The censuses of 1980 and 1990 showed declines in the population of northeastern states and growth in the southern and western states. The result was fewer representatives for the former and more for the latter. Sun Belt voters had more political clout, and their attitudes were taken seriously in elections. Reagan's and Bush's elections in 1980, 1984, and 1988 were based in part on Republican success in these states.

Changes in the Cities

In all sections of the country, the suburbs continued to grow, both as business centers and as residential areas. More and more service and high-tech manufacturing moved out of the cities and into the suburbs. Once-rural communities on the outskirts of cities became well-to-do suburbs, struggling to keep up with the newcomers' demands for roads, schools, water, and other services.

Many middle-class Americans—especially the Yuppies—moved back to cities in the 1970s and 1980s. Called **gentrification,** this shift created still more problems for the poor. They could not afford the rents that the middle class could afford to pay and were often forced out of their neighborhoods. The concentrated **ghettos** that remained were plagued by ongoing

CUBAN SAILBOARDS TO FREEDOM

In efforts to flee Fidel Castro's Cuba, many have made daring escape attempts. Many have been unsuccessful—even fatal—but Lester Moreno Perez made it in a spectacular way.

On the night of March 1, 1990, 17-year-old Moreno Perez launched himself from a Cuban beach on a sailboard. He sailed for ten hours through shark-infested waters, but began to worry when the sail boom broke and he started to drift aimlessly. Luckily a freighter spotted Moreno Perez and took him aboard. Although his hands and feet were severely blistered, he had survived his 60-mile sail.

crime, drug, and health problems as well as by gang violence.

Cities were feeling increased economic pressure. They developed plans to keep businesses in the city, rather than lose them to the suburbs, and to lure back the employers who had already left. They had only limited success. Worse, however, was the squeeze between a higher demand for social services and shrinking revenues. More and more of the urban population was poor, needing help with food, housing, and health care. The drug problem increased the need for spending, as did the **AIDS** epidemic (see Science and Technology). On the other hand, cities were faced with cutbacks in federal spending and a shrinking tax base.

The result was a growing financial crisis among cities. New York City almost went bankrupt in 1976 and required a federal bailout. It verged on bankruptcy again in 1991. Cleveland, Ohio, was unable to meet payments on its loans in 1978, the first city to do so since the Depression. Other cities faced constant pressure to cut city spending or borrow more.

The White Backlash

The 1970s had seen the rise of **affirmative action** programs, which tried to make up for years of discrimination against blacks, Hispanics, and women. As these programs took hold, some white men especially complained about "reverse discrimination." They argued that jobs were being filled by minorities or women to fill quotas.

Some people took to the courts to protest what they saw as unfair preferences for members of minority groups. Alan Bakke was a white man whose application to medical school had been refused. He sued the school, claiming that a less-qualified minority student had been chosen in his place. In June 1978 the Supreme Court ruled that colleges cannot set strict quotas for the number of minority students to admit and then make admission decisions based on meeting that number. The Court did allow colleges to give special consideration to applicants from minority groups.

The mixed decision was seen as upholding affirmative action but banning quotas. During the Reagan and Bush years, however, the executive branch did not support affirmative action.

Sometimes the backlash was violent. Racial incidents, many in the Northeast, continued to appear in headlines. At Howard Beach, New York, racist white teenagers attacked two black men who were in their neighborhood and killed one of them. Also in New York, a white subway rider shot and paralyzed a black teenager who was apparently mugging him. In New York City's Central Park, a woman jogger was beaten and raped by a gang of young blacks. In a bizarre twist, a man in Boston used racial tensions to cover up a murder. He claimed that his wife had been murdered by black hoodlums, but in reality had done the deed himself. TV viewers saw repeated clips of Los Angeles police officers beating a black man, Rodney King. Each of these cases revealed a continuing tension between whites and blacks.

MIAMI EXPLODES INTO VIOLENCE

In May 1980 three days of rioting began in Miami after an all-white jury acquitted four white police officers of killing a black insurance executive. As a result of the riots, 18 people were killed, 400 injured, and nearly 1,000 arrested.

RIGHTS AND RESPECT

Blacks and women continued their struggles to achieve a fair shake in American society. James Farmer, former head of the Congress of Racial Equality (CORE), summed up this new stage of civil rights: "What we succeeded in doing in the sixties was in dealing with the constitutional issue of rights. We've won that battle. . . . [Now] we're dealing with real equality." Advances were made, but it was a rocky road. Other groups, seeing the partial success of blacks and women, also sought recognition of their special status.

Black Gains in Political Power

Across America's cities more and more African-Americans moved into the mayor's office. The nation's first black mayors had been elected in 1967. By 1991 such major cities as Chicago, Cleveland, Detroit, Kansas City, Los Angeles, New York City, Philadelphia, and Washington, D.C., either currently had black mayors or had been run by black mayors for at least one term.

Blacks also made other political gains. In 1990 Douglas Wilder of Virginia became the country's first black governor. Jesse Jackson, active in the civil rights movement of the 1960s, ran for the presidency in 1984 and 1988. He was very strong in the 1988 primaries; he was runner-up to Michael Dukakis for the Democratic nomination.

Among blacks as a whole, an income gap was growing between those who attended college and those who did not. The recession of the late 1970s and the 1980s boom increased this gap by leaving the poorest and least educated behind. They faced joblessness and poverty. The unemployment rate for young black men reached Great Depression levels of 25 percent or more. The single-parent family became increasingly the way of life in the inner city. Children were left to

▼ Harold Washington (left) was elected the first black mayor of Chicago in 1983. Douglas Wilder was sworn in as governor of Virginia in 1990.

WOMEN IN THE MILITARY

Since 1976, when women were first permitted to enter the military service academies, they have gradually increased their numbers in the armed forces. In 1989 women made up about 11 percent of the military.

In August 1989, 20-year-old Kristin Baker made history as the first woman to be chosen First Captain of the Corps of Cadets at West Point. As the academy's highest-ranking cadet, she was in charge of 4,400 cadets—90 percent of them male.

The careers of female officers are generally limited by rules that restrict them from combat. Combat command is the traditional path for advancement. But the Gulf War showed that the line between combat and noncombat duty can be blurred. One female soldier died in that conflict, and another was taken prisoner. Many thousands more served with distinction.

fend for themselves while their mothers sought service jobs to pay the bills.

Minority children often attended schools plagued by gang violence and drugs. Tight school budgets reduced the possibility of providing special programs. Survival won out over education. In these situations only the exceptional child dreamed of going on to college. Black college enrollment declined from its peak in the early 1970s. The road out of the ghetto still seemed long and hopeless.

There were positive changes in the black community as well. In the late 1960s and early 1970s black leaders lamented the lack of role models for black children. In the 1980s there were many—black managers, professionals, technical workers, and government officials, in addition to prominent artists, entertainers, and sports stars in the public eye.

Changing Women's Concerns

"I am disgusted by this move by the United States," U.S. District Judge Patrick Kelly said on August 6, 1991. He was referring to the Justice Department's decision to side with an antiabortion group fighting Kelly's order to keep two Wichita, Kansas, abortion clinics open. Abortion continued to be the most controversial women's issue.

The Supreme Court's 1973 ruling *Roe v. Wade* left the decision to have an abortion to an individual woman and her physician. The opponents of abortion launched a counterattack. Abortion clinics—like those in Wichita—became the site of demonstrations as antiabortion groups tried to block women from entering. Many states passed restrictions on abortion, and antiabortion groups continued to bring challenges of abortion laws to the Supreme Court. Conservative justices appointed to the court by Presidents Reagan and Bush seemed ready in the early 1990s to overturn the *Roe* ruling and ban abortion.

Abortion was not the only women's issue, however. Feminists lost the fight to get the Equal Rights Amendment (ERA) added to the Constitution. But women did succeed in changing some laws and some attitudes. New national attention was focused on concerns long considered women's issues. These included child care, rape awareness, spouse abuse, and sexual harassment.

Women also made some gains in the workplace. They entered many professions that had long been dominated by men, even taking top management posts. But even in 1990 women were still earning only two-thirds of what men earned for the same job. Further, very few gained the highest positions in big business. Management attitudes created an invisible barrier, or "glass ceiling," that limited women's chances to rise up the ladder of major corporations.

New gains spelled new burdens for women as they attempted to balance career with family. More than half of all women worked outside the home, and many of them had young children. Employers slowly began to adapt to women's needs, awarding maternity leave and providing child care. Busy middle-class couples had to find

NEW SURGEON GENERAL

In 1990 Dr. Antonia Novello became the surgeon general of the United States. Born in Puerto Rico, Novello was the first woman and first Hispanic to hold the post.

The Supreme Court Shifts to the Right

▲ Associate Justice Sandra Day O'Connor

Between 1953 and 1969 the Supreme Court under Chief Justice Earl Warren revolutionized society by issuing decisions that ended segregation. Its rulings on the rights of criminals, too, brought major changes. It was also known for championing the First Amendment right of free speech.

Under Chief Justice Warren Burger, appointed in 1969, the Court upheld many of the major decisions of the Warren Court. The Burger Court issued a landmark ruling in the 1973 case of *Roe v. Wade.* That decision found that women had a constitutional right to have an abortion.

As the American public grew more conservative, and as liberal and moderate justices retired, the makeup of the Court changed. Presidents Reagan and Bush were able to appoint conservative judges more likely to carry out a new Court agenda.

In 1981 Reagan made history by appointing the first woman Supreme Court justice, Sandra Day O'Connor. In 1986 Justice William H. Rehnquist became chief justice, and Antonin Scalia was appointed as associate justice. In 1987 Lewis F. Powell Jr., who often cast pivotal votes, retired. Filling Powell's seat brought on bitter debates between the Democratic Senate and the White House. The Senate rejected President Reagan's first nominee, Robert Bork. A second, Douglas Ginsburg,withdrew his nomination amid controversy. A third nominee, Anthony M. Kennedy, was confirmed in 1988.

By the middle of his term President Bush had the chance to appoint two justices. David Souter joined the Court in 1990. Clarence Thomas became the second black justice, in 1991, when he replaced the retiring Thurgood Marshall.

The result of all of these appointments was a conservative tilt to the Court. The new Court handled questions of the separation of church and state differently than in the past. In 1984 a conservative majority upheld a city's right to include a Nativity scene in a public Christmas display. Liberals believed that this decision was wrong because the practice endorsed one religion over others.

The new Court began turning away from the Warren Court's stance on criminal rights as well. In 1986 the Court allowed some involuntary confessions to be used as evidence. Another decision validated evidence obtained in certain cases, on search warrants that were somehow defective.

The main issue, however, was abortion. Ever since the *Roe* decision was handed down, conservatives had tried to overturn it. By the late 1980s the growing conservative power on the Court seemed to be chipping away at the edges of that ruling. In 1989 an important decision in the case *Webster v. Reproductive Health Services* gave states broader rights to place restrictions on abortions. Several states passed restrictive laws, some of which may eventually challenge *Roe.*

The swearing in of Clarence Thomas marked a new turning point. Although Thomas did not reveal his views on abortion during his confirmation hearings, his earlier speeches and writings suggested that he would oppose it. If so, his vote will give the conservatives a clear majority on the Court.

ways of sharing the demands of child care, housework, and careers. Women who headed single-parent families, often on the edge of or below the poverty line, struggled to work at their jobs and raise their children alone.

The Graying of America

People were living longer than ever before. The special needs and burdens of the elderly had to be met. Senior-citizen groups such as the American Association for Retired Persons (AARP) and the Gray Panthers lobbied legislatures on behalf of the elderly. Among other achievements, their efforts resulted in many businesses offering discounts to senior citizens.

People began to realize that a productive life does not magically end at age 65 and that older people should have the chance to work if they choose. Congress passed civil rights laws banning employers from discriminating against older workers. More and more older people delayed retirement or began to work part time.

▼ The Vietnam Veterans Memorial opened to the public in 1982 amid controversy. Some veterans complained that the monument's design—a V-shaped wall of black granite set into the side of a hill—reflected the way America tried to bury the experience of that war. As time went by, however, the moving power of the list of 50,000 Americans killed in the war made the monument very popular. It was designed by Maya Yang Lin, a design student at Yale University.

Retired workers lived on fixed incomes. They relied on Social Security payments from the government, sometimes supplemented by savings or retirement benefits paid by their former employers. Health-insurance plans such as government-funded Medicare covered 98 percent of the nation's 30 million elderly. But the health-care system for the elderly was not perfect. Many lost their savings paying for extended medical or nursing care. Others were brought into the homes of their now-adult children to try to avoid these expenses.

Veterans Speak Out

Those who fought in the Vietnam War felt that they were never appreciated. The unpopularity of that war had rubbed off on the veterans, some of whom felt scorned or ridiculed when they returned home.

In the 1980s and early 1990s more attention was paid to veterans of that war. A landmark event was the dedication of the Vietnam Veterans Memorial in Washington, D.C. A moving monument to those who died in that war, the memorial helped heal the feelings of neglect that the surviving veterans suffered. The country's support for the armed forces during the Gulf War also helped the Vietnam veterans. People began to look on those former soldiers and sailors more favorably.

Many veterans were active in trying to get better treatment for Vietnam veterans who suffered psychological and physical problems during their service. Some veterans had emotional problems. Many were afflicted by nightmares and flashbacks, as well as by depression and guilt.

Others had developed cancers and other serious illnesses. Some blamed Agent Orange, a chemical that had been used to strip the jungles of Vietnam bare of vegetation. The federal government sponsored many studies of the chemical's effects, as veterans demanded that its manufacturers or the government pay for their treatment. A victims' fund was eventually established. In 1989 President Bush created the Department of Veterans Affairs, a cabinet-level agency, to deal with these and other issues.

Rights for the Handicapped

People who were physically handicapped also organized to protect their civil rights. For years they had been looked at with fear and suspicion and confined to back rooms or institutions. New attitudes, along with medical and technological advances, enabled many people to lead more normal lives. With their new freedom they demanded access to public buildings and transportation. New laws required wheelchair ramps and special access, such as elevators, to be provided in all new construction. Civil rights laws and rulings banned discrimination against the handicapped, as they did against other groups.

Gay Rights

Homosexuals first became active on behalf of their own civil rights in the 1960s. The primary aim of gay-rights groups had been the passage of laws to protect them from discrimination in housing or on the job. That changed in the 1980s.

The spread of AIDS raised new challenges to homosexual groups. When the disease was discovered in the early 1980s, it seemed mostly to affect gay men. As a result, some people viewed the disease, which caused death and had no known cure, as a punishment for homosexual behavior. Many in the gay community felt that such attitudes contributed to the inaction of government officials and medical experts in fighting the dreaded new disease.

Gay-rights groups are now active in a number of AIDS-related causes. They constantly remind government officials and health-care workers of the need to continue research into a cure for AIDS. They work to provide humane treatment for those suffering from AIDS, whether they are homosexual or not. And they keep a watchful eye out for any discrimination against AIDS sufferers.

THE COLD WAR AND BEYOND

Starting in the late 1970s, the Cold War heated up. But by the middle 1980s the two superpowers made progress toward arms-control agreements. Then the collapse of communism in Eastern Europe and the sweeping changes in the Soviet Union suggested that an era of tension between East and West was now history.

ANTINUKE PROTEST DRAWS THOUSANDS

On June 12, 1982, no-nukes groups held a demonstration in New York City against the Reagan administration's arms buildup. Police estimated that the huge crowd numbered more than 700,000. The protesters marched 3 miles to Central Park, where they heard speeches promoting nuclear arms control. Five thousand New York police officers were on hand, but not needed, because the demonstration was peaceful.

AMERICAN FIFTH GRADER IS GOODWILL AMBASSADOR

Samantha Smith, an 11-year-old girl from Manchester, Maine, became an international celebrity in 1983. The fifth grader had written a letter to Soviet leader Yuri Andropov. In the letter Smith expressed her fears about the possibility of nuclear war.

Andropov responded, pledging to work toward a peaceful relationship with the United States. In a heady public relations move, he invited young Smith to the Soviet Union. She toured the country for two weeks, being lavished with gifts and treated as a major star. She received a similar welcome when returning to the United States.

Sadly, in August 1985, Smith and her father were killed in an airplane crash. They were flying home from London, England, where she had been filming her television series *Lime Street.*

The End of Détente

President Carter's opposition to Soviet involvement in Afghanistan set the stage for a renewal of tense relations between the two superpowers. The United States helped arm the rebels fighting Soviet troops—a move the Soviets disliked. To underscore his displeasure with the Afghan War, Carter prohibited U.S. athletes from competing in the 1980 Summer Games in Moscow. The Soviets returned the favor four years later, withholding their athletes from the games held in Los Angeles.

Conflict came over other issues as well. The American people expressed support for the Polish Solidarity movement after its first rise in 1980 and during its suppression by the hard-line Communists. President Reagan condemned the Soviets in 1983 when one of their fighters shot down a civilian Korean jetliner, which had strayed over Soviet airspace. All 269 people aboard the plane were killed.

Reagan's hard-line stance toward the USSR was as unacceptable to the Soviets as these Soviet actions were to the United States. Calling for an end to what he considered years of neglect of the nation's defenses, Reagan instituted a renewed arms buildup. Spending on new, high-tech weapons increased. Advanced guided missiles were stockpiled, and radar-avoiding airplanes were developed.

Reagan also introduced a plan to send defensive weapons into space. Called the Strategic Defense Initiative—but more popularly known as "Star Wars" after the hit movie—the plan called for space-based weapons that could shoot down nuclear missiles before they landed. Reagan pushed the program as the best way of ensuring security; Democrats criticized it as an impossibility. The president proclaimed that once these defensive weapons were developed, he would share the technology with the Soviets. The Soviets saw Star Wars as an offensive system and as a violation of a treaty they had signed with the United States. Nor did they believe Reagan's promise to share.

One reason that the Soviets mistrusted Reagan was the force of his anti-Soviet statements. In language that reached back to the height of the Cold War, he referred to the USSR as the "Evil Empire." On another occasion, he joked that the Soviet Union was being outlawed, and "We will start bombing in five minutes." The joke was overheard, and the Soviets could not find it reassuring.

Intervention Abroad

President Reagan took a number of actions to back up his tough talk—although military involvement did not come against the Soviets. Two clashes took place with Libya—first in 1981 when two Libyan jets were shot down, then in 1986 when Reagan ordered two Libyan cities bombed in revenge for a terrorist attack. In 1983 he sent U.S. troops to the Caribbean island of Grenada to remove an anti-American government. In 1987 he took action to try to ensure the smooth flow of oil out of the Persian Gulf by using U.S. Navy ships to escort tankers.

Other U.S. military actions were less successful. In 1982 Reagan had sent U.S. Marines to Lebanon to try to restore order in that land torn by civil war. He was forced to pull the troops out the next year after a terrorist attack on Marine headquarters left 239 soldiers dead.

Under Reagan, the U.S. government was also involved in the conflict between left-wing and right-wing groups in Central America. Fearing a Communist takeover of El Salvador, America sent military aid to that country's government. Democrats opposed the move because the El Salvador government abused the rights of its citizens. Reagan persisted.

In Nicaragua nationwide uprisings followed the murder of an opposition leader in January 1978. Leftists called "Sandinistas" overthrew the ruling Somoza family in 1979. These leftists aligned themselves with the Soviets and Cuba. Once Reagan took office, he gave aid to right-wing anti-Sandinista **guerrillas** (called "Contras"). After Sandinista leader Daniel Ortega was elected Nicaragua's president in 1984, Reagan continued to support the Contras. Congress outlawed aid to those guerrillas in 1984 but lifted restrictions in 1986. Reagan's policy led to the most damaging scandal of his administration, however.

The Iran-Contra Scandal

After Reagan's reelection in 1984, the Iran-Contra affair came to light. The scandal began with secret arms sales to Iran, made with the hope of influencing that nation to help get U.S. hostages released from the Middle East. The profits from the arms sales were then passed on to the Contras. The entire operation presented two problems. The arms sales appeared to contradict Reagan's policy of not making any deals with terrorists to get hostages released. That was merely embarrassing to Reagan; worse, however, was the Contra funding. If true, it was in direct violation of an act of Congress banning any aid to that group.

The public outcry was loud and widespread. A special prosecutor was appointed to investigate those involved in the arms sale, Contra aid, or both. Reagan appointed a review board headed by former senator John Tower. Its February 1987 report found the president not guilty of knowing of any wrongdoing, but it hardly endorsed the administration's actions. The report bluntly criticized the president's management style as "inept." Shortly afterward, Reagan gave a television speech that accepted the report's judgment and took responsibility for the actions of his subordinates.

Senate and House Democrats sniffed a chance to damage Reagan. Committees held televised hearings from May to August of 1987. They learned that a few members of the National Security Council (NSC) staff used secret private operatives to carry out policies; that officials lied to Congress and others; and that the Contras received only some of the diverted money. Former national security adviser John Poindexter admitted that he had ordered the money to be used for the Contras and had not informed the president.

The scandal shook Americans' faith in Reagan and damaged U.S.

THE WHITE HOUSE BASEMENT

A central figure in the Iran-Contra scandal was Marine Lieutenant Colonel Oliver North, who was working for the NSC in the White House. North's role in the affair became clear during congressional hearings. He ran both ends of the scheme that diverted funds from Iranian arms sales to the Nicaraguan Contras. The hearings also revealed that he lied to investigators and destroyed key evidence after the plan became public.

Millions of Americans watched the Iran-Contra hearings on television. Many were struck by how sincerely North believed that he had done the right thing. At the same time, however, Americans were appalled by how much foreign policy had been conducted from the White House basement—behind the backs of Congress and the people.

North's 1989 court convictions for his role in Iran-Contra were overturned in 1991. North still claimed that President Reagan knew about and backed the plan, a claim that others in the administration denied.

► Mikhail Gorbachev (left) and Ronald Reagan sign the 1987 Intermediate Nuclear Forces (INF) Treaty, which ended a whole class of nuclear weapons.

prestige abroad. The Tower committee's report said, "The common ingredients of the Iran and Contra policies were secrecy, deception, and disdain for the law." The report brought to mind the presidential abuses of power from the Johnson and Nixon years all over again.

Summit Success

The renewed chill in U.S.-Soviet relations ended with the rise of Mikhail Gorbachev in the USSR. The first summit between Reagan and Gorbachev, in Geneva in 1985, produced smiles and handshakes, but very little agreement. A second summit between the two leaders in Iceland in October 1986 suggested that progress was possible. On that occasion they nearly agreed on reductions in nuclear missiles. When Reagan insisted on not limiting Star Wars research, the meeting ended with no deal.

In December 1987 the two leaders finally signed an arms-control agreement, which removed all medium- and short-range missiles in Europe. This treaty held promise for the future. It was the first time the superpowers agreed to destroy a class of weapons.

Under President Bush relations with the Soviets continued to improve. Bush had a warm, friendly relationship with Gorbachev, and the two leaders seemed to work well together. The United States appreciated Gorbachev's hands-off policy when the Communist governments of Eastern Europe tumbled. Gorbachev also cooperated greatly in the diplomatic and military responses to Iraq's invasion of Kuwait. Bush, in turn, helped Gorbachev by promoting arms reductions; the Soviet leader wanted an end to the arms race so he could try to revive his nation's ailing economy. Bush also helped Gorbachev by supporting him during an unsuccessful **coup** attempt in August 1991.

The fruit of this friendship was further steps toward arms control. The START talks of 1990 produced an agreement to reduce some nuclear arms and to remove ground forces from Europe. The dramatic announcements of late 1991, when both the United States and the Soviets stated their intention to disarm whole classes of nuclear weapons, signaled that tension was finally being removed.

THE BAY AREA EARTHQUAKE

On October 19, 1989, the San Francisco Bay area was rocked by its second major earthquake in the twentieth century. At least 62 people died, many of them trapped under a collapsed freeway. Part of the Bay Bridge also collapsed. The quake struck just as many Americans were tuning in to a World Series game between two Bay area teams, the San Francisco Giants and the Oakland A's.

THE BABY BOOMERS GROW UP

After the idealism, activism, rebellion, and conflict of the 1960s, the Baby Boom generation reached adulthood—and changed. Young Americans in the 1970s and 1980s tended to focus on themselves and their own needs, rather than on social change.

Many Americans turned to religion. Church and synagogue attendance increased, and people watched evangelists on TV. Some sought guidance in Eastern religions like Zen Buddhism. Many African-Americans became Muslims in an attempt both to satisfy their spiritual needs and forge closer links with nonwhites in other parts of the world.

Self-help books and magazines became more popular with Americans. It seemed that new ways to achieve success, conquer fears, or live longer were published every day. Awareness of drug and alcohol addiction grew, and many people joined programs to overcome substance abuse. The names of celebrities and athletes who suffered from these problems were constantly in the news.

Health and fitness became important priorities to the Baby Boomers—and to Americans as a whole. Memberships in health and fitness clubs soared. People "worked out" through weight lifting, aerobics, running, swimming, racquetball, and power walking to enhance both their well-being and appearance. For the same reason, people also watched what they ate as never before. Diet foods, diet books, and diet fads abounded. Americans ate less red meat and more fruits and vegetables, less salt and fat and more fiber. People turned to salad bars, "lite" foods, and diet soft drinks. At the same time, many Americans' taste for junk food only increased.

The Haves and Have-Nots

The 1970s culture of self-absorption filtered through the business boom of the 1980s to become the 1980s culture of money. People were attracted to the opportunities of the corporate world. New tax laws and the "me" mentality added to the growth of the super rich and approval of wealth. Scandals from Wall Street proved that the pursuit of money could easily undermine business morality.

This was the era of Yuppies and preppies. Young, upwardly mobile professionals talked about having the right job, the right address, the right clothes, the right friends. The newly rich bought large homes and estates. Housing developments bore names that suggested prosperity and prestige. In the booming real estate market, the well-to-do bought land, houses, and condos as investments.

This was the glitzy, attractive side of the 1980s boom. On the other side the picture was not so pleasant. The changing job market resulted in growing inequality between those with money and those without. Foreign competition and increasing automation made for fewer entry-level manufacturing jobs. The service economy created opportunities, but wages there were often low.

"It's the Me-Decade."

—Author Tom Wolfe, speaking about the 1970s

GENERICS DEBUT

The first no-brand generic products appeared on supermarket shelves in 1976. The products, which debuted in Chicago, were meant to offer a cheaper alternative to name-brand goods. They could sell for less in part because they used simple black-and-white packaging and had no advertising costs.

The Use and Abuse of Drugs and Alcohol

The counterculture of the 1960s had brought new acceptance of the use of mood-altering drugs such as marijuana, LSD, and cocaine. Adults condemned their use, but the young promoted it. In the 1980s drugs moved from being a hotly debated form of recreation to a widely acknowledged social problem. Attitudes changed as people recognized the perils that drug use brings.

The media began to be filled with stories of successful Yuppies who wasted fortunes—and—lives on cocaine. Many athletes admitted to drug and alcohol abuse; some were banned from their sports two or three times because they could not permanently shake their habit. Many actors also went public about their addiction problems.

Members of the urban underclass, more and more alienated from mainstream American life, often turned to drugs. Dealing drugs became a way to succeed. Using them was an avenue of escape from a seemingly hopeless existence. In the mid-1980s the cheap and highly addictive "crack" cocaine hit the streets. Overnight, neighborhoods became terrorized by the effects of crack and the violence of crack dealers. Bullets pierced the night as dealers fought over territory. Children were killed in the crossfire. A few respected religious and civic leaders were found to be crack addicts, suggesting the extent of the epidemic of addiction.

Also troubling was the appearance of "crack babies," the children of women who used crack cocaine when pregnant. These poor infants were born addicted to the drug. Health and school officials wondered how they would grow and develop after this horrible start to life.

▼ ▼ ▼

The media began to be filled with stories of successful Yuppies who wasted fortunes on cocaine.

Presidents Reagan and Bush tried to combat the growing use of drugs. First Lady Nancy Reagan started the "Just Say No" campaign to encourage children—and adults—to refuse to use drugs. President Bush declared a "War on Drugs" that featured increased law enforcement. Both presidents also tried to pressure the governments of Colombia and other cocaine-growing countries to clamp down on the drug trade at its source. Experts on chemical addiction criticized these efforts as inadequate. They wanted more resources to fight the underlying causes of addiction and help people recover.

Drug testing also became a hotly debated issue. Questions arose about how legal mandatory drug testing was, but concern over public safety suggested that some controls might be necessary. Many people pointed to accidents caused by train engineers, school bus drivers, and oil tanker captains who were under the influence of drugs or alcohol as reasons for routine testing.

The campaign against drugs moved people to view alcohol use differently. Mothers whose children had been killed in car accidents that involved alcohol use formed Mothers Against Drunk Driving (MADD). Students began Students Against Drunk Driving (SADD). Suddenly, it became accepted to speak out against alcohol.

People going to parties were encouraged to name a "designated driver," who was to refrain from drinking. Public service announcements urged people to avoid drinking and driving and to limit the use of alcohol. These campaigns raised humorous contradictions. Makers of beer said that their alcoholic beverage should be drunk in moderation—at the same time they promoted it as part of the fun life.

As a result children and the working poor, especially women, suffered. Cuts in federal funding combined with state and city financial problems reduced the number of people who could be helped by welfare. Yet continued joblessness kept the number of the needy high.

In the 1980s *homelessness* entered the American vocabulary. Loss of jobs drove people out of their homes. And the high cost of housing meant that even people with jobs sometimes could not afford to buy shelter. Americans were shocked at first to see homeless people in public buildings, in downtown business districts, and in makeshift settlements. The extent of the problem and shortage of government aid led many volunteer agencies to increase their food and shelter programs. The rise of homelessness posed dilemmas for all urban dwellers, who daily weighed pleas for spare change against their own wishes that the problem would disappear.

Issues for the Nineties

By the late 1980s people had come to realize that the world—its resources and its prospects—had limits. The supply of oil or coal was not endless, and the widespread use of chemical fertilizers and pesticides was not without danger. The conservative movement of the 1980s even had most liberals agreeing that there were limits both to what the government could do to solve problems and to how much the government could spend.

But this awareness of limits did not reflect despair, as it had in the late 1970s. The changes of the 1980s were dramatic, and there were certainly many problems to be solved. But Americans had a renewed faith in people's ability to take action and solve problems. Many felt that the collapse of communism endorsed the American economic system and that the Gulf War showed U.S. power could be used effectively in a just cause.

The questions that remained, however, were huge. Could this renewed confidence and hope be turned to use in attacking the many problems that confronted the country? Could the American people find ways to achieve unity but cherish diversity, grow economically but distribute wealth fairly, compete with foreign economies but maintain employment, and expand production but protect the environment? Could solutions to problems in family life, education, drug abuse, and health care be found? Only time would tell.

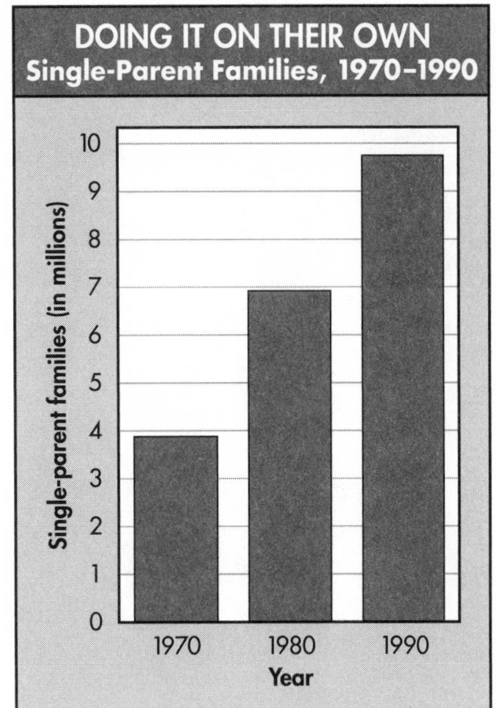

Source: U.S. Bureau of the Census.

◀ From 1970 to 1990, the number of single-parent families in the United States more than doubled.

"The educational foundations of our society are presently being eroded by a rising tide of mediocrity that threatens our very future as a nation and as a people."

—*A Nation at Risk*, the 1983 report of the President's Commission on Education

THE WORLD

Since 1961 the Berlin Wall had divided the German city and stood as a grim symbol of the Cold War. An entire generation grew up in its shadow. East German border guards shot many people trying to cross from East to West Berlin. The Wall scarred the German psyche, and it loomed as a threat of future conflict. And then, miraculously, the gates were opened on November 9, 1989. The barrier between East and West Germany was removed. Within days Germans were walking on the rubble of the fallen Wall (above) and chopping chunks out of the Wall to keep as souvenirs.

Between 1976 and 1991 tremendous changes occurred throughout the world. In Europe and the Soviet Union, one Communist dictatorship after another fell, toppled by the will of the people to have political freedom and better economic opportunities. Democracy was on the move in Communist China, too. In that land, however, its advocates suffered brutal repression. The nations of Latin America had better success. Many of them overthrew dictators. Even that bulwark of tyranny, South Africa, took steps to loosen the bonds that shackled its black people.

But the rising tide of freedom did not bring the end of conflict. Wars flared in the Middle East and elsewhere. Many of these were bloody civil wars fueled by centuries of ethnic or religious hatred. Minority populations in countries all over the world demanded their own land and the chance to govern themselves. These calls for nationalism that began with the twentieth century were still strong as it drew to a close.

AT A GLANCE

- Global Village, Global Challenges
- The Collapse of Communism
- Planning for Europe '92
- Turmoil in the Middle East
- Conflict and Change in Africa
- Asia: Land of Giants
- Democracy in Latin America
- The Challenges Facing Canada

DATAFILE

World population	1975	1988
Total	4.1 bil.	5.1 bil.
Africa	415 mil.	610 mil.
Asia	2.4 bil.	3 bil.
Australia and Oceania	21 mil.	26 mil.
Central and South America	322 mil.	430 mil.
Europe	474 mil.	496 mil.
North America	239 mil.	272 mil.
USSR	255 mil.	284 mil.

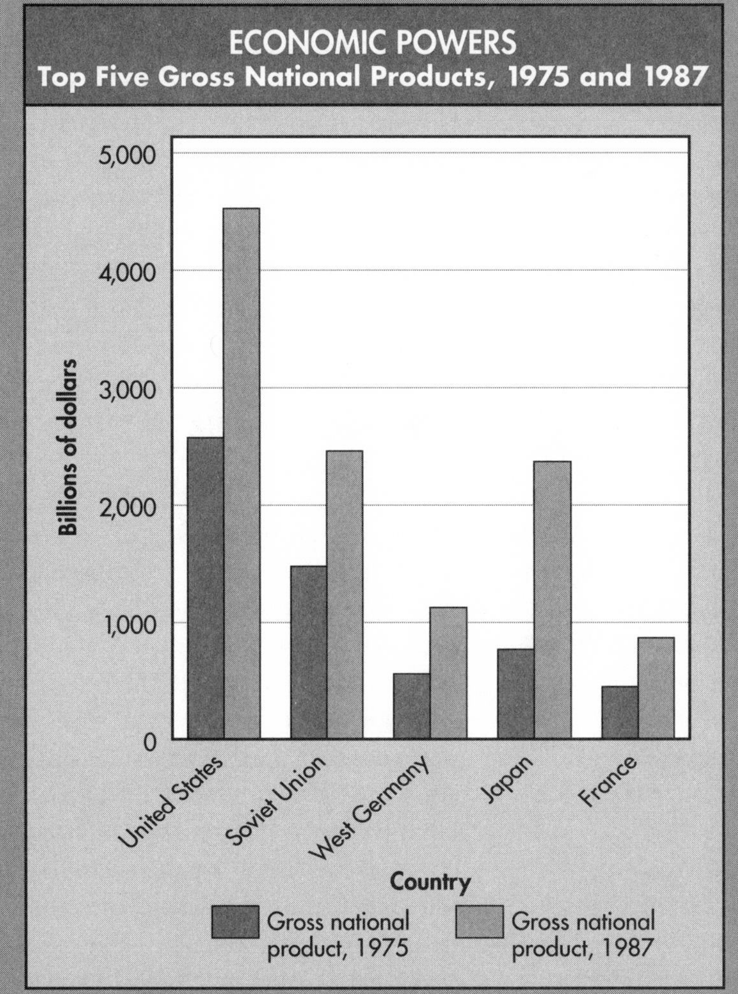

Source: *Statistical Abstract of the United States, 1990* and *1986*.

GLOBAL VILLAGE, GLOBAL CHALLENGES

Many people have come to use the term *global village* to describe our world and its people. But the phrase is very puzzling. How can the globe—the vast sphere of water and land that is the earth—be a village, when it is home to more than 5.5 billion people? The key to this puzzle is in the human relationships of a typical village, where everyone knows everyone else and people face many of the same kinds of problems.

In the global village, then, people all over the world are increasingly exposed to the same information—and share the same concerns. High-tech satellite communications and jet travel have made the world's people aware of their neighbors around the globe in dramatic new ways. Billions of people can now watch the same events on television. News, ideas, and fads spread quickly from country to country and continent to continent. The term also suggests ways that the people of the earth are related by their common needs. All people want personal safety, economic security, good health care, and personal freedom. Finally, the term emphasizes that the fate of all the world's nations, regions, and peoples are increasingly linked.

Together the people of this global village face a number of serious challenges. Pollution, shortages of water and other natural resources, ethnic and religious conflict—these and other problems

WORLDWIDE NEWS

The links forged by global communications were dramatically evident in three events during 1991. In January satellite pictures of the bombing of Baghdad, Iraq, showed the opening of the Persian Gulf War on live television. In August Soviet president Mikhail Gorbachev tracked the progress of the resistance to a coup aimed at toppling him by listening to Britain's BBC radio broadcasts. At the end of the year, the U.S. television networks carried—live—the historic resignation speech of Gorbachev.

challenge the human race. Some problems are new, having developed within the past 15 years, whereas others have been present for the entire century, or even longer. But the cooperation of all is needed to make the village a safe and healthy place in which to live.

A New World Order

September 1, 1989, marked the fiftieth anniversary of the start of World War II. It was one of the few days since that date in 1939 that no full-scale international war was being fought anywhere in the world. Although peace did not last, the moment symbolized a subtle yet decisive shift in the balance of world power. A planet once dominated by two military superpowers—the United States and the Soviet Union—gave way to a global village led by a number of economic powers. Many of those powers represent regional forces, rather than single nations.

"The U.S. and the USSR," wrote one observer, "now have far less to fear from each other than they have to fear not only from their internal problems, but from events over which they can have little control—from unrestrained growth of population in large parts of the world, from the global environmental changes that have become such a threat, from the likely emergence of new nuclear weapons states."

The challenges to the new world order are daunting. The gap between industrial nations and the impoverished **Third World** is growing rapidly. The high-tech Western economies have been able to provide their citizens with a moderate standard of living. On the other hand the Third World has remained a realm of grinding poverty, hunger, disease, infant mortality, and unemployment. In 1989, for example, well over 1 billion people in the Third World were seriously ill or malnourished. Thirty percent of the African population suffered from malnutrition and disease, including AIDS. Rapid population growth continues to fuel the problems of the Third World.

"It is obvious . . . that the use or threat of force no longer can or must be an instrument of foreign policy. This applies above all to nuclear arms."

—Mikhail Gorbachev, 1988

Global Economy

The 12 nations of the European Community (EC) have set January 1, 1993, as the date for establishing a linked economic system free from **tariffs** and other trade barriers. These nations will form the world's largest trading bloc. The former Communist nations of Eastern Europe have shown interest in joining the EC. Across the Atlantic the United States and Canada established a free-trade agreement in 1988. The United States and Mexico were discussing a similar agreement, signaling the possibility of a huge North American trade zone.

These changes show the increasing integration of the global economy during the 1980s. More and more businesses built factories and sold their products in more and more countries. Businesses from various nations also worked together to create factories and make products. The value of U.S. exports, for example, jumped by more than 65 percent during the 1980s, and its imports nearly doubled. As a result of this global trend, disputes over trade barriers often drew more international concern than did border feuds.

Global economic interdependence has also brought problems, however. **Recessions** now affect many nations at the same time, as the world community discovered during the recession of 1980 to 1982. Nations worried about foreign companies controlling jobs or finances in their own countries. Balance of trade or debt difficulties dogged many nations. For example, the United States was the world's largest creditor nation in 1980. It had become the world's largest debtor nation by 1990, triggering serious challenges for American industry.

The difficulties of many Third World nations showed that high debt can be painful. To help them repay the billions of dollars in debt they owed to Western banks, many of these nations had to impose policies to slow economic growth. But these measures, which included higher prices and fewer social services, harmed their large populations of poor people.

Global Politics

The global village faced other challenges as well. Efforts to control the spread of nuclear weapons have not been completely successful. The United States and Soviet Union took steps to reduce their nuclear arsenals. But at the same time other countries were starting nuclear-weapons programs of their own. Europe and North America feared that these nations might not be controllable in their use of such weapons. Biological and chemical weapons were a growing fear as well.

Bloody civil wars—the worst ones in Lebanon, Afghanistan, Ethiopia, Sri Lanka, and Yugoslavia—erupted as ethnic and religious groups fought to establish separate states. With nations more interconnected than before, these civil wars took on an international flavor, sometimes through terrorism. Arab terrorists exploded Pan Am flight 103 over Lockerbie, Scotland, in 1988, killing all 259 people on board and 22 on the ground. Western hostages were held for years in Lebanon.

▲ Police and fire fighters investigate the wreckage of Pan Am flight 103 in Lockerbie, Scotland.

Violence also increased because of the international drug trade, exacting a high social and human toll. During 1989 alone, for example, assassins killed 50 judges in Colombia.

Global Ecosystem

During the 1980s many nations in the global village realized their common need to protect the environment. Pollution is a worldwide fact. Seas, lakes, and rivers on all continents have been fouled by industrial, medical, and human waste. The burning of forests in the Third World has resulted in

HOSTAGES RELEASED

Late in 1991 a chapter in world terrorism seemed finally to end. Pro-Iranian groups in Lebanon released—over the course of a few months—the last Americans and Britons being held hostage. Some had been taken seven or eight years before. UN secretary general Javier Pérez de Cuéllar, in his last year in office, played a significant role in the hostages' release.

ecological disasters, including the loss of millions of acres of tropical rain forest.

As a result of auto and industrial pollution, the air in some world cities—among them Los Angeles, Mexico City, Tokyo, and Budapest—has become almost unbreathable from smog and pollution. Air pollution can cause worldwide climate changes in a phenomenon called the **greenhouse effect.** Scientists warned that pollution may warm the atmosphere, which could cause a catastrophic 2-foot increase in sea levels by the year 2090.

Acid rain was another environmental problem that knew no political boundaries. Air pollution in the United States was helping to kill trees in Canada and the northeastern United States. Similar effects were being seen across national borders in Europe. Scientists urged political leaders to work together to find global solutions to these problems.

Greenpeace's Environmental Activism

The international environmental group Greenpeace, begun in 1969 in Canada, drew widespread attention for its work during the 1970s and 1980s. Greenpeace used direct and nonviolent actions to halt what it saw as environmental threats, such as commercial whaling, toxic waste dumping, the buildup of nuclear arms, and the clubbing of baby seals.

In 1988 one protest took place outside the home of British prime minister Margaret Thatcher. The two activists in the photograph wore protective clothing and displayed a one-year-old dead seal that may have been contaminated in the North Sea.

THE COLLAPSE OF COMMUNISM

Perhaps the most surprising development of the era was the downfall of communism and dictatorships in Eastern Europe and the Soviet Union. Since 1918 in the USSR and since the late 1940s in Eastern Europe, dictatorships had kept a firm grip on power in nine countries. From the middle of 1989 to the middle of 1991 they were swept from power in almost all of the countries of Eastern Europe and even in the Soviet Union, which ceased to exist as a country by the end of 1991.

The flood of democracy began in Poland. In August 1989 Poland inaugurated its first non-Communist prime minister since World War II. Between that event and the end of the year, overwhelming public pressure led to the driving out of hard-line Communist regimes in Hungary, East Germany, Bulgaria, Czechoslovakia, and Romania. For good reason the miraculous last half of 1989 has been called "The Autumn of the People." By 1991 even the Soviet Union had turned against communism. Even more surprising than these changes was the ease with which they took place.

The Soviet Union

"We are not abandoning our convictions, our philosophy or traditions, nor do we urge anyone to abandon theirs," said Soviet president Mikhail Gorbachev in a historic address before the United Nations General Assembly in 1988. "Let everyone show the advantages of their social system, way of life or values—and not just by words or propaganda, but by real deeds."

Despite Gorbachev's bold statement, what was becoming clear about the Soviet system was not the advantages of communism, but its shortcomings. Under Leonid Brezhnev, who led the nation from 1964 to 1982, industrial output had lagged, and the economy slipped into serious decline. Brezhnev's adventure into Afghanistan, where he started a ten-year commitment of Soviet troops, accomplished little and became a kind of "Soviet Vietnam." After Brezhnev's death Yuri Andropov (1982–1984) and Konstantin Chernenko (1984–1985) led the Soviet Union. Neither managed to alter the course of economic decline.

Gorbachev's ascent to power on March 11, 1985, however, brought changes. Gorbachev, a brilliant and tough politician, quickly assessed his country's economic weaknesses. Gorbachev wrote: "The Soviet Union is the world's biggest producer of steel, raw materials, fuel, and energy, but it suffers from shortages of these crucial goods because of waste and inefficiency. Our rockets can fly to Venus with amazing accuracy," he added, "but many Soviet household goods are of extremely poor quality."

His words were not news to the Soviet people. They often stood in lines for hours to buy basic items like coffee and soap. They waited months or even years to buy shoddy appliances and poorly built cars. The central Soviet government made all the economic decisions. People had little incentive to work hard and produce high-quality goods.

Gorbachev's bold plan to reverse the Soviet decline was revolutionary. To revive the economy his program of *perestroika* (or restructuring) removed many economic decisions from the central government and gave them to plant managers and consumers. His policy of *glasnost* (or openness) allowed free speech and ended censorship by the Communist party. He even made plans for *demokratiztsiya* (democratization), which would gradually allow Soviet citizens to choose officeholders.

The Soviet people embraced *glasnost* with enthusiasm. For the first time in Soviet history, political issues were discussed freely in the press, on radio and television, and in debates at Communist party headquarters, in factories, and on farms. Even the initial skeptics agreed that steps toward democracy had come, too. In 1989 Soviet citizens voted in virtually free elections for the new Soviet parliament. In 1991 voters in the Russian republic elected a president—Gorbachev's rival Boris Yeltsin. Those millions of people were now ruled by an elected leader for the first time in their history.

The new openness had more painful effects as well. Old ethnic

THE STRUGGLE FOR AFGHANISTAN

In 1979 thousands of Soviet troops were sent to Afghanistan, and a puppet regime was installed to suppress rebels in the Muslim population. Although the United States and other Western nations did not take overt action against the Soviet Union, they did not condone its occupation of Afghanistan.

Throughout the countryside, resistance forces waged guerrilla warfare against Soviet troops, who were not prepared for that kind of fighting. As was the case in the Vietnam War, Soviet efforts in Afghanistan proved unsuccessful. Finally, in 1988, under Soviet president Mikhail Gorbachev's direction, Soviet troops were withdrawn from Afghanistan.

Mikhail Gorbachev: Leader Without a Country

"He's a master of words, a master of the art of politics and diplomacy. . . . He's hard, he's tough, he's strong." That was the view of former Speaker of the U.S. House of Representatives Thomas P. "Tip" O'Neill Jr. after a 1985 meeting with Soviet leader Mikhail Gorbachev. The next few years would prove just how perceptive O'Neill's evaluation was.

Gorbachev, a soft-spoken but very direct communicator with an engaging sense of humor, was unlike prior Soviet leaders in many ways. Aged 54 when he took power in 1985, he was the youngest head of the Soviet Union since Joseph Stalin and the first to have graduated from a university. A member of the Communist party since 1971, Gorbachev became a full member of the ruling Politburo in 1980 and head of the Communist party in 1982. He had a master politician's sense of how to play to the crowd and the media—at least in the nations of the West, where he was very popular. His wife Raisa, who holds a Ph.D. in philosophy, played a much more public role than previous Soviet leaders' wives.

The biggest difference between Gorbachev and past Soviet leaders was his vision of the Soviet Union's relationship to the rest of the world. "Today the world's nations are interdependent, like mountain climbers on one rope," Gorbachev said in a 1987 speech in Prague. "They can either climb together to the summit or fall together into the abyss." This view was quite a change from Nikita Khrushchev's vow to the West: "We will bury you."

One of Gorbachev's chief goals was working with other world leaders to achieve peace and security. "The world today is one in which a struggle is under way between reason and madness, morality and savagery, life and death," he explained in a 1986 interview. "We have determined our place in this struggle definitely and irreversibly. We are on the side of reason, morality, and life. That is why we are for disarmament, most notably nuclear disarmament, and for creating a system of general security. This is the only possible way mankind can regain immortality."

Because Gorbachev was very popular in the West, Soviet reactions to the 1991 coup shocked Europeans and Americans. Gorbachev was not as popular at home. His policies had not helped the economy, and shortages of food became even worse under his rule. He had waffled for years between policies favoring reform and those protecting Communist power. Many Soviet citizens blamed him for the coup. The hard-liners who tried to overthrow him were people that he had kept in power.

At first Gorbachev survived, but the forces that he unleashed proved stronger. The Soviet people made it clear that they were fed up with communism, with the Soviet state, and with Gorbachev. By the end of 1991, party, nation, and leader were all gone. On December 25, Gorbachev announced his resignation as leader of the USSR, a nation that—by then—few wanted to preserve. What he would do next was unknown, but it was clear that the people of the USSR—and of Eastern Europe—owed much to his reform policies.

rivalries emerged. The three Baltic republics **annexed** by Stalin in 1940—Lithuania, Estonia, and Latvia—increased their longtime demands for independence. Meanwhile Christian Armenians and Muslim Azerbaijanis fought over land in the mountainous south of the Soviet Union. Other Soviet republics also faced ethnic conflicts or demanded independence.

The End of the Soviet Union

With all these changes the nation's economy worsened. The political situation was dangerous as well. Old-time Communists began to fear the loss of power and privilege. They also worried about the breaking up of the country into many smaller states. In August 1991 these hard-liners, supported by the KGB and the military, launched a **coup** to overthrow Gorbachev. As an anxious world watched, the coup failed, in part because of the courage of a resistance movement led by Yeltsin and the refusal of the army to fire on its own people.

In the aftermath of the coup the old guard lost its power. Gorbachev and the Soviet parliament quickly agreed to grant the Baltic republics their independence and other republics more freedom. Even more remarkable, the Communist party was outlawed. Discredited by years of failure and corruption and hated by a long-suppressed people, the Party seemed to go quietly into the night. But large and well organized, it remained a threat to the fragile Soviet democracy.

In the last months of 1991, the Soviet Union disappeared. One by one, the republics declared independence. Then they formed a loose confederation called the Commonwealth of Independent States. Gorbachev warned that disaster would result from the Soviet Union's breakup. When that breakup happened anyway, he resigned as the president of the now-defunct USSR.

The details of this new confederation were not immediately clear. A central authority was to form a common army and control the nuclear arsenal of the former Soviet Union. But various republics planned to have their own armies as well. Each new state desired economic independence. But the USSR had been built on inter-republic economic links that might prove hard to separate. Ethnic

The Russian Maverick

As Mikhail Gorbachev won over Western nations and gradually reformed the Soviet Union, an aggressive populist politician, Boris Yeltsin (waving above), stole his thunder at home. Yeltsin, who spent three years fighting the Communist party establishment, became the president of the Russian Republic in 1990. He won that election by telling the frustrated Russian people that it was time for a change.

Unlike the more-moderate and smooth-talking Gorbachev, Yeltsin is blunt. He proved that bluntness during the August 1991 coup, when he flatly refused to accept the hard-liners. This refusal helped defeat the coup and added to his own popularity.

Yeltsin used his widespread support to achieve the independence of Russia and engineer the collapse of the Soviet Union. He vowed to institute a program of radical reform. Early steps were to release all farmland from state control into private ownership and to lift price controls. The world wondered whether Yeltsin would remain popular if these actions produced further hardship.

feeling, which led each republic to desire nationhood, remained a problem as ethnic minorities within the republics demanded their own land. Although Yeltsin was the most powerful leader, he did not control all the republics, whose leaders wielded their own power.

Caught between the desire for independence and the need for coordinated action, the new commonwealth faced an uncertain future.

Eastern Europe

Democracy did not happen in Eastern Europe overnight—although at times it seemed that way. The movement began in earnest in 1980, when a group of determined workers at the Gdansk shipyard in Poland formed the Solidarity trade union. It was led initially by Lech Walesa, who won a Nobel Peace Prize for his efforts. Withstanding a Soviet-led crackdown and harsh martial law in the early 1980s, Solidarity at last forced the Communist government of Poland to hold free elections in June 1989. Solidarity won those elections.

▼ Polish strike leader Lech Walesa is carried on the shoulders of fellow workers in the shipyard after an agreement was signed with the top government negotiator on August 30, 1980.

Encouraged by Poland's success, people in other Eastern European nations rebelled against their Communist rulers. "Our jaws cannot drop any lower," remarked one astonished European journalist as he watched one Communist government after another fall. The world worried that the Soviet Union would move to restore the Communists, as it had done in Hungary in 1956 and in Czechoslovakia in 1968. But Gorbachev steadfastly refused to crush the rebellions. "We have no right, moral or political, to interfere in events happening there," he proclaimed to a relieved world.

Events moved even faster in Hungary than in Poland. Less than four months after its parliament agreed to permit independent political parties, Hungary's Communist leader had been overthrown and the nation's border fences torn down. On October 23, 1989, a cheering crowd gathered in the capital of Budapest to hear leaders proclaim the non-Communist Republic of Hungary and announce plans for free elections.

The Berlin Wall—perhaps the most tragic, poignant symbol of Communist Eastern Europe—crumbled on November 9, 1989. This move by the Communist East German government followed weeks of protest by crowds of up to half a million people in several East German cities, most notably Leipzig. Free to travel into West Germany, East German crowds continued to protest until the Communist leaders stepped down. A new government announced that free elections would be held the following spring.

By mid-November 1989 the flourishing freedom movement in Bulgaria forced Communist leader Todor Zhivkov to resign. Czechoslovakia's Communist party was deposed on December 10, after months of rallies and protests. Only in Romania did the transfer of power turn bloody. Violent street battles between prodemocracy forces and President Nicolae Ceausescu's private security forces cost between 7,000 and 10,000 lives. At the climax of the "Christmas revolution," rebels captured Ceausescu and his wife, sentenced them to death in a secret trial, and executed them immediately.

By the dawn of the 1990s the postwar shape of Europe had been radically changed. Gorbachev's move toward reform, openness, and democracy in the Soviet Union had spawned revolutions in Eastern Europe. But tough days filled with new challenges remained ahead. The new democracies needed to modernize their economies and take their place in the new world of the 1990s.

Ethnic conflict also threatened a number of these nations. Slovaks resented what they saw as domination by Czechs, for instance. But the most bitter conflict came in Yugoslavia, a nation of many ethnic groups with old grudges against each other. The site of nationalist fervor that had exploded into World War I, Yugoslavia was torn by a civil war that began in 1991 and seemed without solution.

One Germany, Again

A year of dramatic upheaval in Eastern Europe reached an exciting climax on November 9, 1989. That day the East German Communist regime lifted all travel and emigration restrictions on its citizens. Within hours, thousands of Germans from both the East and West gathered at the Berlin Wall. Some sat atop the barrier that had separated the city since 1961. Others streamed through to greet friends and family. Many dared to dream: was it possible that the tide of change could end the political division of Germany as well?

Behind the Iron Curtain: The Fall of Communism in Eastern Europe

Date	*Country: Events*
Jan. 1989	**Hungary:** Parliament allows independent parties.
May 1989	**Poland:** Solidarity union legalized. **Hungary:** Barbed-wire border with Austria opened; Communist leader Janos Kadar ousted after 33 years.
June 1989	**Poland:** Solidarity sweeps first open parliamentary elections.
Aug. 1989	**Poland:** Solidarity's Tadeusz Mazowieki becomes first non-Communist prime minister since World War II. **East Germany:** Citizens begin escaping to West through Hungary and Czechoslovakia.
Sept. 1989	**East Germany:** Hungary allows free access to West Germany for East Germans, triggering flood of refugees.
Oct. 1989	**Hungary:** Republic declared. **East Germany:** Street protests mount in cities; Egon Krenz takes over Communist party leadership from unpopular Erich Honecker; over 200,000 have now fled country.
Nov. 1989	**East Germany:** Berlin Wall opened. **Bulgaria:** Communist leader Todor Zhivkov resigns after 35 years.
Dec. 1989	**East Germany:** Communist leadership steps down. **Czechoslovakia:** Communist party falls; reformer Vaclav Havel becomes president. **Romania:** Popular uprising defeats forces of Nicolae Ceausescu, Communist president since 1967; Ceausescu and wife executed; former Communist Ion Illiescu becomes president.
Jan. 1990	**Yugoslavia:** Communist party allows formation of other political parties. **Poland:** Communist party dissolved.
Mar. 1990	**East Germany:** Free elections (first ever). **Hungary:** Free elections.
May 1990	**Romania:** Free elections (first since 1937).
June 1990	**Bulgaria:** Free elections; communists win majority under name of Socialist party. **Czechoslovakia:** Free elections (first since 1946).
Oct. 1990	**East Germany:** East Germany and West Germany reunite after 45 years; capital of Federal Republic of Germany moves to Berlin.
Dec. 1990	**Poland:** Lech Walesa elected president.
July 1991	**Yugoslavia:** Croatia and Slovenia declare independence; country becomes engulfed in civil war.

Terrorist Attack on the Pope

Karol Wojtyla, a Pole, was elected pope in 1978. He took the name John Paul II to honor his predecessor. He was the first non-Italian pope since the sixteenth century and the first Polish pope.

Since the beginning of his papacy John Paul has visited countries throughout the world, making him the most widely traveled pope ever. His visits are greeted by large and enthusiastic crowds.

On May 13, 1981, Pope John Paul was shot while driving in his open-topped vehicle among 10,000 pilgrims in Vatican City. He was rushed to a hospital, where a five-hour operation saved his life. The would-be assassin was a Turkish terrorist, who was tried, convicted, and sentenced to life imprisonment.

The pope quickly recovered and resumed his worldwide travels.

It happened sooner than anyone could have imagined. In less than a month West German chancellor Helmut Kohl proposed a plan to unite the two Germanys. But Kohl insisted on waiting to negotiate details until after East German elections in March 1990. He supported "the right of the German people alone" to choose their form of relationship.

In those elections the conservative Alliance for Germany won by a huge margin. Supported by Kohl, the Alliance favored rapid reunification of the two Germanys. That change took place at a dizzying speed. On May 18 finance ministers of East and West Germany signed a treaty to create a unified monetary system based on the West German currency, the mark. By July the two nations had merged their economic systems.

Finally, at midnight on October 2, 1990, the reunification of East and West Germany was complete. The new nation is known as the Federal Republic of Germany, formerly the official name of West Germany. It has Europe's largest population, 78 million. It also boasts the largest European economy, producing more than $1 trillion of goods and services each year. The new nation's military has more than 600,000 troops, 8,000 tanks, and 800 combat planes. Once again, a strong Germany dominates central Europe.

Yet questions remain. Can the German economy take on the staggering burden of the former East Germany's outdated industries, massive unemployment, and widespread pollution? Can the East Germans be moved into that economy without suffering? Will a united Germany dominate the EC? What role will once-aggressive Germany, now part of NATO, play in the postcommunist world?

PLANNING FOR EUROPE '92

The idea of a "United States of Europe" is not new. In fact, a French statesman put forward a plan to unite Europe shortly after the end of World War II. In the late 1980s that dream began to become a reality. The economic union called the European Community (EC) began to plan for a free-trade zone in Western Europe. "Europe '92" was on everyone's lips, because 1992 was the year that this historic union would begin.

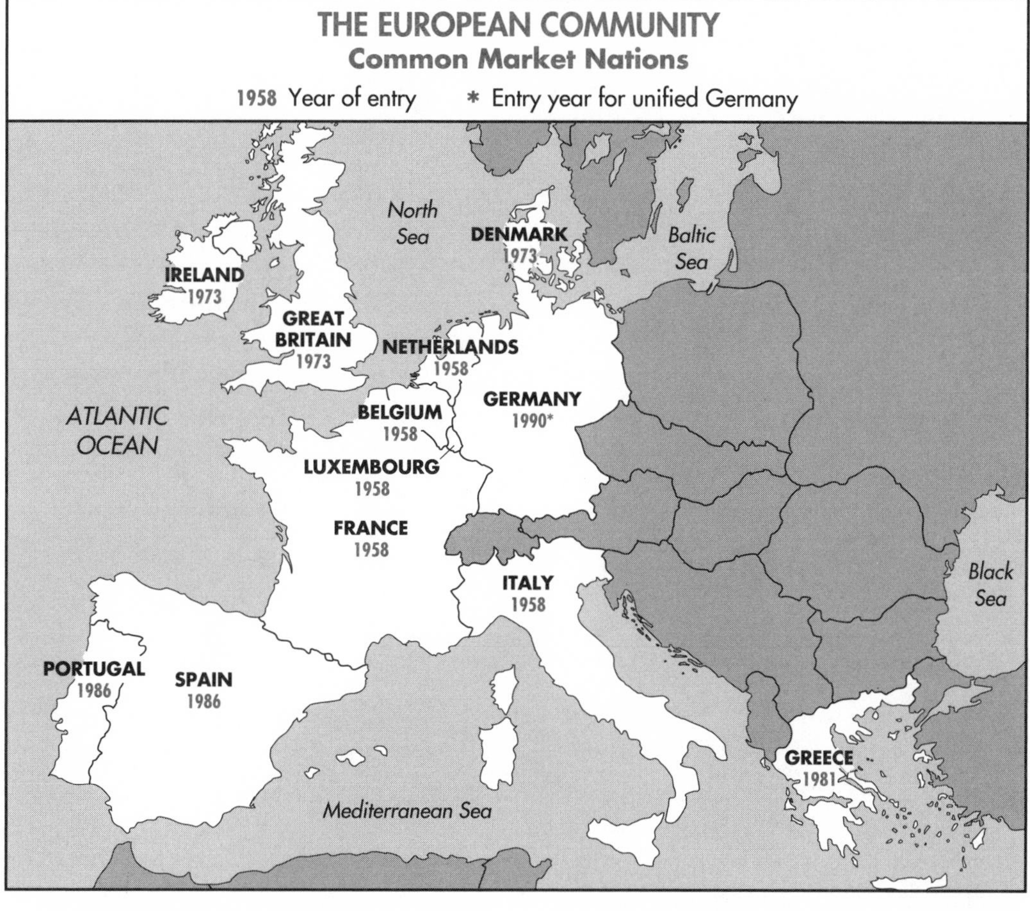

◄ The European Community is composed of 12 countries. Although West Germany was one of the original countries in 1958, it was not until 1990 that all of Germany became a part of the economic union.

The EC was formed of 12 nations of Western Europe. It began in 1958 as an organization called the Common Market. The first members were Belgium, France, Italy, Luxembourg, the Netherlands, and West Germany. Its goal was to join the economies of these nations by removing tariffs and other trade barriers. Three other nations—Denmark, Ireland, and Great Britain—joined in 1973. Greece was added in 1981 and Spain and Portugal in 1986.

In the mid-1970s the move toward a united Europe gained unstoppable momentum. In 1978 member nations established the European Monetary System, which made currency exchange rates more stable and created an official European currency unit. The following year member nations held their first direct elections to select representatives to the European Assembly. This legislative body was to make laws that all member nations would obey.

During the 1980s the march toward European unity was led—and sometimes opposed—by three key leaders of Western Europe. Margaret Thatcher, the Conservative prime minister of Great Britain from 1979 until 1990, was a forceful leader. She advocated free trade among EC nations, but feared that Britain's identity might be lost in a united Europe.

She especially opposed the creation of "an area with no internal frontiers" called for by the Single European Act of 1986. She feared that such openness would give

WAR IN THE FALKLANDS

The Falkland Islands, located in the South Atlantic east of the southern tip of South America, have been the object of disputes between Great Britain and Argentina since the 1700s. Armed conflict between the two countries was avoided for decades, but on April 2, 1982, Argentine forces seized the islands.

Britain responded by sending a fleet and imposing a sea blockade around the islands. During the first few weeks of fighting, the British seized one of the islands and sank an Argentine cruiser.

Before the end of May the British had a strong hold on East Falkland and were advancing on Stanley, the islands' capital. The war was over on June 14 when Argentina surrendered. In 74 days of fighting, 256 British soldiers and 712 Argentine soldiers died.

drug traffickers, illegal immigrants, and international terrorists free access to Britain. Many Britons agreed with her EC policy for some time. But she was forced to resign in 1990 in part because her nation had become more willing to unite with Europe. Her successor, John Major, leaned more than she in that direction.

French president François Mitterrand, the Socialist leader of France since 1981, enthusiastically supported the EC. Reelected in 1988 to a second seven-year term as president, Mitterrand used his diplomatic skill to press for greater economic unity of EC nations. At the same time, he reformed the French welfare and banking systems, **nationalized** key industries, and decentralized many government functions.

Helmut Kohl, since 1990 the chancellor of the unified Germany, emerged as a leading spokesman

Margaret Thatcher: The "Iron Lady"

▲ Margaret Thatcher waves from the steps of No. 10 Downing Street after arriving officially to take up residence.

Her admirers called Margaret Thatcher the "Iron Lady" because of her unbending will and forceful leadership. Her opponents called her by other names, including "Attila the Hen" and "Thatcher the Milk Snatcher." The latter dates from early in the 1970s, when—as secretary for education and science—she abolished a free-milk program for schoolchildren. One reporter described her as "perhaps the most admired, hated, fascinating, boring, radical, and conservative leader in the Western World."

Whatever she was called, Thatcher left a clear mark on Britain and the world. Trained as a research chemist, Thatcher served as prime minister from 1979 until 1990, the longest continuous period in British history anyone has held the post. The Falkland Islands War of 1982, in which Great Britain defeated Argentina, helped her remain popular.

Her conservative views, known as "Thatcherism," led her to cut taxes, remove government wage and price controls, end subsidies of inefficient industries, and sell many state-owned businesses and housing units. Her success in curbing the strength of Britain's powerful labor unions is viewed by the British business community as her most lasting achievement. But her direct, sometimes abrasive style offended some people. On the global scene, Thatcher's close relationships with U.S. presidents Ronald Reagan and George Bush, and Soviet president Mikhail Gorbachev, made her a potent force in international affairs.

Always, she carried in her wallet these words of Abraham Lincoln, her manifesto: "You cannot strengthen the weak by weakening the strong. . . . You cannot help men permanently by doing for them what they could and should do for themselves."

for Europe in the 1990s. Given Germany's history of aggression, however, many in other countries viewed with concern his calls for increasing German independence on certain economic and military matters.

As Europe approaches the critical date of 1992, it faces a decade of promise and challenge. With a population of more than 300 million, the EC makes up the world's richest free-trade zone and enjoys great opportunities for economic growth. But problems loom as well. A number of member nations must deal with ethnic groups who demand separate states. These groups appear in Northern Ireland, Corsica, and the Basque region of Spain in particular. Another problem is the thousands of refugees that arrive every day from Eastern Europe, Africa, and the Middle East. Also, the crippled economies of Eastern European countries demand help.

The changes in Eastern and Western Europe during the 1980s were breathtaking. But hard work remains to be done to make Europe secure and to keep its people free and its unity lasting.

TURMOIL IN THE MIDDLE EAST

The Middle East has always been a political hot spot. The region is home to the human family's most persistent ethnic and religious feuds. Jerusalem, for example, is a holy city for three world religions—Judaism, Christianity, and Islam. Palestine is regarded by both Jews and Arabs as their ancient homeland. In addition, the Persian Gulf and the Suez Canal are crucial shipping lanes for merchant ships of all nations, especially since two-thirds of the world's petroleum reserves lie in the Middle East.

A Time of Change

Between 1976 and 1991 this region remained troubled. No major war erupted between Israel and its Arab neighbors. But the area nevertheless was the site of violence and strife. Civil war plagued Lebanon, and internal protests rocked Israel. Iran and Iraq fought a long and bloody war, and Iraq suffered defeat at the hands of a **coalition** of nations led by the United States. Terrorism sponsored by the Palestine Liberation Organization (PLO) and by pro-Iran Muslim groups in Lebanon struck innocent people around the world.

Political alignments shifted. The United States became mindful of the need to protect the supply of oil, much of which was controlled by Arab nations. Thus, it began to shift from a strongly pro-Israel policy to a more balanced view. Under Gorbachev, the Soviet Union began to shift from its strong pro-Arab position to a more balanced stand as well. Iran moved from being a staunch U.S. ally to a bitter enemy and from there to an uncertain status. Iraq shifted from U.S. friend to enemy.

Most hopeful, the period saw prospects for peace. Egypt's Anwar Sadat and Israel's Menachem Begin signed a peace treaty in 1979. In this agreement—the Camp

BENAZIR BHUTTO LEADS PAKISTAN

In December 1988 Benazir Bhutto became the first elected leader in Pakistan in more than a decade—and the first woman leader of a modern Islamic nation.

Bhutto, the daughter of slain prime minister Zulfikar Ali Bhutto, was educated at Radcliffe College in the United States and at Oxford University in Great Britain. She returned to Pakistan in 1977, just before her father was overthrown in a coup. Two years later her father was executed, and Benazir Bhutto swore to avenge his death.

She was repeatedly arrested and detained for her opposition to the military dictator General Mohammad Zia ul-Haq. Finally Zia put an end to martial law and called for elections. When Bhutto's party won a majority, she became prime minister.

Bhutto faced huge challenges in office. When she was unable to deliver on her promises for prosperity, education, and social change, unrest began. It grew into violence, which spread into many areas. Finally, Pakistan's president dismissed Bhutto and called for a new government to be formed. Bhutto tried to regain the post in a 1990 election, but lost.

"Ring the bells for your sons. Tell them that those wars were the last of wars and the end of sorrows."

—Anwar Sadat, 1977

"The time of the flight between Cairo and Jerusalem is short . . . [but] the distance between them . . . until yesterday, quite large. . . . Sadat passed this distance with heartfelt courage . . . . We, the Jews, know how to appreciate this courage."

—Menachem Begin, 1977

David Accords—Israel gave back all of the Egyptian territory it had taken after the 1967 war. But that nation's longtime refusal to consider returning any other land or to allow the creation of a new state for Palestinian Arabs hampered other efforts at peace.

Finally, U.S. secretary of state James Baker arranged a peace conference for October 1991. It was planned to include all interested parties—Arabs, Israelis, and Palestinians—and to address all issues. The initial meetings—in Madrid, Spain—produced no major breakthroughs for peace. Observers were encouraged, however, by some signs of compromise from a number of parties. Also hopeful was the fact that all participants agreed to join in further talks.

Revolution in Iran

After a period of westernization in the 1960s and early 1970s, the Iranian people grew restless under the harsh rule of Shah Mohammad Reza Pahlavi. By 1979 the shah, a close ally of the United States, was driven from power. In his place was a fundamentalist Muslim religious leader, Ayatollah Ruhollah Khomeini. The new leader declared Iran an Islamic republic. Bitter at American support for the shah, he labeled the United States the "Great Satan."

▶ After Shah Mohammad Reza Pahlavi was driven from power in Iran, demonstrators pulled down the statue of his father, Reza Shah.

Inflamed by intense anti-U.S. sentiment, Iranian students seized the U.S. embassy in Tehran in November 1979. The ayatollah ordered that the 52 American inhabitants in the embassy be taken hostage. These Americans were held for more than one year, destroying the presidency of Jimmy Carter and inflaming passions against Iran. They were not released until Ronald Reagan was sworn in as president.

Meanwhile a 1980 border dispute with Iraq's president Saddam Hussein over control of a key waterway erupted into a full-scale war—which lasted eight years. To the surprise of experts, Iran's somewhat ragtag army fought the Iraqi invaders with great skill. Despite losing a million troops, Iran's tenacity—and American-built jets purchased in the days of the shah—forced Iraq to accept a UN-sponsored cease-fire.

The devastation caused by the war, however, along with the anti-Western economic policies of the ayatollah, almost destroyed the Iranian economy. When Khomeini died in 1989 he was replaced by a more moderate regime. Those leaders took immediate measures to strengthen ties with the West and rebuild the war-torn nation.

Israel and the *Intifada*

The promise of peace raised by the Camp David Accords was lost soon afterward. Prime Minister Begin took three steps that the Arabs viewed as hostile. First was a 1980 announcement that the entire city of Jerusalem—occupied by Israel since 1967—was now Israel's. Second, in 1981, Israel claimed legal and political authority in Syria's Golan Heights, also taken in the 1967 war. Finally, throughout the period, Begin promoted Israeli settlements in the occupied West Bank (Jordan had controlled the West Bank from 1948 to 1967 and considered it Jordanian territory). In response, the PLO resumed bloody terrorist attacks against Israeli targets. Israel fought back, invading PLO bases in Lebanon (1982) and bombing PLO headquarters in Tunisia (1985).

Palestinian anger at Israel exploded in the 1987 *Intifada*, an uprising against Israeli control. Before long, the *Intifada* developed into a deadly daily ritual. Arabs hurled stones and Molotov cocktails at Israeli soldiers or civilians. Soldiers responded with tear gas or bullets or both. Clashes between demonstrators and soldiers led to death. In 1987 Jordan gave up its claim to the territory. *Intifada* leaders declared a Palestinian state.

The United States has been actively involved in a search for peace in the Middle East. Traditionally, however, both sides have refused to sit down with each other. Political conflicts within Israel block concessions that the Arabs want. Also, rising tides of Jewish immigrants from Ethiopia and the USSR—who are often settled in occupied territories—make the situation more difficult. The U.S. efforts for peace have in some cases angered the Israelis, who feel that they are being abandoned.

Earthquake Kills Thousands in Armenia

On December 7, 1988, an earthquake struck the Soviet republic of Armenia, killing 55,000 people and destroying whole cities. Soviet president Mikhail Gorbachev cut short his visit to America to lend aid to the Armenian people.

In the photograph above, an Armenian child riding a donkey and his father walk alongside the debris of a house one month after the earthquake.

The Destruction of Lebanon

Lebanon, once a jewel at the east end of the Mediterranean Sea, has been destroyed by repeated conflict. For 15 years a bloody civil war has engulfed the nation. The war pitted the mostly Muslim Nationalist Movement against the mostly Christian Lebanese Front.

Over time, however, the conflict drew in many outsiders. The PLO fought on the side of the Muslims. Syria, failing to recognize Lebanese independence and claiming the territory as part of greater Syria, sent troops but kept changing sides. Israel sent soldiers and warplanes on a number of occasions.

"This is the first day of the government of God."

—Ayatollah Khomeini, 1979

Their goal was to destroy PLO bases in southern Lebanon. In their wake, they left a Christian army in the southern region of the country. Even the United Nations sent forces, although their job was to maintain the peace.

Meanwhile constant fighting reduced the once beautiful capital city of Beirut to rubble. Its population shrank from 1.5 million to 150,000. Most of the people simply fled for their lives. The Christian president-elect of Lebanon, Bashir Gemayel, was assassinated in a bombing in 1982. The following year hundreds of Americans died when Muslim terrorists blew up the U.S. embassy and the headquarters of a Marine peacekeeping force.

The carnage reached a peak in 1989 when Christian general Michel Aoun launched a "war of liberation" against Syrian forces, now backing the Nationalists. Between March and November nearly 1,000 people died. Among them was Rene Moawad, a new president. He, too, had been assassinated, after serving only 17 days in office.

When Aoun was defeated in late 1990, however, peace seemed possible once again. Omar Karami became prime minister of a new government of national reconciliation. But Lebanon's bloody disputes and the regional conflicts surrounding it will not be resolved easily.

▼ During the Gulf War all of Kuwait's 950 producing oil wells were set on fire or damaged by Iraqi sabotage or allied bombings.

The Persian Gulf War

Iraq added another violent chapter to the often-bloody saga of the Middle East. In August 1990 Iraq, under President Saddam Hussein, invaded Kuwait, a tiny but wealthy Arab neighbor to the south. Hussein accused Kuwait of conspiring with the United States to hold down the price of petroleum. Iraq desperately needed higher oil revenues to pay its debts and rebuild its economy after the long war with Iran.

International reaction was swift and decisive. Within weeks, a U.S.-led coalition of Western and Arab nations began a massive military buildup in neighboring Saudi Arabia. The force eventually included more than 800,000 troops opposing the million-man Iraqi army.

In November the United Nations authorized "all necessary means" to oust Iraq from Kuwait. It set a deadline of January 15, 1991, for Iraq to leave or suffer the consequences. As the deadline approached, the consequences became clear. President Bush rallied the support of other world leaders to back the use of force. The U.S. Congress voted to approve the use of force against Iraq as well. There was a flurry of diplomatic activity as the deadline neared, but Iraq's Saddam Hussein steadfastly refused to give up his hold on Kuwait.

On January 16, coalition forces began a devastating air assault—code-named Operation Desert Storm—against Iraqi positions in Kuwait and southern Iraq. They also attacked Iraqi communications and other facilities in the capital of Baghdad and other cities. The air attack went on at a furious pace for more than a month, with thousands of missions flown every day. By destroying Iraq's radio communications and bombing runways, the forces were able to control the air and fly at will.

The ground phase of the campaign began on February 23. It lasted a mere 100 hours, as coalition forces swiftly encircled the Iraqis. The attack left more than 100,000 Iraqi soldiers dead, thousands of tanks and vehicles destroyed, and thousands of Iraqi civilians dead. Iraqi soldiers surrendered in thousands. President Bush declared a cease-fire on February 27. The coalition got the remaining Iraqi troops to leave Kuwait and restored that country's government.

The postwar situation was confusing, however. Bush had hoped that the Iraqi people would overthrow Saddam Hussein and thus stopped short of an invasion of Iraq. But U.S. failure to support rebellions that sprang up shortly after the war ended left Hussein still in power. A skillful survivor who may still have some devastating weapons, Hussein remains a serious obstacle to lasting peace in the region.

CONFLICT AND CHANGE IN AFRICA

Between 1957 and 1968, 37 nations gained independence in Africa, a region long dominated by European powers. Once free from foreign rule, however, the new nations faced many problems, including undeveloped economies, widespread disease, and drought-induced famines. In the 1980s the World Health Organization estimated that 160 million Africans suffered from malnutrition and disease, including AIDS, a disease that is **epidemic** in some African nations.

Civil War and Famine

Another deadly problem for Africa was a bloody chain of civil wars. The fighting paralyzed economic development; produced mass starvation, hunger, and disease; and forced millions to become refugees. The Ethiopian government, led first by Emperor Haile Selassie, then by communist president Mengistu Haile Mariam, had fought independence rebels in the provinces of Eritrea and Tigre since 1962. In 1991 the rebel forces finally seized control of the capital city, Addis Ababa, and set up a new government.

In the meantime, however, millions of Ethiopians died in combat or from combat-related famines. Droughts in 1984–1985 and 1989 added to the suffering. The problem became worse with Mengistu's 1990 decision to block delivery of relief supplies in an effort to starve out the rebels.

THE IRAN-IRAQ WAR

Throughout the Persian Gulf War the United States was vocal about its opposition to Iraqi leader Saddam Hussein. What many Americans did not realize, however, was that the United States supported him during the Iran-Iraq War in the 1980s.

Iraq started the war on September 17, 1980. Hussein announced that a long-standing border agreement was void and mounted a full-scale invasion of Khuzistan, an Iranian border province. His goal was to seize oil-rich territory and to weaken the power of Iran's Ayatollah Khomeini.

Iran resisted the invasion, and two years later Iraq withdrew. It tried to gain a cease-fire, but the Iranians answered with their own invasion. The war, which lasted eight years, was bloody and hurt the economies of both countries. Oil and port facilities were shattered in the fighting.

In Sudan a civil war between the Muslim majority and the Christian minority began in 1983. As many as 1 million refugees uprooted by the fighting died from hunger, 250,000 in 1989 alone. By the end of 1989, 2.2 million refugees had abandoned their homes in southern Sudan, Ethiopia, Eritrea, and Chad. They had little hope for peace—or even for survival. Governments in the region had few resources, war further disrupted farm production, and the prospect of new droughts and more fighting clouded the future.

A civil war between the leftist government and right-wing **guerrilla** forces began in newly independent Mozambique in 1976. The U.S. government estimates that the right-wing guerrillas, in an effort to terrorize the population, killed 100,000 people between 1987 and 1989. They also destroyed the economy by burning farms and towns.

New Hope in South Africa

South Africa, a wealthy standout on this generally poor continent, also endured a struggle for political change. But the results may be more promising.

Since 1912 the black-led African National Congress (ANC) has fought to end the all-white government's control of the nation. Although they constitute only 5 million of South Africa's 31 million people, white South Africans retained power. The keystone of their power was **apartheid,** a system of legal segregation and discrimination. Blacks could not vote or travel freely. They were forced to live in wretched housing in all-black "homelands," which were territories that the whites decided blacks could call their own. Black workers were restricted to dangerous mining jobs and menial service jobs.

During the 1970s defense of and opposition to apartheid became more organized and violent. In 1976, for example, 400 people died when riots erupted in Soweto and other black townships. The government jailed many critics, including Stephen Biko. When Biko died the following year in police custody, a storm of international protest was unleashed.

When P. W. Botha became prime minister in 1979, he began a decade-long program of slow reform. His government made black labor unions legal for the first time. Laws restricting the movement of blacks were repealed in 1986, and blacks were granted limited property rights in some areas. Yet the homelands policy continued, and in 1987 a new constitution denied blacks the right to vote in national elections.

The situation remained tense. Several times during the mid-1980s the white government declared a state of emergency to put down the rising tide of black protest. International pressure to end apartheid grew. More and more nations imposed economic boycotts and political sanctions on South Africa.

In 1989 F. W. De Klerk replaced Botha as prime minister. After a cautious start, De Klerk moved more aggressively to remove the laws that he called the "cornerstones" of apartheid. Among these was the very foundation of the system—the law that forced people to

FIRST RIOTS IN SOWETO

Violent uprisings occurred during the summer of 1976 in the black township of Soweto, near Johannesburg, South Africa. In June, 2,000 secondary school students went on strike to protest the required use of the Afrikaans language—the language of one group of the dominant whites in South Africa. A demonstration was broken up by the police, and a 13-year-old boy was shot and killed, triggering violence in Soweto and elsewhere.

By the end of June nearly 1,300 people had been arrested. Property damage in Soweto was estimated at $20 million, and almost every public building had been destroyed.

register as white, black, or colored. The last official apartheid law was repealed in June 1991, although apartheid still exists in the electoral system, which denies blacks the vote.

De Klerk also opened up political avenues for blacks. He lifted the 30-year ban on the ANC, released 1,500 nonviolent political prisoners, and ended most press censorship. Yet the white government remains. While a new constitution is being debated, whites are reluctant to yield their power to the black majority.

In fact, conservative whites have started a proapartheid backlash. And even as De Klerk met with black leaders to discuss a new political order, a long-standing feud continued between two black

Nelson Mandela: Antiapartheid Crusader

◀ Nelson Mandela and his wife, Winnie, salute supporters as he leaves Victor Verster Prison after almost 27 years of imprisonment.

February 11, 1990, was, in the words of a South African radio announcer, "the moment that a majority of South Africans, and the world, have been waiting for." Nelson Mandela, sentenced in June 1964 to life in prison for his unrelenting crusade to abolish apartheid in South Africa, emerged from the Victor Verster Prison Farm near Cape Town, free at last. As he waved to the crowd of wildly cheering supporters, a broad smile spread across his face. Then he raised his clenched fist in the sign of victory.

Mandela joined the African National Congress (ANC) in 1944, four years before the white National party came to power and legalized apartheid, South Africa's system of racial segregation. For 20 years Mandela worked tirelessly toward the ANC's goal of "a free, independent, united, democratic and prosperous South Africa." The white government charged him with sabotage, treason, and conspiracy and jailed him for life.

During his 27 years of imprisonment the former heavyweight boxer and long-distance runner never lost hope. "I know that my cause will triumph in the end," he told a visitor. Mandela became the world's most celebrated political prisoner, a symbol of hope in the fight to end apartheid in South Africa and injustice around the world.

After his release Mandela played a key role in negotiating with De Klerk to abolish South Africa's apartheid laws. He also worked to end the bitter fighting between the ANC and the rival Zulu-based Inkatha movement.

groups. The ANC, led by Nelson Mandela, and the Inkatha movement, led by Zulu chief Gatsha Buthelezi, both sought to be the power to represent the nation's blacks. Fighting among the supporters of the two groups left many dead.

ASIA: LAND OF GIANTS

During the 1970s and the 1980s Asia became a land of giants. Japan's giant economy became the world's leading producer of manufactured goods. China's giant population grew restless under the iron hand of its Communist government. India's giant democratic system threatened to fall apart under pressure from its diverse ethnic and religious groups. All three nations had to confront problems caused by rapid population growth. Many experts believe that the economic future of Asia, which has 56 percent of the world's people but only 30 percent of its land, will be determined by the ability of Asian nations to limit population growth.

Japan and the Mini-Dragons

Japan, whose economy expanded more than 10 percent a year from 1954 to 1972, continued its amazing growth. It developed superior auto, steel, and electronics industries. Led by the probusiness Liberal-Democrats, Japan's economic and trade success made it an increasingly powerful force in global affairs. By 1988 it provided more aid to developing nations than did any country in the world.

Japan's trade policies were under increasing pressure from other industrial nations, however. The United States, in particular, tried throughout the period to get the Japanese to open up their own markets to foreign goods and to restrict the level of exports. Japanese automakers responded by building auto plants in the United States. But the debate over trade policy continued to plague relations between the two nations.

Domestic politics in Japan were in turmoil. A series of financial scandals upset the Japanese government. A number of ministers were forced to resign because they were involved. Growing calls for political reform threatened the longtime rule of the Liberal-Democrats.

South Korea, Taiwan, Hong Kong, and Singapore—the "mini-dragons" of the Pacific Rim—also flexed their economic muscles. Aided by close business relationships with Japan, each became an industrial power in its own right during the 1980s. South Korea, under military rule from 1972 to 1979, endured a difficult transition toward more democratic rule in the 1980s.

The changes to come in Hong Kong were even more profound. In 1984 China and Britain signed an agreement to return full control of Hong Kong to China by 1997.

Southeast Asia

Other nations in the region, including Thailand, Malaysia, Indonesia, and the Philippines, moved more slowly toward indus-

WEALTHY GET WEALTHIER IN JAPAN

By the late 1980s economic fairness was breaking down in Japan. Soaring real estate values, rising stock market prices, and deregulation were all factors in these changes.

A small group of rich people was becoming richer, and the middle class was being squeezed out. A vacant lot cost about 40 times an average person's income—keeping many people, especially the young, from owning property. A three-bedroom apartment in a good district sold for as much as $7 million to $9 million.

trialization. Dictator Ferdinand Marcos ruled the Philippines from 1965 until he was driven out in 1986. The Philippine people then placed in power Corazon Aquino, the widow of an opposition leader who had been assassinated. Economic turmoil and social unrest continues, however, as President Aquino struggles to consolidate her power. The Philippines also showed renewed **nationalism**. In 1991 the Philippine Senate refused to extend the agreement that allowed the United States to lease land for two military bases.

Conflict over Democracy in China

With more than 1 billion people as of 1982, China is the most populous nation on earth. The year 1976, when China's longtime Communist leader Mao Ze-dong (Mao Tse-tung) died, was a turning point for citizens of the Asian giant. An oppressive era of extreme communism and the radical Cultural Revolution ended. A more moderate leader, Deng Xiaoping, took firm control. Under his rule, China made impressive advances in reforming its stagnant economy. He sought investment and technical assistance from Western nations, including the United States. By 1990 China enjoyed a $10 billion trade surplus with the United States, a sign of its growing economic might.

Deng also took steps to reduce tensions with the Soviet Union. He sent tens of thousands of Chinese students to study abroad. He was not prepared, however, to reform the basic structure of China's political system. Foreign visitors and

Political Terror in Southeast Asia

In 1973 a jubilant President Richard Nixon announced to a war-weary America: "We today have concluded an agreement to end the war and bring peace with honor in Vietnam and Southeast Asia." The treaty may have ended U.S. involvement, but it did not end the fighting in the region. The U.S.-supported regimes in Cambodia and South Vietnam could not survive alone. The Cambodian capital of Phnom Penh fell to the Communist Khmer Rouge on April 17, 1975. Saigon, the capital of South Vietnam, fell to the Communist North Vietnamese two weeks later. For some of the people of Southeast Asia, however, their decade-long nightmare grew worse.

This time, however, the horrors came from within. Dictator Pol Pot and his Khmer Rouge forces led a reign of terror in the once-peaceful kingdom of Cambodia. In a drive to create a radical socialist society, they drove city dwellers into the countryside and killed entire families in rural areas. The Khmer Rouge murdered at least a million Cambodians. The Vietnamese invaded Cambodia to do away with Pol Pot—a former ally—in 1979. They departed in 1989 after 10 years of civil war, leaving Cambodians fearful of Pol Pot's return. Finally, in 1991, a peace treaty that included both the Khmer Rouge and Prince Norodom Sihanouk was signed—to be supervised by the United Nations.

▼▼▼

After decades of civil war, political horrors continue to haunt Southeast Asia.

In the 13 years after the Vietnam War ended, more than 1.5 million Vietnamese people fled the Communist regime. Some left legally, but others left as "boat people," in junks, sampans, and fishing vessels. After long stays in Asian refugee camps, about half made it to the United States, but the rest remained without a home. Many were murdered by Thai pirates as they drifted on the high seas. After decades of civil war, political horrors continue to haunt Southeast Asia.

returning students brought Western ways into China. People began to demand more political freedom.

In the late 1980s student groups across China held rallies to promote democracy. The movement spread, and on March 4, 1989, more than 100,000 students and workers staged a march in Beijing to demand democratic reforms. Two weeks later, during a visit by Soviet leader Mikhail Gorbachev, students gathered again to protest. At Beijing's Tiananmen Square, in front of the Great Hall of the People, protesters demanded the removal of Deng and other hard-line Communist leaders.

After a week of student defiance, Deng ordered the army to remove the students from the square. Television pictures, press photos, and newspaper accounts shocked and horrified the world. Infantrymen with automatic weapons shot students. Tanks rolled over helpless bodies. Five thousand students died. Similar attacks were staged in other cities. Some world leaders protested the action with words and economic sanctions, but to no avail. Deng and the hard-liners remained in power.

Religious Conflict in India

Violence also upset India, Asia's largest democracy, during the 1980s. Sikhs in the Punjab region tried to win more autonomy. In 1984, after several years of violence, Indian troops invaded and desecrated the Golden Temple at Amritsar, a Sikh holy place. Indira Gandhi, who served as prime minister from 1971 to 1977 and 1980 to 1984, was assassinated by Sikh bodyguards in response to the army's outrage. In March 1991 her son Rajiv, who had been prime minister after his mother's death, was assassinated as well. As in the Middle East, ethnic and religious conflict persists.

In the meantime India's continuing population explosion slowed the nation's industrial gains. Economic problems led many professionals to leave India, taking their skills elsewhere.

▼ Violence erupted in both China and India in the 1980s. In China more than half a million prodemocracy protesters filed into Tiananmen Square (left) over a month before students were massacred there. In India (right), Prime Minister Indira Gandhi is shown talking to her son Rajiv just a few weeks before she was killed at her residence by two Sikh members of her personal bodyguard force.

DEMOCRACY IN LATIN AMERICA

Since their origins in the nineteenth century, the nations of Latin America have suffered a painful tug-of-war between dictatorship and democracy. This period was no different. Latin America was ruled mostly by military dictators at the end of World War II. A democracy movement in the 1950s left only four military governments in power by 1959—an all-time low. These new democracies were unable to solve the region's most serious problems—poverty, hunger, illiteracy, and unequal distribution of wealth. Eight of them fell to military dictatorships in the mid-1960s. By the 1970s only four Latin American democracies remained: Costa Rica, Mexico, Colombia, and Venezuela.

The Debt Crisis

During these turbulent years many leaders became convinced that industrial development was the key to peace and prosperity. Governments borrowed huge sums of money from banks in the United States and Western Europe to finance economic growth. They sank even deeper in debt during the energy crisis of the 1970s. Oil-poor nations, such as Brazil and Argentina, needed more loans to buy petroleum to fuel their factories and vehicles. Oil-rich nations, such as Venezuela and Mexico, borrowed money to search for more oil and to modernize their industries.

The world recession of the early 1980s caused demand for Latin American products to fall. The region's export earnings declined sharply. At the same time, interest rates skyrocketed. The combined result was disastrous. Brazil, for example, saw the interest payments on its foreign debt shoot from $2.7 billion to $9.2 billion in only three years. And Brazil had no money to pay this interest.

The nations were desperate for relief. In 1985 Peru announced it would limit its debt payment to 10 percent of annual export earnings—about one-third of what it owed. By the early 1990s Latin American nations were still struggling to find ways to pay their debt.

Civil Wars and Renewed Democracy

In addition to economic problems, the region endured several violent civil wars. Some were fought between rival political groups, others between government authorities and powerful drug lords. The civil war in Colombia, ongoing since 1948, was fought first by the Conservative and Liberal parties. Then the M-19 movement, supported by Cuba and other revolutionary groups, entered the conflict. Since the mid-1980s the government has fought against large, well-trained armies maintained by Colombian cocaine dealers. In 1989 the United States sent military advisers and equipment to help fight this drug war.

In Peru the left-wing Shining Path movement has fought savagely against the democratic government of President Alan Garcia. A decade-long war in Nicaragua between U.S.-backed Contras and the ruling Sandinista government

TREATIES GIVE CONTROL OF CANAL TO PANAMA

In 1978 the United States and Panama signed two treaties concerning the Panama Canal. The first guaranteed the canal's neutrality after the year 2000. The second stated that the United States would supervise operation of the canal, with growing Panamanian involvement, until the year 2000. In that year, Panama assumes full control of the canal zone.

President Carter declared that the treaties marked the beginning of a new era of mutual respect and partnership between the two countries.

▲ Using everything from slingshots to automatic weapons, young Sandinista guerrillas battle the forces of right-wing dictator Anastasio Somoza in 1978. The Sandinistas overthrew Somoza the following year.

ended in 1988 as the result of a peace plan presented by Costa Rica. The Reagan administration used Soviet support of the Sandinistas to justify its intervention in the dispute. When Violeta Chamorro defeated the Sandinista president in a stunning 1990 election upset, Nicaragua moved toward democracy. As with other nations, however, Nicaragua had serious economic problems to solve before peace could be ensured.

The civil war in El Salvador, which left 70,000 dead during the 1980s, reached a blood-soaked stalemate between the Cuban-backed leftist guerrillas and the oppressive, U.S.-backed right-wing government. The Salvadoran government and its opponents entered into negotiations in 1991. But the power of the army and the wealthy ruling elite may block a peaceful solution to this conflict.

Democracy did return to some Latin American nations during the 1980s. In 1989 Chile held its first free presidential elections in 16 years. Patricio Aylwin defeated the candidate put forward by General Augusto Pinochet, the dictator from 1973 to 1989. The same year Brazil also held its first direct presidential election in 28 years. After long military rule, both Argentina and Uruguay held their second round of free elections during the 1980s.

Democracy fared less well in Panama, however. Dictator Manuel Noriega voided a 1989 presidential election to stay in power. That December, U.S. troops invaded. They captured Noriega, who was wanted in the United States on drug trafficking charges. They also installed in office the man who won the voided election. Noriega's ties to the CIA and his possible involvement in the Iran-Contra scandal, however, complicated his U.S. trial on drug charges.

Like its Latin American neighbors, Mexico struggled under a heavy foreign debt and a high inflation rate. As a result, the power of the Institutional Revolutionary Party (PRI), which had dominated Mexican politics since 1929, declined. Mexico appears to be moving toward a more democratic multiparty system.

Mexico still suffers from economic problems, however. Thousands of Mexicans leave for the United States each year, seeking better jobs. The free-trade agreement that Mexico is discussing with the United States holds some promise for the future of Mexico's economy.

THE CHALLENGES FACING CANADA

Canada is the second largest country in the world in size. But its population is only 26.5 million, just slightly higher than that of California. The people of Canada have drawn on the rich natural resources of their country—vast timberlands and large deposits of oil, natural gas, and minerals—to build a modern, prosperous economy. Canada's increasingly close economic relationship with the United States posed challenges and potential benefits to both nations.

Three main challenges faced Canada's leaders in recent years. When Liberal party candidate Pierre Elliott Trudeau became Canada's prime minister in 1968, he faced strong pressures from French Canadians to preserve their way of life. Many believed that their French-speaking culture could be preserved only through greater political autonomy. The citizens of Quebec were particularly insistent: "master of our own house" was the slogan of many in the 1960s. In 1976, the Parti Quebecois, a group committed to making Quebec an independent republic, won Quebec's provincial elections.

Although the people of Quebec voted down a proposal for political independence in 1980, the issue persisted. Even a 1982 constitutional reform begun by Trudeau failed to put the issue to rest. Brian Mulroney of the Conservative party became prime minister in 1984 and inherited the problem. He reached an agreement with Quebec three years later. Called the Meech Lake Accord, it recognized Quebec as a "distinct society" with the right "to preserve and promote" its identity. The Accord failed, however, because one Canadian province, under native Indian pressure for similar recognition, withheld approval. The status of Quebec remained unsettled.

Mulroney had far more success in dealing with another issue: Canada's economic relationship with the United States. Canada sells 78 percent of its exports to the United States. Thus, it was angered by trade restrictions and tariffs imposed by the Nixon administration in the early 1970s. After long negotiations Mulroney and President Reagan signed a Free Trade Agreement in 1988. The agreement will end all taxes and trade restrictions between the two nations by the year 2000. It also advocates joint Canadian-American business ventures and lifts controls on trade in key energy products, such as oil, natural gas, coal, uranium, and electricity.

Canada's third challenge is an environmental one. Acid rain has damaged Canadian forests and killed fish in 14,000 Canadian lakes. Much of the damage is caused by waste from power plants and autos in the United States. Finally, in 1989, after ten years of discussions between the two nations, President Bush agreed to cut the U.S. output of emissions that cause acid rain by almost 50 percent before the year 2000. This agreement, along with the free-trade pact, promises to improve an already close relationship between the two nations.

DEATHS

- Mao Ze-dong, Chinese leader, 1976
- Golda Meir, Israeli prime minister, 1979
- Marshall Tito, Yugoslavian leader, 1980
- Leonid Brezhnev, Soviet leader, 1982
- Yuri Andropov, Soviet leader, 1984
- Konstantin Chernenko, Soviet leader, 1985
- Nicolae Ceausescu, Romanian leader, 1989
- Emperor Hirohito, Japanese emperor, 1989
- Ayatollah Ruhollah Khomeini, Iranian leader, 1989
- Ferdinand Marcos, Filipino leader, 1989
- Andrey Sakharov, Soviet scientist, 1989

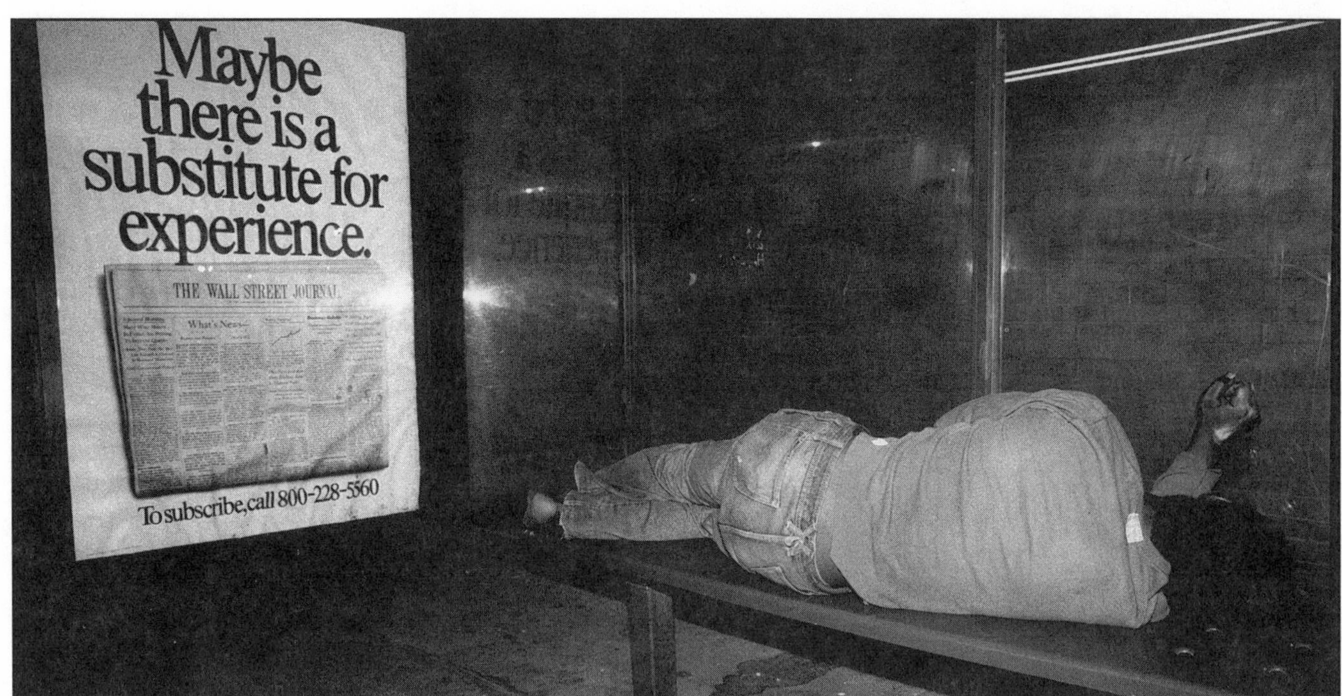

BUSINESS AND ECONOMY

From the mid-1970s to the early 1980s America was mired in a deep recession. When the economy began recovering after 1982, the wealthy and upper middle class prospered while many middle-class and poor Americans had incomes that stayed the same or decreased. As the standard of living fell for many, the gap between the rich and poor grew.

While federal cuts in welfare hurt the unemployed, the demand for unskilled labor fell. Those who could find jobs were often forced to work for low wages and no benefits. Increasing inflation continued to cut into wages, and many workers, especially women and minorities, lived in poverty. Meanwhile, housing prices shot up rapidly.

The homeless population in America soared. By 1990 more than 3 million Americans lived in the streets. Homelessness spread from cities and towns into rural areas that had lost major industries. All over America, soup kitchens and charities sprang up to help this new group of Americans.

On the other side, the greatest economic gains of the 1980s occurred among the richest 5 percent of the population. Almost 100,000 people were worth more than $10 million. And many upper-middle-class Americans who counted themselves in the top 20 percent enjoyed the benefits of the "booming" economy as they earned fortunes from investments, rents, bonuses, and businesses.

AT A GLANCE

- The Economic Roller Coaster
- Companies Experience Changes
- Challenges Facing Industry
- America's Transportation Problems
- The Changing Job Market

DATAFILE

Wealth and productivity	1976	1988
Gross national product	$1.8 tril.	$4.9 tril.
Per-capita income	$6,655.00	$16,497.00
Trade balance		
Imports	$123.5 bil.	$440.9 bil.
Exports	$115.2 bil.	$322.2 bil.
Dow-Jones average	1,014.79	2,168.57
Raw steel output (net tons)	128.0 mil.	99.9 mil.
Auto factory sales	10.1 mil.	10.6 mil.
Labor force	**1979**	**1988**
Total	98.8 mil.	121.7 mil.
Male	58%	55%
Female	42%	45%
Unemployment rate	5.8%	5.5% (1989)
Union membership	13.6 mil.	14.1 mil.
Government	**1976**	**1989**
Federal spending	$371.8 bil.	$1.1 tril.
National debt	$73.7 bil.	$161.5 bil.

MARKET BASKET
Retail Prices of Selected Items, 1983

Bread (1lb.): **$0.54**

Three-minute phone call (New York to Denver): **$0.77** (1991)

Milk (½ gal.): **$1.13**

Car (Toyota Celica Supra): **$18,106.00**

Woman's dress: **$120.00**

Movie ticket: **$3.00**

Man's suit: **$395.00**

Sony Discman **$248.00**

Postage (1st class, 1 oz.): **$0.20**

Electricity (per kilowatt hour): **$0.07**

Economy

THE ECONOMIC ROLLER COASTER

Take the rate of **inflation,** add to it the rate of unemployment, and the result is the "discomfort index"—a measure of national economic pain. In 1965 the index stood at about 6 percent; by 1970 it had climbed steadily to about 11 percent. After a short decline the index shot upward once again. By 1980 it was approaching 20 percent. Many Americans had to live with the deeply disturbing possibility that they might lose their comfortable way of life.

The Sluggish Seventies

Although the nation faced less social upheaval during the 1970s than in the 1960s, the serious economic troubles of the late 1960s carried over into the 1970s. The high costs of the Vietnam War added to President Lyndon Johnson's spending for social programs stretched the economy to its limits. High government spending pushed up the rate of inflation, which was already high. Huge price hikes by the Organization of Petroleum Exporting Countries (OPEC) also contributed to high inflation. **Recession** hit the United States auto industry when consumers fought high gas prices by buying more fuel-efficient foreign cars. Industrial productivity climbed an average 3.3 percent a year between 1947 and 1965, which increased business profits and reduced the cost of products to consumers. In contrast, productivity increased only 0.2 percent between 1976 and

NEW WORDS

golden parachute
junk bond
leveraged buyout
Reaganomics
voodoo economics
white knight

1980—a clear sign of a faltering economy.

Despite two recessions the average American's real income rose 28.5 percent during the 1970s. But household and business debt increased even more, from $94 billion to $328 billion. This sharply rising debt threatened the nation's economic health. Experts endlessly debated the cause of the weaknesses. Some said it was too much government spending, some said it was too little. Others blamed it on too many regulations, too much foreign competition, or too little investment. Many experts proposed plans for recovery, but no one could give guarantees that they would work.

President Jimmy Carter, who took office in 1977, believed inflation to be a greater threat to the nation's economic vitality than either recession or unemployment. To reduce the number of dollars "chasing" the nation's goods and services, Carter made reducing federal spending a top priority. Unfortunately, the spending cuts also increased unemployment. To stimulate the economy Carter eliminated oil price controls, convinced Congress to ease federal control of the nation's banks, and removed regulations on the airline, trucking, and railroad industries. Despite his many efforts the economy was a shambles by 1980.

The Changing Role of Government

Carter's unsuccessful attempts to stimulate the economy opened the door for a dramatic shift in the role of the federal government. For almost 50 years the nation's presidents had followed the strategy advocated by British economist John Maynard Keynes. To stimulate a nation's economy, argued Keynes, the government should increase spending, which creates additional demand for goods and services. Keynes favored raising taxes to fund the spending, arguing that as the economy improved, people's income would rise to cover the increased tax burden.

This view of government's active role in the economy had been popular in the 1960s. In the 1980s, however, more-conservative government leaders shifted attention from social concerns to economic policies. If the economy were healthy, the new thinking suggested, then everyone would be better off. On the other hand, if the economy were to falter, not even the government could provide enough food, shelter, and jobs for everyone.

The Rise of Reaganomics

Ronald Reagan supported this view of government in the 1980s. When he took office in 1981 Reagan promised to make a "new beginning" in the war on economic stagnation. His advisers referred to his approach as **supply-side economics;** critics called it a return to the failed "trickle-down theory" of President Herbert Hoover's era. When George Bush competed against Reagan for the Republican presidential nomination in 1980, Bush called these economic theories "voodoo economics." But later, as Reagan's vice president, Bush supported the policies.

The main feature of Reagan's plan was a five-year, $750 billion tax cut, the largest in the nation's history. The cuts reduced personal income taxes by 25 percent over three years and the maximum tax rate on all income from 75 to 50 percent. The plan, approved by Congress in 1981, benefited mostly wealthy people and corporations. Reagan believed that they would use the money they saved on taxes to build new plants, create new jobs, and make new products. Over time this renewed supply-side economic activity would "trickle down" to benefit the middle classes and even the poor.

The other part of Reagan's attack on economic problems was "to check and reverse the growth of government." Believing that government was too involved in American life, Reagan continued Carter's move to reduce government regulation of business. He also asked Congress to cut billions of dollars from social programs, including school meals, welfare **subsidies,** Medicare, and Medicaid.

Was the "Reagan Revolution" successful? In mid-1981 the nation slipped into a recession that lasted two painful years. Sales of houses dropped sharply. Auto sales fell to their lowest point in two decades. One-third of the nation's factories and mines stood idle. By late 1982 unemployment topped 10 percent, the highest rate since 1940. Farmers and business people were especially hard hit. Unable to make payments on high-interest loans, businesses declared bankruptcy by the thousands. During one week in 1982, 572 businesses failed—the most in a single week since the Great Depression of the 1930s.

By the end of 1982, however, the economic tide turned. Interest rates dropped from a high of 21.5 percent to 10.5 percent, and inflation fell from 12.4 percent to less than 7 percent. Businesses could again afford to expand production. Consumers could afford to increase their spending. The stock market took off like the space shuttle. American companies embarked on a "feeding frenzy" of **mergers** and **acquisitions**. In many cases big corporations used financial pressure to force weak companies to sell out.

Good News and Bad News

Reagan's economic policies radically reshaped the financial landscape of America, but not in every respect for the better. For example, the nation's **gross national product** (GNP) doubled during the 1980s, from \$2.7 trillion to \$5.3 trillion. But the nation's debt almost tripled to its highest point

▼ Although the national debt fell from 1976 to 1979, it skyrocketed in the 1980s to its highest level ever.

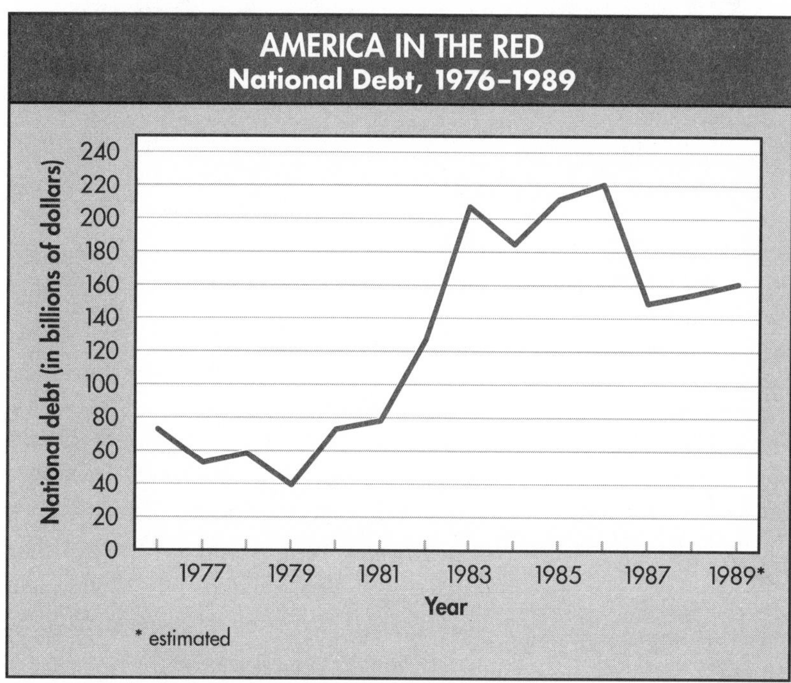

Source: U.S. Office of Management and Budget.

ever. Both Congress and the president made repeated attempts to reduce the national debt, but without success. The prosperity of the 1980s, in other words, was fueled in large part by borrowed money. The new economic policies led to far more **deficit spending** than the old Keynesian economic policy ever had. Year after year, the nation's debt rose as the government spent more than it took in in taxes. The deficits continue to climb, and someday Americans will have to pay for the cost of the 1980s.

During the 1980s America produced new millionaires by the thousands each year. Also, the income of the top 20 percent of American families increased by more than $9,000, to nearly $85,000. But the bottom 20 percent of families saw their income drop by $576, to a meager $8,880. In short, the economic policies of the 1980s increased the differences between the rich and the poor. The rich got richer as the poor got poorer.

Although 20 million new jobs were created, many were low-paying service positions such as serving food in restaurants, cleaning hotel rooms, and working in dry-cleaning businesses. International trade increased in the 1980s, but the United States suffered from a growing **trade deficit.** In 1980 the United States was the world's largest lender; now it is the world's largest borrower. Reagan's policies were continued by the Bush administration, which faced another recession in 1990 to 1991. The United States is still searching for economic policies that will bring an improved living standard to more of its people.

SNEAKER SALES EXPLODE

The 1980s witnessed a fantastic boom in the sales of athletic shoes. As Americans became increasingly fitness conscious, as manufacturers created high-tech shoe designs, and as fashion styles changed, sneaker sales skyrocketed.

Nike and Reebok International Ltd. held the top two spots in the business, and by 1989 newcomer LA Gear was number three. Inflatable shoes that increased ankle support and shoes with honeycomb padding similar to that found in space shuttle seats were sold to willing buyers.

Multimillion-dollar advertising campaigns featuring sports heroes and other celebrities enticed consumers to pay $110 for a pair of Nike "Air Jordans" or $170 for "The Pump" by Reebok. In 1989 the worldwide sports shoe market was worth $7 billion.

Corporations

COMPANIES EXPERIENCE CHANGES

"We all have to have a little greed to progress," corporate takeover specialist Carl Icahn once told a business group in Chicago. "That's a virtue in business." Icahn, famous for his strong-armed takeover of Trans World Airlines (TWA), was a driving force behind the frenzy of corporate takeovers, mergers, and acquisitions that dominated the nation's corporate life in the 1980s. He symbolized the spirit of the era.

What motivated Icahn and others to treat companies like pieces on a chessboard? "What really turns me on is the excitement of it all," he said. Then he added: "I don't care who wins—as long as I do."

The Game of Business

For American corporations, the period between 1976 and 1991 included both crushing recession and dramatic expansion. This economic roller coaster speeded up an already-existing trend toward uniting corporations. Some strong companies bought out weaker competitors. Others expanded by buying companies that supplied them with materials or distributed their products. Still others used their profits to purchase companies in entirely new industries. Weak companies, faced with the threat of bankruptcy, often merged with wealthy corporations.

None of this business activity was new, but it became almost an obsession during the 1980s. Starting in the mid-1970s groups of investors would identify a company

Crisis in the Savings and Loan Industry

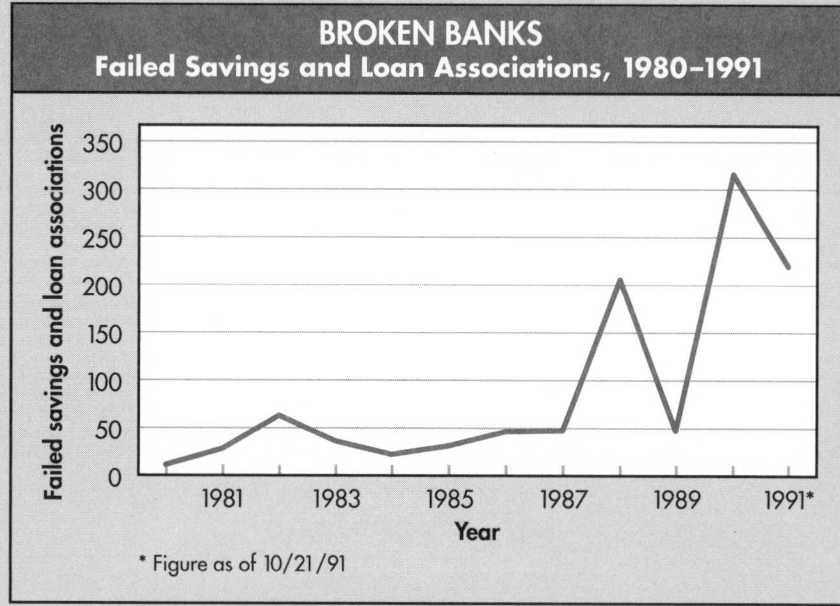

Source: Office of Thrift Supervision, Resolution Trust Corporation.

◄ Although the number of failed savings and loan associations fell temporarily after deregulation in 1982, their numbers skyrocketed in the late 1980s. Overall, the number of failed S&Ls climbed from just 11 in 1980 to 315 in 1990.

For decades, the savings and loan (S&L) industry was a safe, tightly regulated business. Most S&Ls offered savings accounts that paid individual depositors a modest 5.25 percent rate of interest on their money. S&Ls then lent out the depositors' money in the form of home mortgages and other loans. It was a simple and virtually risk-free business because all deposits were insured by the federal government.

In the 1970s, however, interest rates rose to record levels. Depositors could earn far more by investing their money in Treasury bills or money-market funds than by keeping it in an S&L. No longer satisfied with the low 5.25 percent interest, people took their money out of S&Ls. Many S&Ls went out of business. In response to this downturn, the Reagan administration eliminated many of the regulations on the S&L industry so they could compete with other financial institutions.

Changes in the industry came suddenly. Many S&Ls began to offer much higher interest rates to attract new depositors. But as money poured in, the S&Ls made high-risk, high-yield loans. Almost overnight, the S&L business became a high-flying, high-growth, high-risk industry. It just as quickly turned into a national nightmare, as one S&L after another closed its doors.

What went wrong? First of all many S&Ls lent money to individuals and companies for risky real estate ventures and start-up businesses in growth industries. When these ventures failed, the businesses could not repay their loans. Then, when the S&Ls were unable to pay their depositors, the government, through the Federal Savings and Loan Insurance Corporation (FSLIC) and other federal agencies, had to step in and "bail out" the failing S&Ls. To complicate matters, some S&L managers and owners even made loans to themselves and their friends—loans they never paid back.

The amount of money lost was staggering, but the federal government was obligated to cover most depositors' losses. The government agency in charge of the S&L cleanup estimates that the S&L fiasco may cost American taxpayers more than $500 billion—a sum equal to about $2,000 for every citizen. The economic scandal has caused many Americans to question the wisdom of the **deregulation** of important industries.

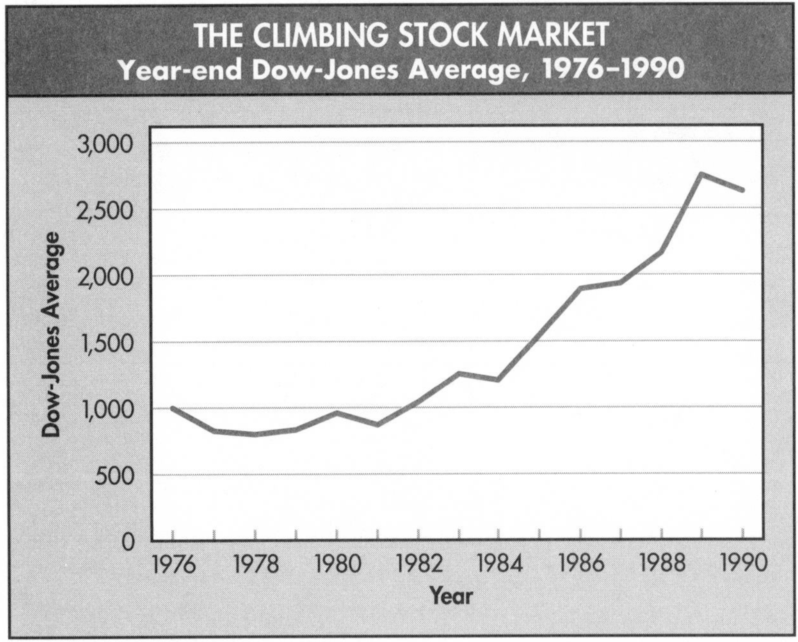

Source: Dow-Jones Public Inquiries.

▲ The Dow-Jones industrial average is the most widely followed indicator of stock-market activity. Although the 1987 year-end closing does not vary widely from 1986 and 1988, the stock market plunged a startling 508 points on October 19, 1987. That day set a record as the worst day in the history of the New York Stock Exchange.

they believed was badly managed or undervalued. Then they would buy enough of the company's stock to launch a "hostile takeover." Sometimes they split the company into several pieces, selling the parts for more than they had paid for the whole. In other cases they kept the company whole and resold it later at a profit.

The trend turned into an explosion, however, with the perfection of a maneuver known as the **leveraged buyout** (LBO). Icahn, for example, quietly bought a small amount of stock (usually 5 to 15 percent of the total stock, but 25 percent in the case of TWA) in a target company. Then he informed the company's managers of his intention to buy more, a move that usually sent the price of the company's stock skyrocketing. At that point, Icahn had several options. He could sell his stock holdings for a hefty profit. Or he could force the company to borrow huge sums of money to buy back his shares at an inflated price—a move that became known as "greenmail" (a legal form of blackmail).

Some companies, when faced with a hostile takeover, sought to merge with a friendly company, known as a white knight, that could save them. TWA, for example, tried to merge with Frank Lorenzo's (another corporate raider) Texas Air Corporation. TWA hoped that the resulting company would be too big for Icahn to buy. The strategy failed, however, and Icahn was able to buy a majority share of TWA stock and seize control of the company.

Business Debts Rise

Where did Icahn and his fellow raiders find the billions of dollars to play this game of corporate chess? Much of the money for LBOs came from so-called junk bonds issued by investment bankers to their customers on behalf of the raiders. The raiders had to pay a high rate of interest because the bonds were not backed by any specific assets. So, whether the takeover succeeded or failed, target companies often faced a heavy debt load.

In 1981 when fewer than $10 billion of leveraged buyouts were announced, American companies owed an average debt equal to 30 percent of their total value. By 1988 when leveraged buyouts topped $200 billion, corporate debt had jumped to 52 percent of the companies' total value. This fast-rising business debt combined with the federal government's huge debt to put the entire economy in jeopardy.

Saddled with huge debts, many companies were forced to put profits into loan repayment. This money might otherwise have been spent on modernizing equipment, developing new products, and other activities that make companies more profitable in the long run. Consequently, American industries found themselves less competitive in global markets than ever before.

The huge gains enjoyed by raiders and shareholders often came at the expense of American workers. When companies merged they often eliminated duplicate operations—and thousands of jobs. If a company reorganized after a hostile takeover, it often cut jobs and shut down less-profitable operations. In many cases raiders also refused to honor a company's labor-union contracts, a tactic that unions were often helpless to resist. Financial experts predict that the legacy of corporate debt from the 1980s will

Vast Fortunes Are Made on Wall Street

◄ Michael Milken (center), king of junk bonds, is escorted to Manhattan Federal Court in New York.

"Greed . . . is good. Greed is right. Greed clarifies, cuts through and captures the essence of the evolutionary spirit. . . . Greed—mark my words—will save the U.S.A."

This passionate opinion, voiced by the fictional corporate raider Gordon Gekko in the 1987 movie *Wall Street*, captures the spirit of excess that dominated the nation during the 1980s. Many top college graduates became merger-and-acquisition specialists, investment bankers, and stockbrokers. Others resisted the lure of power and wealth for two additional years to attend business school and emerge with a Master of Business Administration (M.B.A.) degree.

These creative financial wizards took advantage of decreasing government regulation and devised new ways to make money. They seldom developed better products, services, or companies. Instead, they used questionable financial maneuvers to add to their wealth. High-yield junk bonds were used by some corporate raiders like Ivan Boesky as financing to get huge corporations through leveraged buyouts.

Many people who worked on Wall Street made vast fortunes. Michael Milken, king of junk bonds at the firm of Drexel Burnham Lambert, set the record. He made $550 million in 1987—just before he was charged with and convicted of 98 counts of fraud and other misdeeds.

RISE AND FALL OF DONALD TRUMP

If any figure symbolized the 1980s, it was real estate tycoon Donald Trump. Some thought him a hero or a self-made man, whereas others claimed he was an egomaniac with falsified financial records. His personal life was the mainstay of tabloids and gossip columns.

Trump's reputation for financial wizardry began in the mid-1970s. In New York City he was recognized as having a magic touch—buying seemingly worthless properties, rebuilding them, and making huge profits. His lavish lifestyle began to falter somewhat in 1990. Trump tried to sell his Trump Shuttle airline, his yacht, and other properties to raise cash quickly. Though mired in multimillion-dollar interest payments and negative publicity, Trump still appears destined to come out ahead.

hurt the competitiveness of many American corporations well into the 1990s.

The Entrepreneurs

Not all the economic activity of the 1980s involved giant, billion-dollar corporations. Small corporations created jobs much faster than big corporations cut them. By 1989 the 500 top-selling corporations in the United States had eliminated 2.7 million of the 21 million workers they employed ten years earlier. But total U.S. employment climbed from 99 million to 115 million over the same period, thanks mainly to jobs created by new, smaller corporations. During the recession of 1980 to 1981, for example, companies with fewer than 100 employees created more than 90 percent of all new jobs.

Some of these new companies were run by **entrepreneurs** who had lost their jobs as high-level managers because of corporate takeovers or reorganizations. Others were high-tech innovators, such as Apple Computer founder Steven Jobs and Microsoft's William Gates III.

▶ Apple president John Sculley is surrounded by Apple cofounders Steven Jobs (left) and Steve Wozniak (right) at the unveiling of the new briefcase-size Apple IIc computer in 1984.

Economic and social changes provided other business opportunities. Large corporations, eager to trim costs, called in small specialty firms to provide everything from secretarial to janitorial services. Two-income families increased the demand for day-care centers, restaurants, and quick drive-through auto maintenance centers. Constant advances in computer technology gave rise to a large software industry.

Industry

CHALLENGES FACING INDUSTRY

Everyone recognized that the 1980s had been a time of profound change for American industry. The world had entered the information age. Global economic markets, stiff foreign competition, and high-technology manufacturing had created new challenges for the world's leading industrial powers. Could America respond quickly enough to keep up with rival economic superpowers like Japan and the European Community?

Manufacturing Industries

The most important worldwide economic change was a shift away from low-technology methods of making steel, building autos, and manufacturing consumer goods. Slow to adapt to this change, U.S. companies learned some lessons the hard way. For example, Japanese auto companies seized a major portion of the American small-car market during the energy crisis of the 1970s. American steel manufacturers had to compete against modern, highly automated companies in South Korea and Japan that produced steel that was cheaper and often of higher quality. Other manufacturers were forced to abandon businesses they had pioneered—robotics, televisions, videocassette recorders—because foreign competitors produced these products faster, better, and more cheaply.

To compete in this new global industrial era, American manufacturers had to adopt new, high-technology approaches. These included computer-aided design and manufacturing, computerized inventory systems, and high-tech communications with suppliers and customers. Corporate spending for research and development climbed about 50 percent during the 1980s as companies looked for new ways to build better, cheaper products. Companies also widened their research horizons by cooperating with major universities and foreign laboratories.

These changes had a permanent impact on American society. During the recession of the late 1970s and early 1980s, auto and steel plants in the Northeast and Midwest laid off tens of thousands of workers. Some moved south or west to find employment in the high-tech industries of the Sun Belt. For example, dozens of computer companies set up research facilities and manufacturing plants in the Carolinas, Texas, and California. The spectacular growth of California's "Silicon Valley" region symbolized the aggressive surge of America's new high-tech industrial companies.

An Information Economy

New inventions and processes also altered the American economy in another way. By the 1980s the widespread use of advanced microcomputers and sophisticated communications links changed how companies ran their operations and dealt with their customers. As affordable computers became more powerful and computer networking more commonplace, companies gained almost instant access to valuable information. A grocery-store checkout terminal, for example, could relay detailed sales information to a central computer, which would automatically adjust the store's inventory and compile orders for suppliers. Banks used computerized data links to offer their customers attractive new services, such as full-featured 24-hour bank machines and bank-at-home capabilities.

▼ New inventions, like the laptop computer below, changed the way American companies operated and workers did their jobs in the 1980s and 1990s.

1980s FIGURES

In 1980 the U.S. federal budget deficit was $73.8 billion, and the U.S. trade deficit was $19.7 billion. American assets held by foreigners were $500.8 billion.

By 1989 the budget deficit had grown to an estimated $161.5 billion, and the trade deficit to $119.8 billion. More than $1.7 trillion in U.S. assets were held by foreigners.

The information explosion also created new business opportunities for high-tech entrepreneurs. On-line services, such as Prodigy and CompuServe, offered subscribers access to information, games, shopping, and more in only seconds. A home-based environmental consultant, for example, could, in a few minutes, scan dozens of electronic newspapers nationwide for stories about water pollution.

The information revolution also spawned an enormous software industry, as well as companies specializing in computer and communications systems design. Computer and communications services such as these became available to people around the world, creating a "global village" in which people could contact those in other countries instantly.

A Global Economy

This period also saw a rapid expansion of global trade. Americans bought televisions from Japan, steel from South Korea, machine tools from Europe, clothing from Southeast Asia, and oil from the Middle East. The western Pacific Rim nations, or the Asian nations that border the Pacific Ocean, became the fastest-growing trade region in the world. The shipping of goods between the United States and the Pacific Rim made Los Angeles the nation's largest trading center by the late 1980s.

Not only did foreign firms sell their products in the United States, but they also began to buy American companies and set up their own plants here. During the 1980s the Japanese bought control of Rockefeller Center, Columbia Pictures, and much of Waikiki Beach in Hawaii. By 1989 one of eight "American-made" cars was built in a U.S. plant owned by a Japanese company. Foreign investors owned U.S. corporations valued at almost $1 trillion.

At first Americans seemed to resent this flood of foreign products and investments. Yet they continued to spend billions of dollars on inexpensive, well-made foreign goods. As people purchased more imports, the nation's trade deficit increased.

American firms adopted a new strategy: "If you can't beat them, join them." Ford Motor Company, for example, bought 25 percent of Mazda and joined with Volkswagen to set up a truck-manufacturing plant in Latin America. By 1989 American businesses earned $553 billion from their overseas operations. Of course, when these and other American companies moved their plants in the United States to foreign countries where labor costs were lower, American workers lost their jobs.

▼ Hundreds of Soviet customers stand in line at Moscow's first McDonald's, which opened in January 1990.

Transportation

AMERICA'S TRANSPORTATION PROBLEMS

Both the automobile and airline industries faced difficult challenges during the 1970s and 1980s. The U.S. auto industry declined because of foreign competition and production and labor problems. The deregulation of the airline industry produced chaos, and many carriers went bankrupt or suffered heavy losses.

In the 1990s transportation continues to be problematic as roads, rails, and mass transit need costly repairs and revitalization.

The Automobile Industry

Roger Smith, chairman of General Motors (GM), minced no words in his gloomy early-1980s assessment of the U.S. auto industry: "We're . . . in trouble and we've got to start doing things differently. We're behind our foreign competition right now in quality, in technological design, in plants and facilities, and, yes, even in our own management." He continued: "In 1980, the little girl with the lemonade stand . . . made more profit than all of us—GM, Ford, Chrysler, and AMC together."

Lee Iacocca: A Success Story

Lee Iacocca was an unlikely hero. The son of Italian immigrants who settled in Allentown, Pennsylvania, Iacocca's "brains, bluster, and bravado" took him to the vice presidency of the Ford Motor Company at age 36. Ten years later, in 1970, he became president of Ford. During those years Iacocca was Detroit's most colorful figure. As head of the celebrated Ford Mustang program, he became a legend in automotive history as well.

In 1978 Iacocca took over as head of the ailing Chrysler Corporation, which was on the brink of total collapse. He negotiated a controversial "bailout"—a $1.5 billion loan guarantee from the federal government. He also cut the company in half to keep it alive. A super salesman himself, Iacocca advertised on TV to sell his cars. "You can go with Chrysler," he boomed with utter confidence and conviction, "or you can go with someone else—and take your chances."

The results astonished even Iacocca's most ardent supporters. In April 1984 Iacocca reported a whopping $705 million profit for the first quarter of that year, more than Chrysler had ever made in an entire year. "The time has come to restore the confidence of the American car buyer in American technology, American workers, and American cars," declared Iacocca.

IACOCCA FOR PRESIDENT bumper stickers began to appear. His 1984 autobiography sold more than 6 million copies worldwide. By the late 1980s, however, stiff competition and product safety concerns lowered Chrysler's profits and dimmed Iacocca's reputation. Like other auto manufacturers, Chrysler faced an uncertain future in the 1990s.

▶ In the 1980s Japanese automakers began building more of their cars in the United States. Here workers in the quality assurance department check automobiles at a Honda plant in Ohio.

No one disagreed with Smith. The impact of the mid-1970s recession and energy crisis had devastated the auto industry. American consumers rushed to purchase reliable, energy-efficient foreign cars. In response, U.S. automakers embarked on fast-paced catch-up programs to design and build cars to compete with the imports. At the same time, however, foreign manufacturers began to improve small cars with advanced designs, engineering, and reliability. By the mid-1980s many energy-efficient foreign cars matched their American counterparts in performance and luxury.

As sales of foreign cars in America soared, so did industry calls for limits on how much another country could import and sell in the United States. In 1981 the Reagan administration asked Japan to voluntarily limit to 1.68 million its shipments of cars to the United States. To bypass this restriction, the Japanese built manufacturing facilities in the United States: Honda in Ohio, Nissan in Tennessee, and Toyota in California. By 1983 U.S. automakers recognized that cooperation with their foreign rivals could benefit everyone. GM's joint venture with Toyota in 1983 was the first of many such cooperative efforts in the 1980s.

By the mid-1980s major U.S. automakers were thriving again, as buyers responded to the manufacturers' "renewed commitment to quality." Automakers spent a higher percentage of their profits on developing high-quality cars and high-tech manufacturing plants at home and overseas. Many new car models, such as Ford's Taurus, proved immensely popular with American buyers. GM invested several billion dollars in Saturn, a new car made by a new GM subsidiary. But carmakers faced tough new challenges during the recession that began in 1990, as sales slowed dramatically.

CONRAIL TAKES OVER AILING RAILROADS

April 1, 1976, marked the birth of the Consolidated Rail Corporation (Conrail). The U.S. government created it from six bankrupt railroads in the Northeast. During Conrail's first five years of operation, the federal government invested $3.3 billion in it. However, the rail line lost $1.3 billion during that time.

In 1981 the Northeast Rail Service Act allowed Conrail to cease its small commuter service and devote itself solely to freight service. This change, plus the initiation of cost-cutting measures, helped Conrail turn a profit.

The Airline Industry

The 1978 Airlines Deregulation Act was a landmark event for the airline industry, once tightly controlled by the federal government. The act ended federal control of air routes in 1982 and of fares in 1983. At first deregulation produced chaos in the industry, which had enjoyed record profits in 1978. New, small airlines, such as People Express and British-owned Laker Airways, began to offer passengers lower fares to more cities than many established airlines. People Express, a favorite with college students, flew passengers from New York to North Carolina for only $19. As a result, the number of total passengers soared, but per-passenger revenue dropped sharply.

One established air carrier, Braniff International, chose to meet these new challenges by expanding rapidly and slashing its fares by 40 percent. When American Airlines matched Braniff's fares, however, the two fell into a fare war, which proved disastrous for Braniff. The carrier filed for bankruptcy in 1982 and went out of business. Even the airlines that survived suffered heavy losses. USAir, for example, lost $233 million in 1990.

Most major airlines tried to stem their losses by adopting a route system of one or more major "hub" cities with many "spoked" flights from other cities feeding the hubs. In many cases airlines also forced labor unions to renegotiate their contracts. By the late 1980s the airline industry had become profitable once again—with fewer big airlines. But takeovers, mergers, and bankruptcies continued as carriers tried to find innovative ways to survive.

Future Transportation Needs

As many frustrated drivers know all too well, the nation faced a costly transportation crisis in the 1990s. Despite completion of the interstate highway system in 1991, the nation needs to invest an estimated $315 billion in the 1990s to restore its crumbling highways. Bridge repairs alone may cost another $72 billion. The repairs will place an added burden on state and federal governments. Some experts predict that taxes on gasoline and other taxes will have to be increased to provide Americans with the road system they want.

Work

THE CHANGING JOB MARKET

During the 1970s working people waited impatiently for inflation to stop shrinking their paychecks. During the 1980s they waited for the prosperity of the Reagan revolution to "trickle down" from corporations and the wealthy to them. Neither happened quickly, although prices rose only 64 percent in the 1980s compared with 103 percent in the 1970s. Yet from 1977 to 1988 the real income of most Americans either stayed the same or showed a net loss after taxes.

For the first time since World War II, most American workers faced a drop in their standard of living. Many women joined the workforce, pushing companies to adjust to the needs of two-income families. Flexible working hours, job sharing, and telecommuting became popular options for working parents. Telecommuting workers could stay at home and send their work to the office over telephone lines. Personal computers, modems, and fax machines made such new working arrangements possible. Most people, however, continued to work in offices or factories.

To help families even further, Congress passed a bill in 1990 encouraging companies to provide day care for employees' children. President Bush vetoed the bill, however, claiming that it would financially burden U.S. companies.

Large firms continued to provide extensive benefits for their employees. Many low-paid and part-time workers, unfortunately, saw their sick pay, insurance, pension

"The ultimate GM coat of arms will feature a robot dressed in a kimono seated in front of a word processor."

—Ben Bidwell,
Chrysler executive, on GM's enterprises with Japan, 1985

HOW DID WE MANAGE WITHOUT . . .

Many recent innovations in technology and communications have transformed American businesses. The following list presents some evolutions in American office technology.

FROM ledgers written in red and black ink . . . TO spreadsheets and other accounting software.

FROM manual typewriters and erasers or correction tape . . . TO word processors and laser printers.

FROM the United States Postal Service . . . TO fax machines or express-mail next-day services.

FROM carbon paper . . . TO photocopiers.

FROM thumbtacks and staples to attach notes . . . TO self-stick removable notes.

FROM filing cabinets and manila folders . . . TO computer disks and databases.

FROM desks and chairs . . . TO ergonomic workstations.

Consumer Power in the American Marketplace

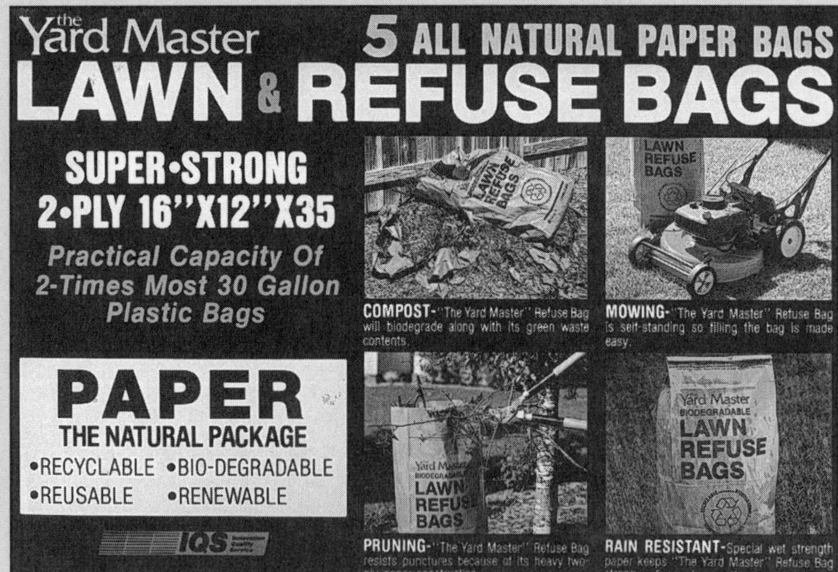

◄ American manufacturers have responded to consumer pressure to make products that are recyclable and biodegradable.

In 1979 presidential candidate Ronald Reagan declared, "Free enterprise is becoming far less free in the name of something called consumerism." He said he wanted to "get government off our backs." Reagan believed that competition alone would do a better job of regulating American industry than government could.

Some American consumers disagreed. They feared that companies would place profit before responsible business practices and product safety. The consumer movement of the previous decades had led to increasing demands for close inspection of products and the companies that made them. For example even after Reagan had been president for two years, most Americans strongly opposed cutting back the powers of the federal government's Consumer Product Safety Commission.

More and more, consumers demanded not only product safety and quality, but also corporate responsibility. They insisted on answers. For example they asked: Which companies were doing business in South Africa, where the racist policy of apartheid systematically discriminated against blacks? Which companies tested their products on animals? Which manufacturers were seriously damaging the nation's air and water quality? Which tuna processors used nets that captured and killed dolphins along with tuna?

Armed with answers to these and other questions, American consumers exercised their power in the marketplace. They used their buying power to force companies to stop many practices that harmed people, animals, and the environment. By 1990, for example, major American tuna processors, reacting to consumer pressure, agreed to buy only fish caught with nets from which dolphins could escape.

Consumers also pressured manufacturers to improve product quality and safety. Consumer concerns about chemicals used in farming led to greater demand for organic produce and natural foods. Many companies reduced the amount of product packaging they used in response to consumer concerns about the wise use of natural resources and the problem of waste disposal.

Faced with mounds of garbage, Americans also pushed recycling programs. Many cities and towns began to collect glass and plastic bottles, old newspapers, and aluminum cans to be recycled into new products.

plans, and paid vacations disappear. By the mid-1980s a study found that 16 million workers—over 15 percent of the workforce—lacked medical insurance. Concerns over the high cost and availability of medical care became major issues in the 1990s.

Overall, the good news during the 1980s was that 20 million new jobs were created. The bad news was that most new jobs were low paying, many in rapidly expanding service industries. At the same time, however, many companies increased the educational requirements for their entry-level workers.

The job market changed in other ways as well. Foreign competition and economic recessions reduced the number of factory workers employed by steel, auto, and other heavy industries. Many other workers lost their jobs because of corporate reorganizations. The increased use of automated equipment and high-tech manufacturing methods also cut out many industrial jobs. Government employees faced an uncertain future, as financial crises forced many agencies to cut budgets and jobs.

Because of these changes, the period from 1976 to 1991 saw a sharp decline in the influence of labor unions. Many business leaders argued that unions made American industry less competitive with its foreign rivals.

President Reagan fueled antiunion sentiment when he fired the nation's air-traffic controllers and demolished their union in response to their 1981 strike. Several hundred major strikes occurred each year during the mid-1970s. By the late 1980s the number of strikes had dropped to about 50 a year. The migration of people and businesses from the North to the South and Southwest also hurt unions. Southern states are traditionally more hostile to organized labor.

Not coincidentally, the percentage of the workforce represented by unions fell substantially during the 1980s. As a result of their diminishing influence, union negotiators focused their energies on keeping as many industry jobs for their members as possible.

Union workers were not the only group endangered by the economic changes of the era. The number of farm families declined as well. In 1970 there were about 3 million farms in the United States, averaging about 375 acres each. By the end of the 1980s the number of farms had dropped to 2.2 million, but the average size of each farm had increased to more than 450 acres each. For the most part farming was a high-tech operation run by large agribusiness companies. One farm in Illinois, for example, used a computer to record exactly how much food each of its steers ate.

American workers in the 1990s, experts conclude, will need to be more highly trained than ever before. For highly trained workers, the prospects for employment are more promising by far in the 1990s than in either the 1970s or 1980s. Because of a sharp decline in the birthrate, nearly 40 percent fewer people will be entering the workforce in the 1990s than in the 1970s. Although the American economy faces major challenges in the 1990s, there is also the promise of growth and progress.

1980s INCOME AND EMPLOYMENT FIGURES

In 1980 there were 4,114 Americans who reported $1 million or more in adjusted gross income. At the same time, 29.3 million lived in poverty. By 1989 the number of Americans with $1 million or more in adjusted gross income had shot up to 57,603. The number living in poverty rose as well during the decade to reach 31.5 million.

Meanwhile the percentage of all employees belonging to labor unions dropped significantly in the 1980s, from 23 percent in 1980 to 16.4 percent in 1989.

SHORTAGES OF WORKERS PREDICTED

The National Science Foundation has predicted that by the year 2000 the United States labor force will be short 540,000 scientists and engineers. Shortages of professors in the humanities and social sciences are projected for the late 1990s.

SCIENCE AND TECHNOLOGY

When astronaut Neil Armstrong took "one giant leap" onto the surface of the moon in 1969, it seemed to many Americans that the wonders of modern technology were limitless. If science could put a person on the moon, people declared, it could do anything.

Twenty years after conquering space, this sense of optimism about the benefits of science and technology remained. Along with it, however, was a greater awareness of the risks of living in a high-tech world. Escaped gases from refrigerators, air conditioners, and aerosol spray cans helped create a hole in the earth's protective ozone layer. Nuclear power plants produced tons of highly toxic waste. Pollution from power plants fueled by coal and petroleum fell to earth as acid rain, damaging forests and killing fish in lakes and streams. Environmental disasters, such as the Exxon Valdez *oil spill in March 1989 (above), killed large numbers of fish and wildlife and fouled clean waters. Could science and technology eliminate these problems and clean up disasters before they seriously damaged the earth and its inhabitants?*

Scientists confronted serious human health-care and environmental issues. AIDS became a worldwide epidemic—hard to detect, difficult to treat, and seemingly impossible to cure. Malnutrition haunted much of the Third World, made more deadly by civil wars and long-term droughts. People in industrialized nations generally had enough to eat, but faced a health-care crisis as costs of medical care skyrocketed. Along with new challenges, scientists and engineers also had new triumphs. The technological success of the period was the personal computer—a stunning machine that revolutionized American work and leisure.

AT A GLANCE

- A Planet at Risk?
- Technical Gains and Human Losses
- The PC Revolution
- Looking for Answers to Fundamental Questions
- Triumphs and Tragedy in Space

DATAFILE

Science

Life expectancy at birth	1976	1990
Males	69.1	72.1
Females	76.8	79.0

Top five causes of death, 1976–1989

1. Heart disease 2. Cancer 3. Cerebrovascular disease 4. Accidents 5. Lung disease

Technology

Miles of paved roads

1979 .... 3.2 mil. 1987 .... 3.5 mil.

Passenger miles traveled, 1988

Railroad .... 5.7 bil. Air .... 4.1 bil.

Households in 1989 with . . .

Electricity	100%
Telephone	94%
Indoor plumbing	97%

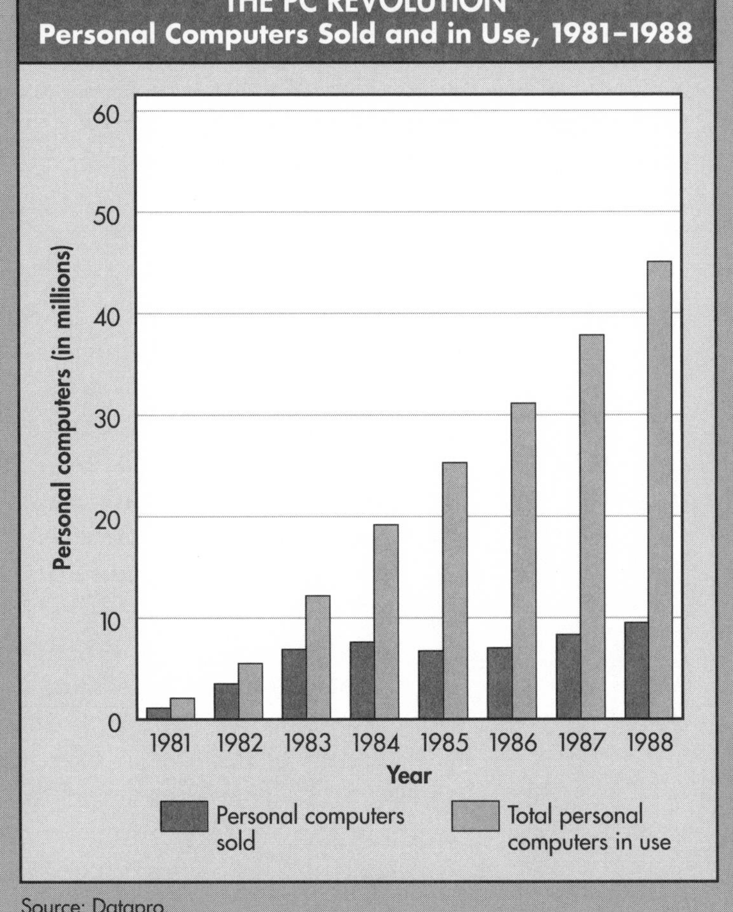

Source: Datapro.

Environment

A PLANET AT RISK?

In centuries to come the 1980s may be remembered as the decade the environment hit the headlines. Ozone depletion, the **greenhouse effect, acid rain,** toxic wastes—these problems became key international issues. Once the concern of only a few environmentalists, the health of planet earth soared to the top of everyone's list of important concerns.

Ozone Depletion

During the 1970s scientists became increasingly concerned that **chlorofluorocarbons** (CFCs) were destroying the ozone in the earth's atmosphere. The ozone layer, a thin shield of gas in the atmosphere high above the earth, helps screen out the sun's ultraviolet rays. These invisible rays cause skin cancer and may weaken the immune system. At first scientists disagreed about the seriousness of the widening hole in the ozone layer.

By the mid-1980s most scientists agreed that damage to the ozone layer was severe. In 1987 color images beamed to earth from a satellite clearly showed that a hole in the ozone layer above Antarctica had expanded. Worldwide pressure to end all use of CFCs mounted. In 1989, 80 nations agreed to ban the use of CFCs completely by the year 2000.

Satellite photographs taken in 1991 showed the hole growing more rapidly than predicted, however. Scientists urged a speedup in plans to phase out use of CFCs.

TOXIC WASTE CAUSES TRAGEDY

In Niagara Falls, New York, the residents of the Love Canal neighborhood discovered that their homes had been built on a toxic-waste dump. The land had been a dump and landfill for a chemical corporation. A school and housing development were built on the filled land in 1953. Seventeen years later toxic liquids began to leak through the clay cap that sealed the dump. Poisonous chemicals polluted the soil and groundwater.

The Environmental Protection Agency (EPA) declared the town unfit for human habitation, and the people were evacuated. Their houses were boarded up, and the town was surrounded by a fence. The New York State government and the federal government provided the families of Love Canal with funds to help them move.

The Greenhouse Effect

In October 1987 an iceberg 2,500 square miles in area and 750 feet thick broke off from the Ross Ice Shelf in Antarctica. Some scientists concluded that the polar ice cap was shrinking because of a gradual rise in the temperature of the earth's atmosphere. Four years earlier the U.S. Environmental Protection Agency (EPA) had predicted that the average world temperature might rise by 9° Fahrenheit before the end of the twenty-first century.

The cause, according to the EPA, was a rapid rise in carbon dioxide from autos and power plants burning fossil fuels, such as coal and oil. The carbon dioxide in the atmosphere trapped the sun's heat, leading to a "greenhouse" effect. To make matters worse, the earth was losing its tropical rain forests, which help the atmosphere by absorbing carbon dioxide and giving off oxygen. The long-term impact of global warming could be disastrous, scientists warned. They feared rising sea levels, rapid expansion of desert areas, and steep declines in crop yields.

▼ Acid rain is killing forests in northern and central Germany and Czechoslovakia.

A 1987 conference of 300 scientists from 48 nations called for a 20 percent reduction of global carbon-dioxide emissions by the year 2005. Some scientists, however, suggested that the rise was temporary or that it was caused by a combination of weather and other atmospheric factors.

In 1990 the United States and the Soviet Union cited disagreement among the world's scientists as a reason to block United Nations attempts to set specific carbon-dioxide reduction targets.

Acid Rain

Acid rain develops when factories, power plants, and motor vehicles burn fossil fuels such as coal, giving off sulfur dioxide and nitrogen oxides. The gases can mix with moisture in the air to form sulfuric acid. The mixture falls to the earth as acid rain, which strips plants and soil of vital nutrients and kills fish. Because these airborne gases can be blown thousands of miles, nations must work together to deal with the problem. In 1984 environmental and health ministers from ten nations met in Canada and agreed to cut sulfur-dioxide emissions by 30 percent over ten years. They also called for other nations to join the "30 percent club."

Unlike studies of ozone depletion and the greenhouse effect, the scientific analysis of acid rain and its effect was less controversial. Scientists could easily measure the acidity of lakes and streams. They could also estimate the pollutants in the air. Over time, studies showed that, as cars and factories reduced sulfur-dioxide emissions, acid levels in rainwater dropped.

Waste Disposal

In 1988 two West German ships, the *Karin B* and the *Deep Sea Carrier*, sailed to Nigeria to pick up 21,000 tons of toxic chemicals from Italy that had been dumped in Nigeria by an Italian ship. Once loaded, the two ships set sail—but soon found they had nowhere to go with the waste. They were refused entry by Spain, France, Belgium, West Germany, Great Britain, and the Netherlands. Finally, despite vigorous local protests, the Italian government said the hazardous wastes would be allowed back into Italy.

Although unusual, this event illustrated a trend. The world produced more and more waste—toxic and otherwise—but had fewer and fewer places to put it. Many environmental leaders sharply criticized the move by some industrial nations to ship their wastes to Third World countries, where environmental regulations were less strict. Scientists feared that poor nations would become toxic waste dumps for rich nations. Such dumping did not solve the pollution and waste-disposal problem, but shifted it from the industrial countries to Third World countries.

An Era of Environmental Disasters

Many serious, long-term environmental problems of the era were difficult for people to see: a hole in the ozone layer, destruction of tropical rain forests, contamination of groundwater. Yet many sudden environmental disasters captured headlines. These events drew attention to the potential or actual devastating impact of human activity on the environment.

1979 The failure of a water pump led to the partial meltdown of the radioactive core of a nuclear power plant at Three Mile Island, near Harrisburg, Pennsylvania, increasing worldwide opposition to nuclear power.

1984 A leaking storage tank at an American-owned pesticide plant in Bhopal, India, produced a deadly cloud of gas that killed 2,500 people and left 100,000 with long-term illnesses.

1986 History's most serious nuclear accident occurred when a nuclear reactor near the Soviet city of Chernobyl caught fire. More than 135,000 people were evacuated. Above-average radioactivity was detected as far away as North America.

1989 The United States suffered its worst oil spill when the tanker *Exxon Valdez* ran aground in Alaska's Prince William Sound. The tanker spilled 200,000 barrels of oil. Wildlife in the region and Alaska's large fishing industry suffered from the polluting spill.

1991 During their withdrawal from Kuwait, Iraqi troops set fire to more than 500 oil wells in Kuwait, sending huge clouds of black smoke into the air. It took more than eight months to put out all of the fires.

▲ More than 30 people died as a result of the radiation-releasing fire at the Chernobyl nuclear power station near Kiev on April 26, 1986.

LYME DISEASE DISCOVERED IN CONNECTICUT

In 1976 a mysterious disease struck a large group of schoolchildren in Lyme, Connecticut. Doctors and researchers soon discovered that "Lyme disease," as it was named, was caused by a virus carried by deer ticks.

The disease, a form of infectious arthritis, may begin with any of the following symptoms: a disk- or bullseye-shaped rash, fever, sore throat, chills, fatigue, and nausea. If left untreated it may cause stiffness or pain in the joints, loss of memory, or severe headaches.

Medicine

TECHNICAL GAINS AND HUMAN LOSSES

Medical science made impressive gains during the 1970s and 1980s. New vaccines and inoculation programs virtually eliminated many common diseases such as smallpox, although measles continued to kill 2 million children per year worldwide. Computerized, high-tech trauma centers—emergency rooms designed to treat life-threatening wounds—saved thousands of accident victims. Other advances allowed ever-younger premature babies to survive outside the womb.

Yet the world of medicine also encountered more than its share of difficulties. Medical costs skyrocketed in the United States, from $133 billion in 1975 to $544 billion in 1988. A cure for cancer continued to elude scientists. But among the most troubling medical events of the era was the appearance and rapid spread of a deadly virus.

▼ From 1976 to 1990 annual health expenditures increased almost four times in the United States, making basic health care unaffordable for many Americans.

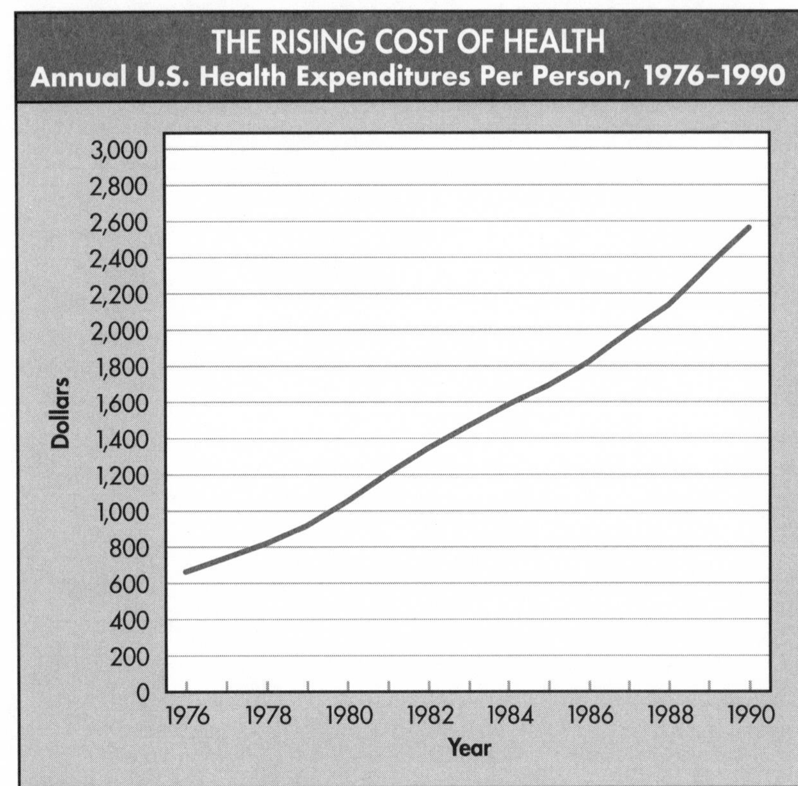

AIDS

At the time the acquired immune deficiency syndrome, commonly known as **AIDS,** was identified in 1981 it was thought to be an infectious disease confined to homosexual men and intravenous-drug users. The disease destroys the body's immune system, so it is not able to fight off other diseases. AIDS was usually fatal within two years of diagnosis. By 1984 researchers at the Institut Pasteur in Paris had determined that AIDS was caused by a virus, later named the human immunodeficiency virus, or **HIV.** They found that the virus was carried in bodily fluids, mainly blood and semen, and spread when these fluids passed from one person to another. People who are HIV-positive have tested positive in a blood test for the virus.

By the mid-1980s the World Health Organization (WHO) declared AIDS a global **epidemic**. It spread most rapidly in Africa and other regions where knowledge of the disease was limited and public health facilities were scarce. In 1990 the WHO announced that, because of rapidly rising infection rates in Asia, Latin America, and sub-Saharan Africa, more than 20 million people would be HIV-positive by the year 2000.

The number of infected individuals in the United States continued to increase as well. By 1990 1 million Americans were HIV-positive, and more than 137,000 were patients with AIDS. The number of new AIDS cases among homosexual men decreased dramatically, while the rate of infection among intravenous drug users held steady. At the same time the percentage of AIDS cases among heterosexual men and women jumped tenfold between 1981 and 1988, a trend dramatized in 1991 by basketball superstar Earvin "Magic" Johnson's announcement that he was HIV-positive.

Researchers struggle to find a vaccine that will protect people against the virus. To date AIDS remains incurable. Some experimental drugs—AZT, DDI, and DDC, among others—offer hope of delaying the start of AIDS for people already infected with the virus. Until a cure is found, however, medical scientists urge the practice of sexual abstinence, safe sex, and the use of safe medical practices as the best protection against infection.

Cancer

A cure for cancer also eluded researchers during the period, and the incidence of cancer continued to rise. By 1990 more than a million new cases of cancer were being reported each year, and 500,000 deaths were attributed to cancer annually in America. But advances in detection methods, new drugs, and sophisticated surgical techniques made more cancers curable. Also, the discovery of links between cancer and lifestyle enabled people to choose ways of living that reduced their cancer risk.

Smoking, for example, was found to be responsible for 83 percent of lung-cancer cases and almost one-third of all cancer deaths.

AIDS Quilt on National Tour

The National AIDS Memorial Quilt was displayed in Denver in 1988 for three days while on national tour. Each square of the quilt bore the name of one person who had died of AIDS. The AIDS quilt, which was the size of two football fields, forced people to consider just how many lives had been lost to the disease. The patches were handsewn by the families and friends of those who had died.

Each year as the number of AIDS cases and the number of deaths increase in the United States, the epidemic remains a frightening medical problem and a difficult political challenge.

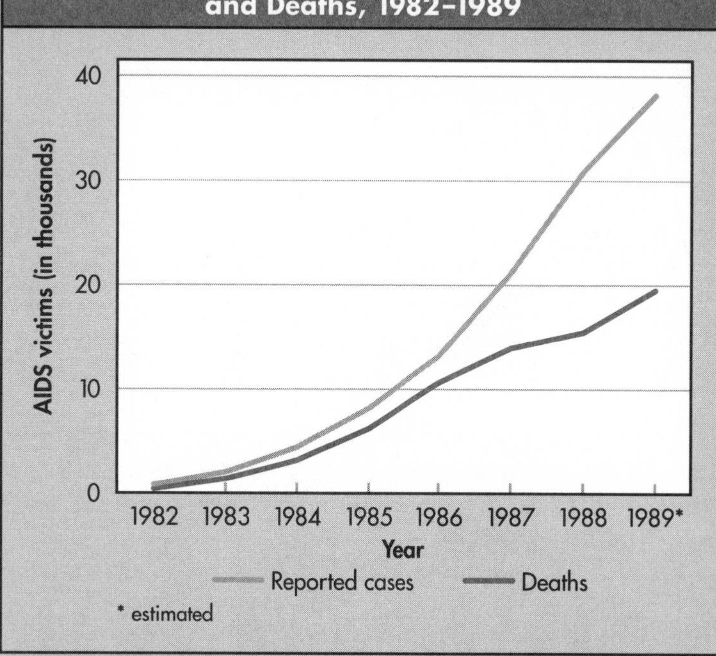

Source: *Statistical Abstract of the United States, 1990*, and *Columbia Medical Encyclopedia*, 1988.

Colon, breast, and uterine cancer occurred more frequently among obese people, and high-fat diets seemed related to the development of breast, colon, and prostate cancer. A diet high in fiber-rich foods, on the other hand, reduced the risk of colon cancer.

Prevention became the watchword. The American Cancer Society and other organizations urged Americans to quit smoking, reduce stress levels, eat a healthy diet, and exercise regularly.

Clark Receives First Artificial Heart

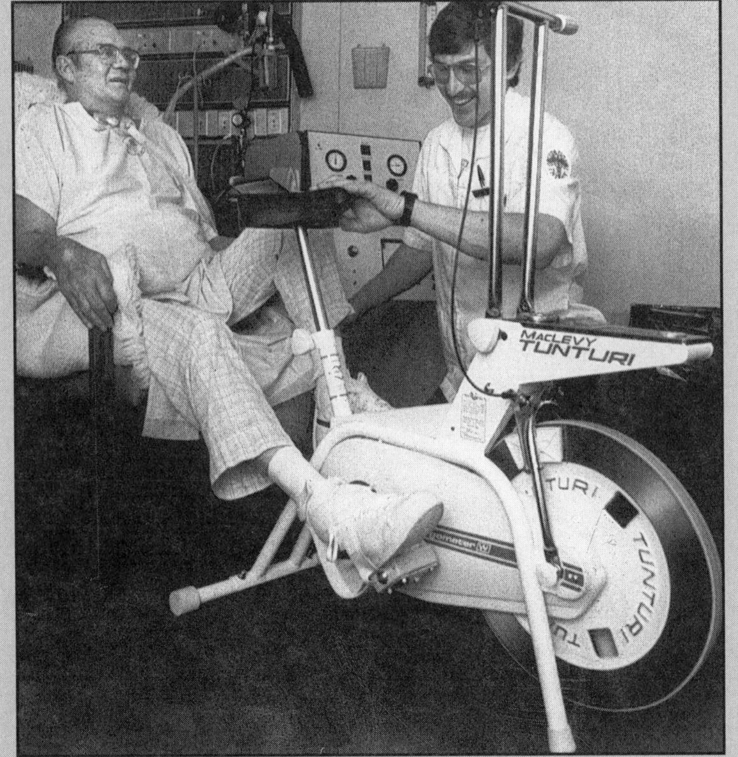

Dr. Barney Clark, a retired dentist, made medical history on December 2, 1982. The 61-year-old patient, who was near death from heart failure, received the world's first artificial heart. The mechanical heart, called the "Jarvik-7," had been successfully transplanted in animals, but Clark became the first human recipient.

Dr. William C. DeVries of the University of Utah Medical Center headed the surgical team that performed the operation. Within a few weeks of the surgery, Clark was able to walk. In March 1983, however, he died of complications. Implants used in other patients were also only temporarily successful, reducing the hope for permanent artificial hearts. But they showed they could be useful as a "bridge" for those awaiting human-heart implants.

Critical Issues

Technological advances in the medical field raised troubling new ethical questions for health-care professionals. Karen Ann Quinlan, a young New Jersey woman who suddenly stopped breathing after ingesting a combination of drugs and alcohol at a party, stayed "alive" with life support until 1980, existing ten years in a coma. But who should decide when to "pull the plug"? A new antirejection drug, cyclosporine, dramatically increased the success of organ transplants and ushered in a new era of transplant surgery. But how should scarce, expensive donor organs be distributed? Innovative "gene therapy" offered hope for curing genetic defects. But what about the possibility and dangers of making genetic "improvements" to human beings? As researchers extended medical frontiers, ethical and legal issues became more complex and troubling.

While scientists tried to sort out these perplexing questions, ordinary Americans began wrestling with a more immediate "health-care crisis." As the cost of medical care soared in the 1980s, insurance companies and the federal government—through Medicare and Medicaid—began to limit the amount they would pay for specific illnesses and treatments. Many small businesses and unemployed people could not afford to pay the ever-increasing cost of medical insurance. By 1991 more than 33 million Americans had no medical insurance at all. Debate raged over reform of the health-care system and the possibility of government-funded health insurance.

Technology

THE PC REVOLUTION

Since the mid-1970s incredibly small, blazingly fast **microprocessors** have revolutionized American homes, businesses, automobiles, and manufacturing plants. This revolution has even changed how Americans spend their leisure time. Computers enable people to do more things more quickly with less effort.

The revolution did not begin in the 1970s, of course. Every five years from 1960 until 1977, the size of the computer was cut in half, without reducing its power. By the early 1970s the invention of the silicon microprocessor had made *smaller, cheaper,* and *faster* industry watchwords. The computer went from the size of a room to the size of a notebook while gaining in power, speed, and reliability.

Personal Computers

The first personal computers (PCs)—small, desktop-sized computers designed for individual use in a business or home—and their software were not developed by giant computer firms. Instead they were primarily the brainchildren of individuals who have since become American business legends, people such as Steven Jobs of Apple Computer and William Gates of Microsoft Corporation. In 1976 Steven Jobs brought out the first Apple PC, a machine he designed in his garage.

When the computer giant International Business Machines (IBM) entered the PC market in 1981, the PC invaded corporate America. The cost of owning a computer dropped at the rate of about 15 percent per year. Even small businesses could afford PCs, which they used in accounting, inventory control, word processing, on-line communications, and information management. By 1983 desktop PCs were becoming a normal part of daily life. In that year alone PCs made their way into over 5 million American homes.

As computers entered the lives of people who had little training and no experience in their use, the demand grew for "user-friendly" programs and machines. Apple Computer introduced the "mouse," which enabled users to work with information on computer disks by moving a small, hand-held device (mouse) instead of typing on a keyboard. Several other companies worked on developing voice recognition, which would eventually allow users to direct computers with spoken commands.

The key to the computer's remarkable success, however, lay in the development of sophisticated software, or computer programs. Computer owners could use their machines in an increasing number of ways. In 1983 more than 1,000 new programs were written for the IBM PC alone. A computer program could be found for writing, drawing, composing music, designing houses, or calculating—practically every type of intellectual activity a user might think of.

Computers Everywhere

The microprocessor has also spawned automatic bank-teller machines, programmable videocassette recorders and microwaves,

RESTING PLACE OF *TITANIC* FOUND

On September 1, 1985, a team of U.S. and French researchers, using a remote-control submarine, discovered the site where the *Titanic* had sunk 73 years before. The exact location of the ship had not been known because the distress signal from the *Titanic* gave imprecise geographic information.

The *Titanic* was found by the *Argo* research submarine, which took pictures and shot videotape of the sunken ship 12,000 feet below the surface of the North Atlantic. Some pictures showed the cargo, luggage, wine bottles, and personal items lying on the ocean floor.

According to the director of the discovery team from Woods Hole Oceanographic Institution in Massachusetts, the *Titanic* wreck was too deep to bring to the surface. Many people agreed that the ship should be left alone in memory of the 1,500 people who died when it sank.

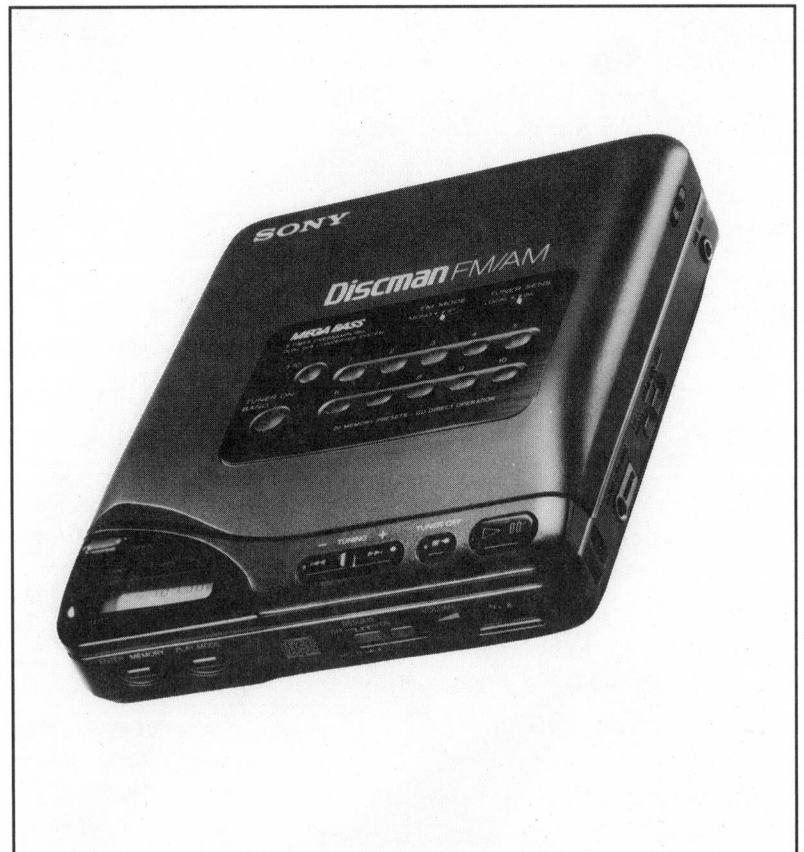

▲ The personal compact disk player is an example of the kind of popular consumer product coming from high technology.

improved auto ignition and fuel-injection systems, hand-held video games, energy-saving thermostats, and cameras that focus automatically. The list of products containing microchips is endless.

Advances in computer technology led to improvements in such fields as robotics and computer-aided design and manufacturing. Super-fast computers encouraged research into **artificial intelligence.** Scientists might yet produce a computer program that simulates the thinking and decision-making processes of the human mind. In the early 1990s rapid advances were being made in creating so-called virtual or artificial reality, a computer-based system for generating three-dimensional images of the real world or an imaginary situation.

NEW WORDS

boot up
camcorder
compact disk (CD)
ecoterrorism
nuclear winter
user-friendly
videocassette recorder (VCR)

Science

LOOKING FOR ANSWERS TO FUNDAMENTAL QUESTIONS

In the last 25 years of the twentieth century, scientists brought sophisticated new tools and advanced supercomputers to bear on many puzzles. They peered into the heavens and explored the activity of subatomic particles. It was a time of dramatic discovery, but the answers to fundamental questions remained elusive.

Exploring the Mysteries of Space and Matter

In 1965 scientists detected a low level of continuous radiation in space. Some astronomers believed the radiation was the remnant from the "big bang," a single cataclysmic event that formed the expanding universe. In 1989 an orbiting laboratory, called "COBE," was launched to make more precise measurements of the radiation. Throughout 1990 COBE took measurements, and scientists searched the data for clues to the first moments of the life of the universe. But results were inconclusive, and the cosmic mystery remained unsolved.

While astronomers peered skyward, physicists probed the inner secrets of matter's building blocks. Huge machines, called "particle accelerators," speeded up tiny bits of matter until they almost reached the speed of light. Then the accelerator smashed the particles against each other with a force that greatly exceeds that of any collision naturally occurring on earth. The goal of this process was to discover what the universe is made of and what the forces are that bind the universe together.

As the century drew to a close scientists made progress in superconductivity research. Scientists have known since 1911 that some substances become "superconductors"—offering almost no resistance to an electric current—at extremely low temperatures. Beginning in 1986 scientists developed new materials that become superconductive at much higher temperatures.

These discoveries bring the goal of room-temperature superconductors much closer. Such materials could transmit electric current without loss, form electromagnets that draw no current, and be used to make batteries that store electric current without energy loss. If they can be developed commercially, superconducting materials could save much energy and greatly reduce pollution.

Mount Saint Helens Blows Its Top

The eruption of Mount Saint Helens on May 18, 1980, was the most violent volcanic event ever to occur in the continental United States. The mountain lies 40 miles northeast of Vancouver, Washington. The volcano had lain dormant since 1857.

Scientists had known weeks in advance that an eruption was due. Despite their warnings many people who lived near the volcano refused to leave their homes. The eruption left 57 people dead; it also caused $2.7 billion of damage, as well as massive destruction to the area's plant and animal life. The explosion blew 1,300 feet off the top of the mountain, leaving a crater almost a mile wide and half a mile deep. The blast sent tons of ash and debris 12 miles into the sky.

Biotechnology Research

A new era in **biotechnology** began in 1980 when the U.S. Supreme Court ruled that "a live human-made micro-organism is patentable subject matter." In other words, if scientists could create new life forms, they could protect their discoveries with patents and reap the profits. Protected by patents, such new life forms could potentially be developed into life-saving and other useful products and sold.

During the 1980s **genetic engineers** used a technique known as gene splicing to produce artificially a variety of organic substances. These included human insulin, which diabetes sufferers lack, and human interferon, a substance produced by the body that some researchers believe may help fight cancer. Both were created from genetically altered bacteria. Gene splicing has shown great promise in the treatment of cystic fibrosis and muscular dystrophy. Also, more recently, researchers in the federally funded $3 billion "Human Genome Project" have made great progress in analyzing the individual components of the human genetic endowment.

Such research raises not only scientific questions, but also moral and legal ones, however. The debate over genetic engineering will undoubtedly be heated in the 1990s.

HUBBLE TELESCOPE FIASCO

NASA endured one more embarrassing failure during the period. Its long-awaited Hubble Space Telescope, placed in orbit by a shuttle crew in April 1990, has a faulty mirror that cuts down on the quality of the images it sends back to earth. NASA may fix the $1.5 billion Hubble—the world's most expensive scientific instrument—on a 1993 shuttle mission.

Space

TRIUMPHS AND TRAGEDY IN SPACE

As the Apollo program came to an end in the early 1970s, the National Aeronautics and Space Administration (NASA) had another goal in view: the flight of a space shuttle, a reusable space vehicle that could return to earth and land like an airplane.

The Shuttle Program

Finally, after extensive testing, the shuttle was ready for space flight. After a frustrating two-day delay, the shuttle *Columbia* lifted off from Cape Canaveral, Florida, on April 12, 1981. The voyage proved that the orbiter could deliver astronauts into orbit and return them to earth. The mission went precisely as planned.

Between 1981 and 1986 the shuttle fleet made 23 more successful flights into space. Each mission demonstrated the versatility of the vehicle some dubbed NASA's "space truck." Astronauts hauled communications satellites into space, deployed research equipment and observation satellites, and performed medical, military, and scientific experiments.

Despite a few glitches along the way, the shuttle program went well—too well perhaps. NASA pushed hard to meet its ambitious schedule of flights. NASA faced stiff competition from the European Space Agency and the USSR, both of which had entered the growing market to launch satellites. In the end NASA tried to do too much too fast. Quality control suffered—with disastrous results.

On the morning of January 28, 1986, tragedy struck the space-shuttle program and the nation. The tenth flight of the orbiter *Challenger* rocketed skyward at 11:38 A.M. Its crew included Christa McAuliffe, a schoolteacher from New Hampshire. She had won a national "teacher-in-space" contest begun in 1984. She planned to conduct two lessons from orbit, then lecture for the following nine months to students across the nation to raise interest in scientific and high-tech careers. As the *Challenger* rose upward, everything appeared normal. Then it disappeared in an immense fireball just 73 seconds after lift-off. At an altitude of less than 10 miles, the explosion occurred in full view of the

Sally Ride: First American Woman in Space

In 1983 Sally K. Ride became the first American woman to travel in outer space. The 32-year-old astronaut took part in the seventh space shuttle mission, which lasted from the 18th through the 24th of June. As the space shuttle lifted off from Cape Canaveral in Florida, cheering crowds chanted, "Ride, Sally, ride!"

Ride received a Ph.D. degree in physics from Stanford University in 1977 and was selected to become an astronaut the following year. Highly regarded for her work in physics, she is also an avid Shakespeare reader, a tennis player, and a rugby enthusiast.

Ride also traveled on the thirteenth space shuttle mission on October 5 to 13, 1984. On this mission she was responsible for successfully launching a satellite that measured solar energy.

In 1986 Ride served on the committee that investigated the explosion of the space shuttle *Challenger*. That same year she also became a special assistant to the administrator of NASA.

◀ The crew members of the *Challenger,* who died in January 1986 when the space shuttle exploded over Cape Canaveral, were (front row, from left) Michael Smith, Dick Scobee, and Ronald McNair; and (back row, from left) Ellison Onizuka, Christa McAuliffe, Gregory Jarvis, and Judith Resnik.

stunned crowd gathered at Cape Canaveral below and millions of people who watched on television. Within hours the explosion was etched into the nation's memory.

NASA halted the program for more than two years while engineers made improvements in the booster rockets that had caused the explosion. The shuttle program itself was also modified. President Ronald Reagan ordered NASA to stop launching commercial satellites. In 1989 NASA announced that it would not permit civilians to fly aboard the shuttle. Flights resumed in September 1988, and by August 11, 1991, the shuttle program had completed 42 missions.

Space Probes

The shuttle did not capture all the space-exploration honors. Long-distance probes, unmanned spacecraft that explore and send back information to earth, traveled the solar system and beyond.

Pioneers 10 and *11* journeyed to the solar system's large outer planets beginning in 1972 and 1973. After flying past Saturn and Jupiter, *Pioneer 10* crossed the orbit of Pluto in April 1983. It continued to transmit data that scientists studied for signs of a tenth planet. *Pioneer 11,* in its sweep past Saturn in 1979, discovered an eleventh moon orbiting the giant planet and two new rings. Two additional Pioneer spacecraft left earth in 1978, giving detailed information about Venus. Two Viking probes launched in 1975 sent pictures and scientific data from Mars.

Two identical *Voyager* interplanetary probes departed from Cape Canaveral in 1977. *Voyager 1* passed above the cloud tops of Jupiter in 1979, flew past Saturn in 1980, then headed out into deep space—the first human-made satellite to leave our solar system. *Voyager 2* had a 1986 rendezvous with the planet Uranus and a 1989 approach to Neptune, where it found six new moons and a series of unusual rings.

CHUNNEL TO END BRITAIN'S ISOLATION

What is more than 32 miles long and will connect the island of Great Britain to mainland France? The Chunnel, or English Channel Tunnel. Begun in December 1987 and due to be completed by 1993, the 32-mile-long Chunnel will be the longest underwater tunnel in the world. It will put an end to Great Britain's physical isolation from the European continent.

Huge boring machines are cutting the Chunnel, which lies 130 feet below the sea bed. When it is finished the Chunnel will consist of three tunnels. Two will be used for high-speed trains. One train will carry passengers, and one will ferry cars, trucks, and their drivers. The third and central tunnel will be used for maintenance and emergency vehicles.

The project, when complete, will cost almost $15 billion. It will enable rail travelers to go from Paris to London in about three hours—a quarter of the time it took before the Chunnel was built.

ARTS AND ENTERTAINMENT

In the early 1980s a fast-food chain ran a campaign inviting Americans hungry for a burger to "Have It Your Way" at their restaurant. The same slogan could have been used to describe arts and entertainment options of the period. The entertainment industry made it their business to give Americans an incredible range of leisure-time choices.

Rapid advances in high technology ignited the explosion of entertainment choices in the 1980s. Through the wonder of satellite communications, Americans with cable television could watch a Michael Jackson music video on MTV (above), a debate on the floor of the U.S. Senate, a football game in Australia, or a civil war in Yugoslavia—all live and in color. Or they could pop a videotape of a hit movie into their VCR, a compact disk into their portable CD player, or a video game into their Nintendo Entertainment System™. Cinemas, network and cable television stations, and music stores offered equally plentiful choices, as producers scrambled to release the next profitable sequel, television series, hit single, or compact disk.

This vast outpouring of entertainment had its limitations, of course. Although the number of choices increased, media ownership and profits were increasingly concentrated in the hands of a few. Many movie and music projects were based more on marketing strategies and profit considerations than on any serious attempt to create fine art. But it seemed that Americans were mostly satisfied with the options offered to them.

AT A GLANCE

- TV Viewers Get More Choices
- Changes in the Movie Industry
- Madonna, Michael, and More
- Instant News Goes International
- The Business of Broadway
- Celebrity and Censorship
- Something to Read for Everyone

DATAFILE

Attendance and sales	1980	1988
Movie attendance (weekly)	23 mil.	21 mil.
Reading material sales (excluding educational)	$16.0 bil.	$25.8 bil.
Home audio/visual expenditures	$22.5 bil.	$52.7 bil.

The press	1980	1988
Number of daily newspapers	1,775	1,670
Circulation	62.2 mil.	62.7 mil.
Number of magazines	10,236	11,229
Circulation	NA	NA

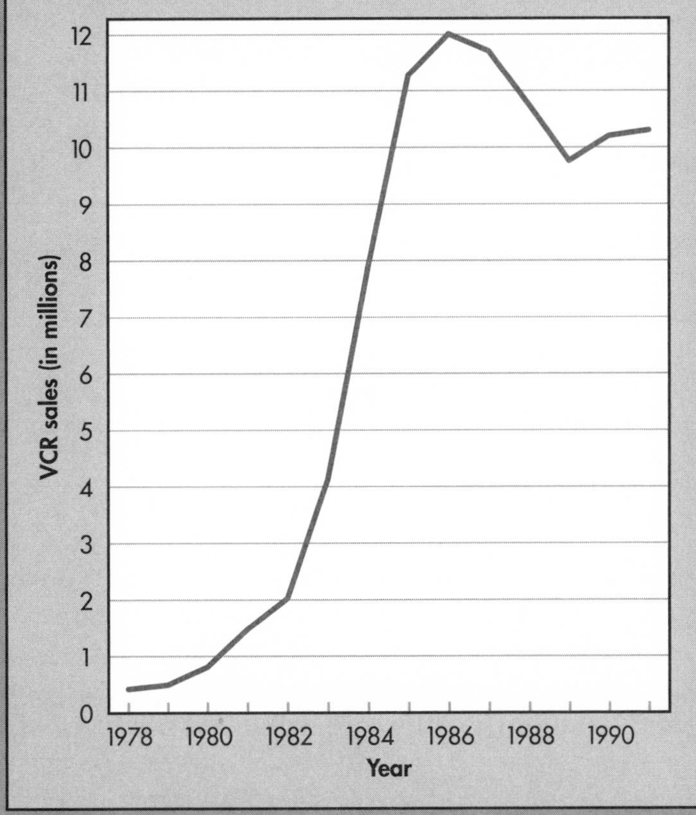

Source: *Electronic Market Data Book,* 1979–1989.

Television

TV VIEWERS GET MORE CHOICES

The 1980s, observed one analyst, was the decade of the remote control. This small handheld device—the size of a deck of playing cards—revolutionized the way people watched TV in the late 1970s and the 1980s. It also symbolized the dramatic change in television programming during the period. During the 1960s and early 1970s the major commercial networks—ABC, NBC, and CBS—largely dominated the nation's airwaves. But by the 1980s viewers were increasingly dissatisfied with look-alike network programs. Americans flicked from channel to channel in search of new and different entertainment.

The Rise of Cable Television

Viewers who subscribed to cable television (fully 50 percent of the nation's households by 1988 and 59 percent by 1990) found a great range of alternative programming. By the late 1980s cable television was as much a part of American life as the morning newspaper. Cable offered something for everyone.

News buffs in the United States and around the world kept up-to-the-minute with Cable News Network (CNN), a 24-hour satellite news network, or its affiliate, CNN Headline News. Viewers could flick to "superstations" in Atlanta, Chicago, or Newark. C-SPAN gave political junkies live access to congressional debates. Viewers could even call in their opinions of current policies and events.

I WANT MY MTV

With a rocket blast-off and the video for the song "Video Killed the Radio Star," Music Television, better known as MTV, hit the airwaves in August 1981. New artists such as Madonna, Cyndi Lauper, and Duran Duran became overnight successes partly as a result of their stylish and clever videos.

Music video styles have influenced the look and pace of other media. Their slick, stylized imagery inspired TV shows such as *Miami Vice,* commercials for Pepsi-Cola, and feature films such as *Flashdance* and *Purple Rain.*

Music fans enjoyed rock and rap videos on Music Television (MTV), adult contemporary tunes on VH-1, and country music on The Nashville Network. Sports fans could watch ESPN any hour of the day or night. They also tuned in to extra-fee sports services, which were available in certain parts of the country. The subscription movie channels—HBO, Cinemax, Showtime, and The Movie Channel, to name a few—had their share of enthusiasts.

By the late 1980s more and more cable systems offered pay-per-view movies and events. With a simple telephone call, viewers could select a movie—often at rates similar to those charged by video rental stores—or a major musical or sporting event. Cable, in other words, was a television viewer's dream come true. And VCRs let people tape and view programs whenever they wished.

Mass Entertainment Reflects Times

The major networks watched with dismay as their share of the nation's TV viewers shrank. As the 1980s progressed it became clear that the networks would never again enjoy the dominance they once had. Viewers had too many options, and their preferences were too diverse for any one channel or network to capture a majority of the audience. In that sense television both reflected and fashioned the social life of the times. America's entertainment preferences revealed its diversity.

There were notable exceptions to this trend. In the 1960s American TV viewers had found a common ground watching such events as President Kennedy's assassination and the *Apollo 11* moon landing.

In 1977 Americans were similarly drawn together by the monumental show *Roots,* a made-for-TV miniseries based on author Alex Haley's search for his African ancestors. One of the eight episodes attracted 71 percent of the television audience, and seven episodes were among the ten highest-rated programs of all time.

Big-time sports events such as the Super Bowl and World Series remained viewer favorites. In 1990 **Nielsen ratings** revealed that 12 of the 25 previous all-time top TV programs were Super Bowl games.

Major news events and crises compelled widespread viewer attention as well. Americans stayed riveted to their sets day and night watching live news coverage of the Persian Gulf War in 1991. Continuing reports from Bernard Shaw, CNN's correspondent trapped in a Baghdad hotel, drew praise and criticism. Live broadcasts of the Senate confirmation hearings of Supreme Court justice Clarence Thomas in October 1991 also captured surprisingly large audiences and prompted a heated, nationwide debate over the issue of sexual harassment.

Except during such crises, however, most of the nation's viewers turned to their sets in search of lighter fare. The glitz and glamour of America's rich took center stage in *Dynasty* and *Dallas,* long-running nighttime **serials** throughout the late 1970s and 1980s. In 1980 nighttime soap opera fans spent an anxious summer waiting to find out who shot J.R., the leading villain on *Dallas*. Even the Turkish parliament reportedly took a recess to watch the revealing first episode of the fall season. That episode of *Dallas* remains the second most widely viewed television program of all time.

As always, situation comedies ("sitcoms") topped the list of America's favorite programs. These TV comedy programs that include the same characters in the same location every week focused mainly on families. The sitcom families of the 1980s, however, differed in important respects from those of the 1960s and early 1970s. In shows like *Married with Children* and *Roseanne*, smart, sassy children who challenged their parents became a comedy staple. Smart-mouthed Bart Simpson, a cartoon character, became a folk hero to children and adults as well.

In the 1980s America's fascination with the lives of the wealthy was reflected in such shows as *Lifestyles of the Rich and Famous*. *The Cosby Show*, one of the decade's top programs, presented a new view: the life and times of a successful, upper-middle-class black family. Other shows featured blended families and single fathers coping with their teenage children.

The new programs of the period showed that producers knew their target audiences well. Some shows were written for the "Baby Boom generation." *The Wonder Years* captured the drama of their youth, while the critically acclaimed *thirtysomething* explored the values and problems of their adulthood.

Film director David Lynch's offbeat *Twin Peaks*, on the other hand, told a bizarre tale of love and death in the Pacific Northwest. Wildly popular at first, *Twin Peaks* saw its audience gradually diminish to a smaller, devoted cult dedicated to solving the mystery of "Who killed Laura Palmer?"

◀ *The Cosby Show* was one of the top programs in the 1980s.

Not all television was escape and fantasy, however. With many women working, they and men were attracted to new types of soap operas. Nighttime drama came of age during the 1980s, with prime-time soaps about police (*Hill Street Blues*), doctors (*St. Elsewhere*), and lawyers (*L.A. Law*).

Also popular with viewers were the daytime confessional talk shows. Phil Donahue, Oprah Winfrey, and Geraldo Rivera became the decade's electronic "confessors." They led their guests and audiences in discussions of such issues as child abuse and incest—the more sensational, the better. Guests on these shows eagerly shared intimate details of their personal lives with millions of viewers. In many ways the decade was

COMEDY GROWS IN POPULARITY

Although Americans have always loved a laugh, comedy grew in popularity during the 1970s and 1980s, particularly on the television scene.

In 1975 NBC debuted *Saturday Night Live,* a late-night show featuring comic actors. The program still airs weekly.

The 1980s then saw the birth of *The Arsenio Hall Show* and *Late Night with David Letterman,* comedy talk shows similar to *The Tonight Show,* a household favorite since 1954.

Cable television became saturated with stand-up comedy programs. Comedy-oriented nightclubs became very popular as well.

a new era for television, showing the powerful medium at both its best and worst.

Film

CHANGES IN THE MOVIE INDUSTRY

The movie industry changed in many ways. The growing popularity of television had a profound impact on the film industry. Between 1945 and the mid-1970s, for example, weekly movie attendance plummeted from 80 million to just over 12 million. The number of films produced each year fell from more than 400 to fewer than 150. In the 1940s Americans spent 80 percent of their entertainment dollars on movies; by the mid-1970s the average had dropped below 50 percent. During the 1980s cable television and video rentals cut even deeper into movie attendance. Some analysts predicted an end to the local cinema.

The movie industry, however, adapted to the times. Major Hollywood studios became primary avenues for film distribution, and many built vast chains of high-tech, multitheater cinemas to show their films. Increasingly studios became part of huge business conglomerates, such as Coca-Cola. This trend accelerated in the 1980s when the Japanese-owned Sony Corporation bought Columbia Pictures and Matsushita Electric Industrial Company Limited bought MCA. Made-for-television movies and TV shows became a major business of Hollywood studios as well. Some produced more material for television than for movie theaters.

Overall, these changes gave rise to two different trends in the industry. On the one hand corporate-owned studios tried to protect profits with big-budget, proven-formula movies starring well-known actors and actresses. This approach led to many predictable **sequels** that sought to capture audiences by relying on tried-and-true story lines and characters. Studios added to their profits by selling merchandise based on movie characters. Movie fans could buy Batman, Ninja Turtle, and Dick Tracy T-shirts and toys. On the other hand, independent, often low-budget producers created movies to fit specialized interests, such as martial arts, rock music, and black culture. The rapid spread of VCRs also created a huge demand for a wide range of videotapes. This latter trend reflected the same growing diversity in entertainment options seen in television programming.

The Epics Come of Age

The year 1977 was important for the film industry and for American moviegoers. In that year director George Lucas released *Star Wars,* the first film in a trilogy of special-effects masterpieces that included *The Empire Strikes Back* in 1980 and *Return of the Jedi* in 1983. Also in 1977 filmmaker Steven Spielberg released *Close Encounters of the Third Kind,* the first of a string of hits that included *E.T.—The Extra-Terrestrial* in 1982, and three films tracing the swashbuckling adventures of an unlikely anthropologist named Indiana Jones.

◀ *Star Wars* (left) was one of the most financially successful movies of all time. In the late 1970s and the 1980s Meryl Streep (right) became recognized as an outstanding actress.

The versatile Harrison Ford starred as Indy in *Raiders of the Lost Ark* (1981), *Indiana Jones and the Temple of Doom* (1984), and *Indiana Jones and the Last Crusade* (1989).

Audiences sat spellbound as they entered the epic worlds of myth and magic created by Lucas and Spielberg. Masterful storytellers, both directors used dazzling special effects and computer-generated graphics, techniques pioneered by Industrial Light and Magic, a Lucas company. Liberal use of these new film techniques also made hits of *Ghostbusters* (1984) and *Batman* (1989).

Movies with Mass Appeal

Audiences flocked to other types of movies as well. Dark stories of horror scared viewers of *Alien* (1979), *Poltergeist* (1982), and a seemingly endless series of *Friday the 13th* movies. The action kings of the era included Clint Eastwood in the tough-cop *Dirty Harry* series, muscle-bound Arnold Schwarzenegger in *Terminator*, and Sylvester Stallone as a boxer in the popular *Rocky* films.

Death, destruction, and the moral questions raised by the Vietnam War attracted the attention of several filmmakers and millions of moviegoers. Michael Cimino's powerful *The Deer Hunter* (1978), Francis Ford Coppola's *Apocalypse Now* (1979), Oliver Stone's *Platoon* (1986), Stanley Kubrick's *Full Metal Jacket* (1987), and Oliver Stone's *Born on the Fourth of July* (1989) helped the nation reflect on the impact of that difficult war.

The dilemmas of everyday life also made their mark. The trauma of divorce emerged in *Kramer vs. Kramer*, a 1979 Academy Award-winning film starring Dustin Hoffman and Meryl Streep, two of the era's most celebrated performers. Troubled families in *Ordinary People* (1980) and mother-daughter relationships in *Terms of Endearment* (1983) evoked tears from empathetic audiences. Dustin Hoffman earned an Academy Award for his portrayal of an autistic man in

ACADEMY AWARD WINNERS: BEST PICTURE, 1976–1990

1976	*Rocky*
1977	*Annie Hall*
1978	*The Deer Hunter*
1979	*Kramer vs. Kramer*
1980	*Ordinary People*
1981	*Chariots of Fire*
1982	*Gandhi*
1983	*Terms of Endearment*
1984	*Amadeus*
1985	*Out of Africa*
1986	*Platoon*
1987	*The Last Emperor*
1988	*Rain Man*
1989	*Driving Miss Daisy*
1990	*Dances with Wolves*

the widely acclaimed *Rain Man* (1988).

Several films captured the drama of young people coming of age. *Saturday Night Fever* (1977), *Flashdance* (1983), *Risky Business* (1983), and *The Breakfast Club* (1985) appealed to young and old audiences.

Woody Allen's wry humor captured many Americans' obsessive concern with self. Critics praised his work on such films as *Annie Hall*, which won the Academy Award for best picture in 1977.

Black and Foreign Films

Black directors, such as the controversial Spike Lee (*Do the Right Thing* and *Jungle Fever*), shocked and entertained, and attracted much larger audiences than ever before. Critics praised the work of newcomer John Singleton, whose *Boyz 'N the Hood* examined life in a Los Angeles ghetto. Black actors such as former *Saturday Night Live* star Eddie Murphy and *The Color Purple* star Whoopi Goldberg also proved popular with audiences and critics.

Spike Lee: Filmmaker with an Attitude

One of the most talked-about films of 1989, *Do the Right Thing*, was the third feature film by 32-year-old African-American filmmaker Spike Lee. It explored the often controversial topic of race relations in the United States. Lee, whose movies were as tough as his name implied, would have it no other way. "Too many people have their head in the sand about racism," he declared.

His film focused on the tensions between a white pizzeria owner and two black youths in Brooklyn, New York. After the sides came to blows, a white cop strangled one of the black youths. The other youth, played by Spike Lee, incited a riot by throwing a trash can through the pizzeria window.

A graduate of New York University's graduate film school, Lee won an award from the Academy of Motion Picture Arts and Sciences for *Joe's Bed-Stuy Barbershop: We Cut Heads* (a film he made while a student). His first feature film, *She's Gotta Have It*, engaged filmgoers with its tale of a woman carrying on affairs with three different men at the same time.

Not everyone applauded Lee for his aggressive treatment of race relations in *Do the Right Thing*. Some feared the film would provoke racial violence. But other people praised its fearless and unflinching treatment of the difficult topic.

The controversy pleased Lee. Commenting on the debate that surrounded *School Daze* (1988), his second feature film, he said, "Something must be wrong if everyone agrees 100 percent on a film I do. I'm an instigator."

Foreign films reached an increasingly wide audience. The German filmmaker Rainer Werner Fassbinder (*The Marriage of Maria Braun*, *Berlin Alexanderplatz*), French director Claude Berri (*Jean de Florette*, *Manon of the Spring*) and Australian Bruce Beresford (*Breaker Morant*, *Tender Mercies*) brought their own distinctive visions to American moviegoers.

Music

MADONNA, MICHAEL, AND MORE

The pop music of the late 1970s and 1980s offered something for nearly every taste. There were radio stations and music stores to please every type of listener. Although the foreign influence was felt more and more in American music, Baby Boomers were making "oldies" popular.

As all of these changes took place, compact disks (CDs) altered the way music was marketed. By the end of 1985 CD players had become a mass consumer item. As portable and automobile CD players appeared on the market, more and more consumers ditched their turntables and swore allegiance to laser sound.

Stars on the Scene

The top-earning U.S. band from 1988 to 1990, according to *Rolling Stone* magazine, was New Kids on the Block. With a two-year income of $115 million, this group of five young white men typified mainstream popular music in the late 1980s. Their formulaic sound was heavy with synthesizers and drum machines, designed to be easily understood and accepted by teenage audiences. Young Americans bought their music as well as their extensive line of New Kids on the Block toys, buttons, posters, and dolls.

At the same time, however, a very different sales event unfolded. The complete recordings of Robert Johnson, a 1920s-era blues singer, sold surprisingly well. Johnson's heartfelt lyrics and soulful tunes had inspired many of the most successful musicians of the 1970s and 1980s, including Eric Clapton, the Rolling Stones, and Dire Straits. Johnson's success signaled a revival of the blues—the roots of rock and roll. For some it also seemed to indicate a movement toward less commercial, more creative sound.

One trend on the pop music scene was the spectacular live stage show. Record companies

BLACK DIRECTORS MAKE THEIR MARK

By 1990 films by and about African-Americans were here to stay. Many black directors have followed the lead of Spike Lee, such as Mario Van Peebles (*New Jack City*), Matty Rich (*Straight Out of Brooklyn*), and John Singleton (*Boyz 'N the Hood*).

Finding financial backing has been the major obstacle for black filmmakers. Lee's first feature film, *She's Gotta Have It*, was shot in just 12 days to keep production costs low. Matty Rich was aided by his mother and sister, who got $16,000 in cash advances from their credit cards to help him buy film stock and to pay a cameraman.

▼ In the 1980s sales of records fell dramatically, whereas sales of CDs rose to more than 286 million.

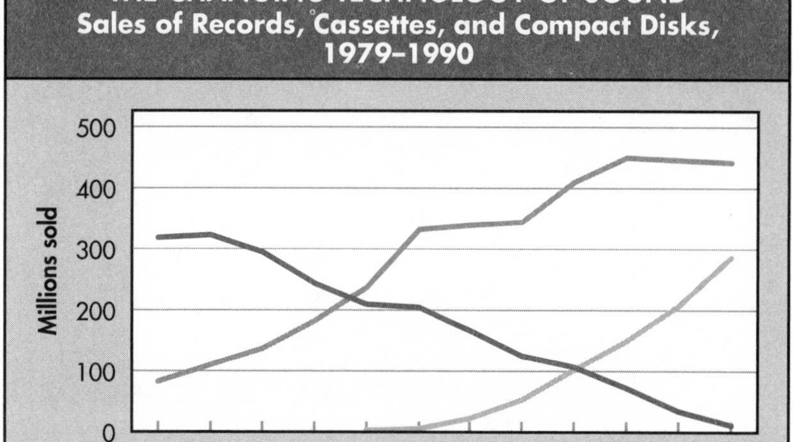

Source: *Inside the Recording Industry: A Statistical Overview 1990 Update*, © 1991 by Recording Industry Association of America, Inc.

SONY WALKMAN CRAZE

Akio Morita, chairman and cofounder of Sony, invented the Walkman portable stereo in 1979. Morita designed the tiny tape player for his three adult children. He sold 100,000 sets in Japan by the end of 1979 and 2.5 million per year by mid-1982.

The instant popularity of the Walkman in the United States took dealers by surprise. In many areas purchasers had to order their Walkmans two or more months in advance.

signed huge contracts with the era's stars. These performers launched heavily marketed albums and then set out on world tours backed by elaborate stage sets, teams of choreographed dancers, dozens of musicians, banks of computerized lights, and special effects wizardry.

Michael Jackson's Grammy Award–winning album *Thriller* (1983), promoted by a lavish coast-to-coast tour, became one of the top-selling albums of all time. The "Thriller" video, created to go with the album, won Jackson and his production crew an unprecedented eight Grammy Awards. The 1984 album *Purple Rain* from Prince, the fascinating musician from Minneapolis, also became a top seller.

"The Dream Is Over"

The world was stunned by the news on December 8, 1980, that John Lennon, a member of the Beatles, one of the most popular groups in rock music history, had been fatally shot. The 40-year-old singer, musician, and songwriter was gunned down just outside his apartment building in New York City by Mark David Chapman, a 25-year-old former mental patient and alleged fan. All over the world public vigils and mourning ceremonies were held to honor Lennon, a cultural hero.

The most popular female singer and pop star of the period was Madonna. Madonna's career took off with million-selling hits such as "Like a Virgin" and "Material Girl." In song, in videos, in movies, and in her live performances, Madonna projected a strong image that reflected the greater independence of women by challenging society's notion of acceptable female behavior.

Rap music, a street form of rhymed poetry spoken rhythmically with music, became popular with both blacks and whites. The social consciousness of Hammer and Public Enemy led an explosion of talented black rap musicians onto the national music scene.

Many other musicians also made their mark on the period. Bruce Springsteen, the popular working-class rocker from New Jersey, had top-selling hits with his albums *Born in the U.S.A.* and *Tunnel of Love.* Millions enjoyed the musical genius of the Irish band U2 on their albums *The Joshua Tree* and *Rattle and Hum.*

Other international musicians also made it big on the American scene, including Britain's George Michael and Phil Collins. Established musicians—Paul Simon, Sting, the Talking Heads, and David Bowie, among other stars—brought African rhythms and South American tunes into their music, giving even mainstream pop a distinctly international flavor.

Using Music for Political Activism

Another musical trend of the period was the rise of large-scale musical political activism. The biggest pop music event of 1985, for example,

◀ Throughout the 1980s Madonna (left) commanded attention for her rhythmic music and sex appeal. In July 1985 "Live Aid" (right) was staged in both London and Philadelphia to raise money to feed people starving in Africa.

was "Live Aid," a cross-Atlantic concert extravaganza to raise money for starving people in drought-stricken Africa. About 72,000 people packed Wembley Stadium in London while another 90,000 assembled in JFK Stadium in Philadelphia. Another 1.5 billion watched the live television broadcast, organized by musician Bob Geldof. The featured musicians included Tina Turner, Mick Jagger, Phil Collins, Robert Plant, Madonna, Bob Dylan, and many more. Together, the two "Live Aid" shows raised more than $70 million for African famine relief.

Other musical benefits for the needy followed, including "Farm Aid" in 1985, the birthday tribute concert to Nelson Mandela in 1988, and Amnesty International's "Human Rights Now!" tour the same year. These events showed that rock and roll could be put to use to better the world.

Media

INSTANT NEWS GOES INTERNATIONAL

During the 1980s the U.S. economy shifted its emphasis. Instant access to accurate information became the primary consideration for most businesses. This new economy that called for more effective communications systems is referred to as "information-based."

The World of News

One symbol of the Media Age, as the 1980s has been called, is undoubtedly the satellite dish. These powerful saucers permitted national newspapers to beam the latest edition of the morning newspaper from their editorial headquarters to printing plants across the country. Roving television news crews could set up mini-satellite relay stations in remote

STUDENT DESIGNS VIETNAM WAR MEMORIAL

When the Vietnam War Memorial was first unveiled, it was the center of much disagreement. Many people disliked the black granite, V-shaped wall, which lists the names of more than 50,000 Americans killed during the war. However, it soon became the most visited site in Washington, D.C. The memorial has a strong impact because the names of those who died are the primary focal point; it does not glorify war in any way.

"The Wall," as it is sometimes called, was designed by a 21-year-old Yale University architecture student named Maya Yang Lin. Her design for the memorial was chosen in 1981 over more than 1,400 other designs. The early controversy over the Wall caused Lin to drop out of college for a time. She later returned and finished her studies at Yale.

DEATHS

Paul Robeson, actor and singer, 1976
Charles Chaplin, actor, 1977
Elvis Presley, singer, 1977
John Wayne, actor, 1979
Thelonious Monk, jazz pianist and composer, 1982
George Balanchine, ballet choreographer, 1983
Tennessee Williams, playwright, 1983
Count Basie, bandleader, 1984
Rock Hudson, actor, 1985
Orson Welles, actor and director, 1985
James Cagney, actor, 1986
Benny Goodman, bandleader, 1986
Cary Grant, actor, 1986
Georgia O'Keeffe, painter, 1986
Fred Astaire, actor and dancer, 1987
James Baldwin, author and playwright, 1987
Andy Warhol, artist, 1987
Irving Berlin, songwriter, 1989
Bette Davis, actress, 1989
Jim Henson, puppeteer, 1990
Theodor Geisel (Dr. Seuss), author and illustrator, 1991

places. Their live signals reached worldwide audiences, as dramatically shown in history's first live televised war: the Persian Gulf War of 1991. As technology improved, so did the demand for up-to-date information.

The late 1970s and 1980s was a difficult period for the few companies that had previously controlled the media industry. Network television news, for example, faced serious competition from its cable rival CNN. In response, networks took a new approach. They signed handsome superstar news anchors to multimillion-dollar contracts, even as they cut their overall news staff. By placing emphasis on the star quality of its reporters and budgets, news shows blurred the line between news and entertainment, and many felt that the news suffered for it.

Although the total daily newspaper circulation remained steady during the period—about 61 million—competition and consolidation put more than 100 daily newspapers out of business. By the mid-1980s newspaper chains and groups—Gannett, Knight-Ridder, and Hearst, among others—owned more than two-thirds of the nation's newspapers. Only about 50 American cities had more than one major newspaper.

At a time when many newspapers were closing, colorful, simplistic, upbeat *USA Today*, the nation's first true national daily, turned a profit for the first time in 1989 after spending eight years and $800 million. By the end of the 1980s it had reached a nationwide circulation of more than 1.8 million, second only to the *Wall Street Journal*.

Other innovative news outlets were also successful. During the Iranian hostage crisis of 1979–1980, ABC added a half-hour news and interview show, *Nightline*, to its schedule after the late local news. With reporter Ted Koppel as host, *Nightline* became one of the 1980s' most dynamic public forums for informed discussion of key social and political issues. It was instrumental in maintaining Americans' attention on the hostages in Iran, and it played an indirect part in Jimmy Carter's 1980 defeat in the presidential election.

National Public Radio raised the caliber of available news programs with its informative and acclaimed *Morning Edition* and *All Things Considered*. On public television the half-hour evening news program expanded to become *The MacNeil-Lehrer News Hour*.

The Magazine Business

Unlike daily newspaper readership, the circulation of magazines increased substantially over the period. In 1977 Americans bought 260 million subscriptions to major magazines, up from 147 million in 1950. More than 300 new consumer and business magazines began publishing in 1977 alone. Many, such as *Skydiving*, *Popular Cars*, *Ballet News*, and *Quest*, appealed to special-interest groups.

A flood of other new titles tempted American readers during the late 1970s and early 1980s, reflecting the diverse themes and interests of the times: *The Runner*, *New Body*, *Bird World*, *Electronic Games*, *Travel Smart*, *Woman's World*, and *City Woman*. The list was as endless as the imagination of America's magazine publishers and the interests of its readers. The total circulation of the nation's periodicals reached a staggering 540 million.

Although magazine circulation grew rapidly, advertising revenues did not. As a result many new magazines stopped publication after only a few issues, unable to attract readers quickly enough to stay in business. Sometimes specialty publications lacked the publicity dollars to reach their target audience. Even well-established magazines, such as *Esquire, Scientific American,* and *Woman's Day,* had to struggle to retain readership and revenues. One reason for this trend: advances in technology—satellite communications, computerized editing of photos, desktop publishing—made it easier for new companies to enter the highly competitive periodical market.

Theater

THE BUSINESS OF BROADWAY

The 1980s witnessed numerous changes on Broadway, the Manhattan home of America's largest theater district, as the cost of producing plays skyrocketed. In 1982 the cost of producing a new Broadway show hit a new high—$5 million—as did the cost of seeing a show—$50. One of the big hits of the season was Andrew Lloyd Webber's *Cats,* an extravagant musical spectacular based on a book of poems by T. S. Eliot. In the opinion of some theater critics, its success related less to its artistic merit than to successful marketing.

▲ More than 6.5 million theatergoers enjoyed *A Chorus Line,* the story of a cast of dancers auditioning and rehearsing for a Broadway show. It ran on Broadway for a record 15 years—more than 6,000 performances, all told.

The longest-running show in Broadway history, *A Chorus Line* debuted in April 1975 and was performed a record 6,137 times before it closed on March 31, 1990. During its 15 years, it brought in nearly $277 million and sustained producer Joseph Papp's nonprofit New York Shakespeare Festival.

But many Broadway theaters stood empty during the era. Several fell victim to the wrecker's ball. Many serious plays fled New York and became the domain of nonprofit and regional theaters.

By 1990 the cost of producing a new show topped $10 million. High ticket prices demanded ever more lavish production effects. The hits of the late 1980s were almost without exception big-budget musicals. *Les Miserables* opened in 1987. In 1988 Andrew Lloyd Webber's *Phantom of the Opera* was the season's smash hit. As the 1990s opened the trend toward musical extravaganzas continued with the musical *Miss Saigon.* But spiraling costs and high ticket prices seemed to push Broadway theater out of the reach of most Americans.

Fine Arts

CELEBRITY AND CENSORSHIP

Artists continued to explore new and varied forms of expression. As in many previous eras they challenged traditional limitations, defied conventional norms, and employed new technologies. Performance artists broke down the boundaries separating art and entertainment. Environmental artists, such as Christo, used the earth's varied landscape as their canvas. Video artists explored the possibilities of electronic imaging.

Art collecting boomed, especially during the prosperous 1980s. Fueled by cash-rich investors, particularly the Japanese, art prices, notably for the so-called Old Masters and the Impressionists, went through the roof. In 1990, for example, a single painting by Vincent Van Gogh brought a record price of $82.5 million.

The greatest art controversy of the decade occurred in 1990, when a Cincinnati museum and its director were **indicted** by a grand jury on obscenity charges related to an exhibit of photographs by the late Robert Mapplethorpe. Seven of Mapplethorpe's 175 photos depicted naked children or homosexual acts. Although a jury ruled that the photos were not obscene, some members of Congress threatened to restrict public funding for the arts.

The incident aroused a heated national debate on the subject of art and censorship. It also reflected the growing conservatism of many Americans.

BEST-SELLING FICTION, 1976–1991

1976	*Trinity,* Leon Uris
1977	*The Silmarillion,* J. R. R. Tolkien
1978	*Chesapeake,* James A. Michener
1979	*The Matarese Circle,* Robert Ludlum
1980	*The Covenant,* James A. Michener
1981	*Noble House,* James Clavell
1982	*E.T.—The Extra-Terrestrial Storybook,* William Kotzwinkle
1983	*The Return of the Jedi Storybook,* adapted by Joan D. Vinge
1984	*The Talisman,* Stephen King and Peter Straub
1985	*The Mammoth Hunters,* Jean Auel
1986	*It,* Stephen King
1987	*Tommyknockers,* Stephen King
1988	*The Cardinal of the Kremlin,* Tom Clancy
1989	*The Joy Luck Club,* Amy Tan
1990	*The Burden of Proof,* Scott Turow
1991	*The Sum of All Fears,* Tom Clancy

Books

SOMETHING TO READ FOR EVERYONE

Those who feared that television would doom America's interest in books breathed a little easier in the 1980s. Books competed with personal computers, CD players, VCRs, and other high-tech leisure activities. But Americans love to read. In 1990 they spent a record $14.7 billion on books, up from $4.1 billion in 1976.

Books Reflect the Times

As in the movie and music industries, tried-and-true formulas dominated publishing. Major publishers showed less willingness to take risks on talented but little-known writers. Publishers competed to sign best-selling authors capable of writing blockbusters. As a result the amount of money spent by publishers for book advances and publishing rights skyrocketed.

In 1981 Bantam paid $3.2 million to author Judith Krantz for *Princess Daisy.* Dell topped this record in 1990, when it paid mystery writer Ken Follett $12.3 million for his next two novels. His best-seller status had been proved by earlier books such as *The Key to Rebecca* and *Triple.*

Book selections reflected the diverse trends of the times. It was the age of "how-to": Robert G. Allen's *Nothing Down: How to Buy Real Estate with Little or No Money Down,* Bill Cosby's *Fatherhood,* and Robert E. Kowalski's *The Eight-Week Cholesterol Cure.* People overcome by the anxiety of the age found inspiration in the folksy advice of Robert Fulghum (*All I Really Need to Know I Learned in Kindergarten*). They were enthralled by the business success of Chrysler's chairman in *Iacocca: An Autobiography* and were uplifted and saddened by the triumph and tragedy of Dr. Martin Luther King Jr. in Taylor Branch's *Parting the Waters.*

But Americans also turned to books for sheer entertainment and escapism. Tom Clancy's technothrillers—*The Hunt for Red October, Clear and Present Danger*—chronicled the last years of the Cold War. The frightening horror stories of Stephen King, the romances of Danielle Steel, and the spy novels of John Le Carré topped best-seller lists. Other readers, seeking challenge, picked up Norman Mailer's masterful *The Executioner's Song,* Saul Bellow's *The Dean's December,* Gore Vidal's impressively researched *Lincoln,* Philip Roth's funny and ferocious *Zuckerman Unbound,* William P. Kennedy's Pulitzer Prize–winning *Ironweed,* or the two final books in John Updike's saga of Rabbit Angstrom, *Rabbit Is Rich* and *Rabbit at Rest.*

New writers also made their mark on the literary scene, including David Leavitt (*The Lost Language of Cranes*) and Jay McInerney (*Bright Lights, Big City*).

The era witnessed a renewed interest in literary diversity. Black voices such as Toni Morrison (*Beloved* and *Song of Solomon*) and Alice Walker (*The Color Purple*), the Chinese-American Amy Tan (*The Joy Luck Club*), and the Cuban-American Oscar Hijuelos (*The Mambo Kings Play Songs of Love*) attracted millions of readers. The popularity of South American authors Gabriel Garcia Marquez (*Love in the Time of Cholera*) and Mario Vargas Llosa (*Aunt Julia and the Scriptwriter*) and Czech writer Milan Kundera (*The Unbearable Lightness of Being*) gave evidence of a greater appreciation of non-American cultures and values.

The Salman Rushdie Affair

The furor surrounding Salman Rushdie's 1989 book *The Satanic Verses* rumbled through the normally quiet world of book publishing like a violent earthquake. The 42-year-old author of two previous novels was born to a prosperous Muslim family in Bombay, India. He completed his education at Cambridge University.

▼▼▼

The Satanic Verses outraged Muslims worldwide.

His first two novels, *Midnight's Children* and *Shame,* reflected Rushdie's deep desire to recognize and integrate his varied cultural influences. *The Satanic Verses* continued this theme. Rushdie used satire and symbolism to examine an individual's relationship to his culture and history. In the novel the fictional scribe Salman modifies the words of God as relayed to him by the fictional prophet Mahound.

Rushdie's best-seller earned him the praise of critics. He was awarded the prestigious British Whitbread Prize for fiction. But *The Satanic Verses* outraged Muslims worldwide. The book was immediately banned in a number of Islamic countries. Ayatollah Ruhollah Khomeini, Iran's fundamentalist Islamic ruler, sentenced Rushdie to death.

Rushdie went into hiding in Britain. Bomb threats disrupted the New York and London offices of Viking Penguin, the book's publisher. Three major U.S. bookstore chains pulled the book from the shelves to protect their employees. Assassins killed one of the book's translators. With no sign from his Islamic critics that their anger is lessening, Rushdie continues to live in hiding.

SPORTS AND LEISURE

A positive sign in sports and leisure during the late 1970s and 1980s was the growth of participation. Americans' concern for health and fitness and the economic boom motivated huge numbers of people to pursue athletics on their own.

In increasing numbers people all over the country played racquetball, walked, did aerobics, biked, and jogged. The New York City Marathon, which began in 1970 with 126 runners, grew to include more than 23,000 runners in 1988 (above).

High technology invaded most playing fields in the 1980s, as it did the rest of American society. Technology did not completely take over sports, but it made its mark. The impact of television on college and professional sports was particularly strong, especially in terms of raising the financial stakes.

For highly paid professional athletes, in particular, more money meant more pressure from team owners and higher expectations from fans. A basketball player earning $100,000 a year could, perhaps, be excused for having a bad game. But when the same player earned $1 million a year, the fans expected top-notch performance all the time.

Some observers mourned the continuing change in sports from a leisure pursuit of enthusiastic amateurs to a high-tech, high-finance, high-pressure industry. Others welcomed the change and called it progress. Whatever one called it, Americans continued their love affair with spectator sports of all types.

AT A GLANCE

- Sports in the Era
- Problems Affect the Olympic Games
- Changes in Baseball
- Basketball's Popularity Grows
- Football Encounters Challenges
- Money Dominates Many College Sports
- Other Sports Enjoy Success
- Americans Pursue Fun with Intensity

DATAFILE

Sports

World records as of 1985	Men	Women
Track and Field		
100 yd. dash	9.0″	10.0″
Mile	3′46.32″	4′15.8″
High jump	7.9 ft.	6.8 ft.
Swimming		
100 m. freestyle	48.95″	54.79″

Leisure

	1980	1988
Average workweek	39.7 hrs.	41.1 hrs.
Attendance		
Baseball (major leagues)	43.7 mil.	53.8 mil.
Football (NFL)	14.1 mil.	17.0 mil.
National parks	60.2 mil.	56.4 mil.
Bicycle sales (units)	8.9 mil.	9.9 mil.

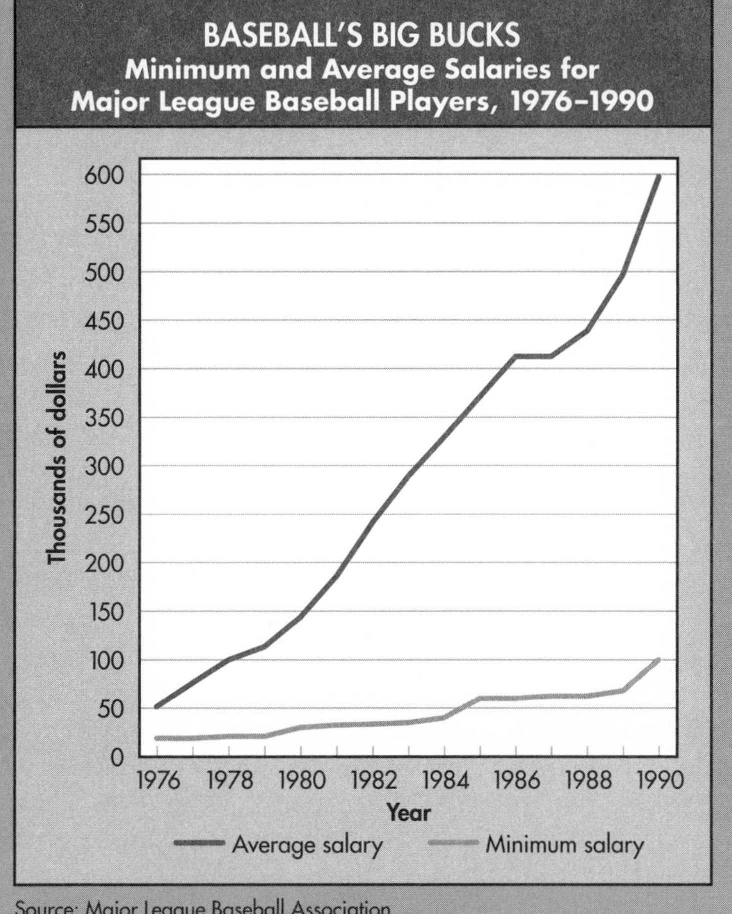

Source: Major League Baseball Association.

Sports Trends

SPORTS IN THE ERA

Between 1977 and 1991 the percentage of personal income Americans spent on recreation almost doubled. That fact suggests how much emphasis Americans placed on sports and fitness during the 1980s.

The Fitness Boom

Many Americans in the 1980s had more leisure time and valued physical fitness more highly, at least in theory. Videotapes and books such as *Jane Fonda's Workout Book* and *Fit for Life* competed with *The Complete Book of Running* and *The Frugal Gourmet Cooks with Wine* for top honors on the best-seller lists.

People needed more than just books to get in shape, of course. They bought millions of pairs of specialized shoes—for running, basketball, racquet sports, or "cross training." Prices often topped $100 a pair. People worked out at health clubs and fitness centers. For many wealthy young professionals such places replaced country clubs as the after-work social center.

Others chose more solitary fitness programs like jogging, power walking, or biking or sought the challenge of competition or the support of others in low-impact aerobics, weight-training, squash, or racquetball. Many adults in the 1980s, it seemed, were trying to get in shape, or at least dressing as though they were. Many children caught fitness fever too, participating in an endless variety of activities from gymnastics to soccer.

AMERICANS EXERCISE FOR HEALTH

In 1960 only 24 percent of Americans exercised for their health. By the mid-1980s at least 47 percent of the U.S. population exercised regularly.

The Business of Sports

Despite widespread participation in amateur athletics, the sports world was increasingly dominated by professionals. Television was largely responsible for this change. All-sports cable networks—ESPN, SportsChannel, and the Madison Square Garden network—along with increased sports coverage by the major television networks created many new outlets for sports programming. Networks willingly paid top dollar to cover sports.

As a result, team revenues increased sharply, and professional athletes began to demand their fair share of the financial pie. Owner-player financial conflict led to strikes in both pro baseball and football. As salaries increased, team owners and coaches pressured athletes to justify their skyrocketing salaries. Some athletes, concerned about job security, turned to **steroids** and even cocaine in a misguided attempt to raise their performance level and value to the team.

Over time, professional sports teams, with their marketing strategies and lawyers, came to resemble large corporations, which in fact they were. By 1990, for example, the New York Yankees received annual revenues of $150 million from television alone.

Team owners used their financial clout to demand that cities build new stadiums and arenas. If cities refused to meet owners' demands, the teams moved to other, more accommodating cities. In pro football the St. Louis Cardinals moved to Phoenix, and the Baltimore Colts moved to Indianapolis. In other cases professional sports leagues capitalized on the sports boom by expanding the number of teams. In 1991 major-league baseball announced that new teams in Miami and Denver would eventually join the National League.

FITNESS FIGURES

In 1980 Americans spent:

- $1 billion on athletic shoes
- $5 billion on health foods and vitamins
- $50 million for diet and exercise books
- $6 billion for diet drinks
- $5 billion at health clubs and corporate fitness centers
- $1 billion for bicycles
- $240 million for barbells and aerobics classes
- $8 billion for sportswear and gadgets

The Olympics

PROBLEMS AFFECT THE OLYMPIC GAMES

Like many other athletic contests, the Olympic Games became a major television event. The International Olympic Committee (IOC) signed huge television contracts in an attempt to pay for the high cost of construction for the games. But as media coverage made Olympic stars household names, it also brought problems to the attention of people around the world.

The Olympics and Politics

It was at the 1976 games in Montreal, Canada, that the word **boycott** entered the Olympic vocabulary. Black African nations, angered that South Africa was allowed to participate in the games, refused to send their own athletes to compete.

The boycotting trend continued in 1980 at the Moscow Olympics. Led by the United States, Western nations, outraged by the Soviet invasion of Afghanistan, stayed away from Moscow in droves. Only 81 nations competed, down from 122 countries in 1972.

The Olympics had been created as an opportunity to put political differences aside in the name of sport. Instead they became a political battleground. The 1984 summer Olympics in Los Angeles were boycotted by the Soviet Union and all but one Eastern Bloc nation, long-standing powers in many of the most popular Olympic sports. Bogged down in yet another dispute with the United States over arms control, the Soviets repaid the United States for its 1980 boycott of the Moscow games.

By 1988, however, the political turmoil was receding. For the first time since 1972, no major political boycott interfered with the games. The fall of South Africa's system of apartheid made the future look even more promising. The IOC decided to invite South Africa to the 1992 summer Olympics in Barcelona, Spain.

Olympic Issues

Two other issues detracted from the Olympic Games. Many nations, most notably the Soviet Union and its satellites, had long sent athletes to the Olympics who were professionals in all but name. Other nations, including the United States, insisted that Olympic athletes be unpaid amateurs.

By the late 1980s, however, the trend toward professionalism was irreversible. The United States allowed professional tennis players to compete on its behalf in 1988 and announced that pros from the National Basketball Association would play on its 1992 Olympic basketball squad.

The troubling alliance of drugs and athletics also blemished the Olympic Games. During the 1988 games in Seoul, South Korea, Ben Johnson, a Canadian sprinter, won the gold medal for the 100-meter dash, setting a new world record. The IOC, however, stripped Johnson of the medal after he tested positive for illegal substances. Nine other athletes were also found guilty of drug abuse, leading to calls for tougher enforcement of drug rules.

▲ U.S. Olympic hockey players celebrate their upset 4 to 3 victory over the Soviet Union in Lake Placid, New York.

Olympic Stars

Despite these distractions the Olympic Games produced many exciting moments. In the 1976 summer games at Montreal, American track-and-field star Bruce Jenner won the decathlon with a record 8,618 points. Montreal also witnessed the emergence of Nadia Comaneci, the 14-year-old Romanian gymnast who earned seven perfect scores and won three gold medals.

In the 1980 winter games at Lake Placid, New York, the underdog U.S. hockey team thrilled the nation with a breathtaking triumph over the heavily favored Soviet hockey team. Eric Heiden, an American from Wisconsin, won all five gold medals in men's speed skating, a sport that had long been dominated by the Scandinavian countries.

"DO YOU . . . BELIEVE . . . IN . . . MIRACLES?"

—Sportscaster Al Michaels, announcing the U.S. Olympic hockey team's 4 to 3 win over the Soviets, February 22, 1980

▶ In 1988 Americans Florence Griffith Joyner (right) and her sister-in-law Jackie Joyner-Kersee collected a total of four track-and-field gold medals in Seoul.

East German skater Katarina Witt dominated the figure skating competition at the 1988 winter games in Calgary, Canada. American diving star Greg Louganis won both springboard and platform diving competitions at the 1988 summer games in Seoul, the second Olympics in a row in which he won both gold medals in diving. Performances such as these continued to appeal to millions of Americans for whom the Olympic Games remain a special—and sometimes magical—competition.

RECORDS SET BY MARY DECKER SLANEY

At the 1984 Olympic Games Mary Decker (later Mary Decker Slaney) achieved the kind of attention no athlete desires. Although most considered her an easy gold-medal winner in the women's 3,000-meter race that year, Decker tripped over South African runner Zola Budd's bare feet. Most people remember Decker, so close to the finish line, sobbing. However, her achievements outshine her fall.

The following year she became the world record holder in the mile for women, one of eight American middle- and long-distance track records she set between 1982 and 1985.

Distance	*U.S. Record*	*Year Set*
800 m.	1′56.90″	1985
1,000 m.	2′34.08″	1985
1,500 m.	3′57.12″	1983
1 mi.	4′16.71″	1985
2,000 m.	5′32.07″	1984
3,000 m.	8′25.83″	1985
5,000 m.	15′06.53″	1985
10,000 m.	31′35.03″	1982

Baseball

CHANGES IN BASEBALL

In the 1970s and 1980s major-league professional baseball enjoyed a revival as attendance shot up. One issue in particular, however, undermined the fans' support—player-owner tension and disputes. And, as such, the main story of the era took place off the field—the development of **free agency.**

The Free-Agency Dispute

As in pro football and basketball, the most heated baseball contest of the 1970s and 1980s was a financial tug-of-war between players and team owners. The battle was waged with legal briefs, court orders, newspaper headlines, strikes, and lockouts.

The issue at hand was simple. Were baseball players bound to the team that first signed them or to which they were traded, as the reserve clause in their contracts stated? Or were the players, as were most other employees, free to take a job elsewhere when their current contracts expired?

In 1975 federal arbitrators struck down the reserve clause. A 1976 agreement between the owners and the Players Association provided for limited free agency. In the wake of this agreement, some team owners went shopping for new players. Outfielder Reggie Jackson, for example, got a five-year, $2.9 million contract by the New York Yankees, who also signed pitcher Jim "Catfish" Hunter to a contract worth $3.5 million over five years.

Could these expensive free agents possibly be worth so much money? Yankee owner George Steinbrenner had no doubts, especially after the Yankees won back-to-back World Series in 1977 and 1978. "We're going to keep spending," said Steinbrenner, "to keep the team winning." He kept spending, but the Yankees did not keep winning. Other teams also stepped up to bid for the best players. Over time the pool of athletic talent was spread more or less evenly among the teams. In fact no team has won the World Series twice in a row since the Yankees did.

The clash between players and team owners peaked in 1981. Salaries had increased in the previous five years to an average of about $175,000. Players, however, wanted a larger share of the television revenues pouring into team bank accounts. For 49 days in 1981 the 650 members of the Major League Baseball Players Association went on strike, forcing the cancellation of more than 700 games. At issue was the owners' claim that they should be compensated when a player left their team. When the dust settled, however, it was clear that the players and their union's head, Marvin Miller, had prevailed.

The settlement of the 1981 strike was not the end of the dispute. In 1990 team owners locked players out of training camp for 32 days in a conflict over **arbitration** and pension-fund issues. For the most part, however, players had already won the battle back in 1981.

As a result salaries skyrocketed during the decade, fueled by ever-higher television revenues and owners' willingness to spend. By 1990 the average major leaguer earned more than $600,000 per year, and the trend showed no sign of weakening. During the 1991 season Pittsburgh Pirate outfielder Bobby Bonilla, who became a free agent at the end of the season, turned down a contract offer from the team for a sum in excess of $4 million per year. Bonilla went on to sign with the New York Mets for an astounding $29 million for five years.

Superstar Players

Baseball was not completely dominated by contract disputes. Despite high ticket prices, more and more fans flocked to ballparks, up from 38 million in 1977 to more than 55 million in 1990. They also tuned in to many games on television, as teams signed contracts with broadcast or cable networks to televise virtually all their games. No team dynasties emerged, but individual players continued to achieve superstar status.

Pete Rose of the Cincinnati Reds, one of the greatest singles

Professional Sports Labor Disputes

Date	*Sport*	*Issues/Effect on Season*
October 3, 1970	Baseball	Umpire pay scale for postseason games/ Games worked by non-union umpires
April 1, 1972	Baseball	Pension-fund dispute/ Season began 10 days late
June 12, 1981	Baseball	Free agency and minimum salary levels/ A third of the season canceled
September 12, 1981	Football	Basic contract provisions/ 7 games of the season's 16-game schedule canceled
August 6, 1985	Baseball	Salary arbitration, free agency, and minimum salary levels/ Games missed were made up as rain-outs
September 22, 1987	Football	Free agency/ Season shortened by 1 game; 3 games played by replacement teams
March 12, 1990	Baseball	Salary arbitration dispute/ Opening of season delayed; missed games made up

Source: *Facts & Dates of American Sports* by Gordon Carruth and Eugene Ehrlich. Copyright © 1988 by Harper & Row, Publishers, Inc.

The Pete Rose Fiasco

Players and fans alike dubbed him "Charlie Hustle" for his all-out play and reckless, head-first slides. But during spring training in 1989 suspicions arose over Rose's activities off the playing field. After several months of investigation, Commissioner of Baseball A. Bartlett Giamatti banned Rose from baseball for life for betting on baseball games.

The 48-year-old Rose, who was manager of the Cincinnati Reds, had retired as an active player in 1986, having set an impressive record as all-time leader in base hits. But his gambling habit encumbered him with a much more questionable distinction. He was only the fifth player in history, and the first since 1943, to be banned from the game of baseball. He was subsequently jailed for tax evasion.

The damaging accusations against Rose first appeared when a check from Rose to a man who was later convicted of receiving and paying off gambling bets surfaced in a gambling raid. Some sources suggested that Rose had used his 1984 World Series ring to pay gambling debts.

Rose never pleaded guilty, but he did sign a document admitting that "the Commissioner has a factual basis" to impose the lifetime penalty. He maintained, however, that he had never bet on the Reds.

Even so, some supporters continued to praise Rose for his singlemindedness—even his initial refusal to admit he had a gambling problem. Others, however, especially young fans, felt hurt by their hero, who had betrayed the game he loved.

hitters of all time, had a career total of 4,256 hits. Lou Brock of the St. Louis Cardinals held the record for stolen bases until 1991, when he was surpassed by Rickey Henderson of the Oakland A's. Wade Boggs of the Boston Red Sox finished the 1989 season with the fifth-highest lifetime batting average in major-league history. Other big hitters also made their mark, including Mike Schmidt of the Philadelphia Phillies and Cecil Fielder of the Chicago White Sox. Pitching standouts included Nolan Ryan of the Texas Rangers, who pitched seven no-hitters and averaged at least one strikeout per inning over 16 seasons, and three-time Cy Young Award winner Roger Clemens of the Boston Red Sox.

Basketball

BASKETBALL'S POPULARITY GROWS

As did other major sports of the period, professional basketball grew by leaps and bounds. The National Basketball Association (NBA) expanded from 9 to 22 teams in the 1970s and added 4 more teams in the 1980s. Millions of new fans flocked to the nation's arenas. Millions more watched at home on television.

Because the NBA's system of choosing players, known as the player draft, gave the worst teams first chance at the best new talent, no team won consecutive NBA titles from 1970 until 1988. There were dominant players and teams during the period, however.

The Boston Celtics ran away with five titles, three of these wins under the leadership of one of the NBA's superior players of the 1980s, Larry Bird. An All-American and College Player of the Year at Indiana State University, Bird won the NBA's Rookie of the Year Award in 1980. Over the course of his professional career, he compiled a remarkable record, averaging 25 points, 10 rebounds, and 6 assists per game.

Michael Jordan, the high-flying Chicago Bulls guard, became the most popular and exciting individual player. He and other stars capitalized on their popularity by endorsing a wide range of products. Jordan's famous grin inspired consumers to buy sneakers, cereal, and soft drinks.

Another basketball star of the 1980s was Earvin "Magic" Johnson. He led the Los Angeles Lakers to five titles, including back-to-back championships in 1987 and 1988. Johnson is probably the finest passer the game has ever known. "Whatever is happening out there," said one of his coaches, "he comes up with a way to win." In 1991 Johnson stunned the world when he retired from the game because of his infection with the virus that causes AIDS.

Football

FOOTBALL ENCOUNTERS CHALLENGES

As did baseball in 1981, the world of pro football suffered a crippling strike in 1982, and for much the same reason. The players in both sports wanted a bigger slice of the financial pie, and they wanted to be allowed to become free agents after their initial contract expired. Unlike baseball players, however, players in the National Football League (NFL) achieved few of their goals. In the long run, only about one-third of the players benefited from the new agreement.

The NFL also faced a stiff challenge on another front. The upstart United States Football League (USFL) began play in 1983, successfully signing several high-profile college players, including Heisman Trophy winners Herschel Walker and Doug Flutie. The NFL itself helped sponsor another start-up league, the World League of American Football (WLAF). With teams in the United States, Europe, and Japan, the WLAF spread American football to enthusiastic fans around the globe.

The San Francisco 49ers dominated football in the 1980s, winning the Super Bowl in 1981, 1984, 1988, and 1989. Joe Montana, the NFL's premier quarterback of the

▲ Los Angeles Laker Earvin "Magic" Johnson (at right) led his team to five championships during the 1980s.

1980s and the highest-rated quarterback in pro football history, led the attack. Montana had "the softest, surest hands you ever saw, an arm that put the ball where he wanted, and a jazzman's ability to improvise," wrote sportswriter Mike Lupica, who called Montana "the best quarterback of all time." Injuries, however, can strike any player. Montana missed the 1991–1992 season with an elbow injury that put his career in jeopardy.

Athletes and Drug Use

◀ In 1986 22-year-old college basketball star Len Bias died of a cocaine overdose shortly after being drafted by the Boston Celtics.

In October 1991 Dallas Mavericks' player Roy Tarpley was banned permanently from the NBA, under terms of the Anti-Drug Agreement between the league and the NBA Players Association. After treatment on two previous occasions for drug dependence, Tarpley missed two team practices and refused to take a drug test. In such cases the NBA agreement stipulates that the test must be considered positive. Tarpley's punishment was permanent dismissal from the NBA.

Tarpley's predicament was neither new nor unique. Amateur and professional athletes alike reacted to the high-pressure, win-at-any-cost atmosphere of the 1980s by turning to drugs. College basketball standout Len Bias died of a cocaine overdose. New York Giants' defensive end Lawrence Taylor suffered a highly publicized bout with cocaine addiction. Star Canadian sprinter Ben Johnson was stripped of his 1988 Olympic gold medal in the 100-meter dash after testing positive for steroids.

Steroid use was a pressing Olympic issue—estimates pegged steroid use by Olympic athletes at 50 percent or higher. Professional sports also wrestled with the problem of performance-enhancing drugs. As many as 40 percent of pro football players, according to a 1989 estimate, used steroids. By the early 1990s, however, most professional and amateur sports leagues had enacted strict drug-testing measures that deterred athletes from using drugs. Evidence of drug-induced health problems also discouraged athletes from taking them. For example, steroids can cause liver failure, mood swings, and shrunken testes.

College Sports

MONEY DOMINATES MANY COLLEGE SPORTS

College sports faced a serious dilemma in the 1980s. Were varsity athletes, particularly those in headline sports such as basketball and football, mostly athletes or mostly college students? The tension between sports and academics had hounded college sports programs for decades. But television contracts offered to top basketball and football schools in the 1980s raised the stakes.

With tens of millions of dollars in revenue on the line, coaches and athletic directors felt intense pressure from fans to sign top high school prospects and produce winning teams. In the pressure cooker of big-time college sports, some stepped over the line. Coaches or alumni booster clubs working on their behalf offered cash, cars, and other illegal incentives to attract talented players.

The wrongdoings did not go unnoticed or unpunished, however.

In the late 1980s the National Collegiate Athletic Association (NCAA) sentenced Southern Methodist University's football team to the "death penalty"—no competition in the sport for two years. The NCAA had uncovered recruiting violations at the school. University of Oklahoma football coach Barry Switzer and University of Nevada at Las Vegas basketball coach Jerry Tarkanian, whose Runnin' Rebels won the 1990 NCAA basketball championship, also faced punishment for recruiting violations and other misdeeds.

College Sports Remain Popular

Despite the many scandals, the popularity of college sports surged. Exciting games and dazzling athletes, showcased in the NCAA basketball tournament, were one reason why. No sports fan soon forgot the thrill of seeing Magic Johnson and Michigan State edge out Larry Bird and Indiana State for the 1979 national championship. The dramatic one-point 1982 triumph of the University of North Carolina Tar Heels, led by the incomparable James Worthy and Michael Jordan, over the Georgetown Hoyas was watched by millions of viewers. In 1983 the upstart North Carolina State Wolfpack clawed out a last-second victory over the mighty University of Houston. In sports, anything seemed possible. The "Final Four," as the semifinals and finals of the NCAA championship are called, became one of the highlights of the annual television sports calendar.

Beginning in the late 1980s the women's basketball Final Four competition was also televised, marking an increased interest nationally in women's college sports. Under federal pressure in most cases, funding for women's sports increased substantially over the period. However, it still lagged far behind that of men's sports.

College football also benefited from the popularity of televised sports. In addition to expanded TV coverage of regular season games, the 1980s witnessed an explosion of postseason bowl games.

Sports

OTHER SPORTS ENJOY SUCCESS

As Americans' interest in professional and college baseball, basketball, and football grew, so did the popularity of other sports, including tennis, boxing, golf, yachting, and bicycle racing. Worldwide television broadcasts that featured these sports attracted millions of viewers.

Tennis

For almost ten years Martina Navratilova dominated the sport of women's tennis. By the late 1980s, however, talented young players had emerged to challenge her longtime reign. Germany's Steffi Graf, for example, won both Wimbledon and the U.S. Open championships in 1988 and 1989, although Navratilova regained the Wimbledon title in 1990.

In men's tennis Jimmy Connors remained competitive throughout the period, winning three times at

DEATHS

Jesse Owens, track-and-field star, 1980
Joe Louis, boxer, 1981
Satchel Paige, baseball pitcher, 1982
Paul "Bear" Bryant, college football coach, 1983
Jack Dempsey, boxer, 1983
George Halas, founder and coach of Chicago Bears, 1983
Johnny Weissmuller, swimmer, 1984
Roger Maris, baseball outfielder, 1985
Carl Hubbell, baseball pitcher, 1988
Victor Davis, Canadian swimmer, 1989
Doug Harvey, hockey player, 1989
Billy Martin, baseball player and manager, 1989
Sugar Ray Robinson, boxer, 1989
Bobby Davies, basketball player and coach, 1990
Hank Gathers, basketball player, 1990
Rocky Graziano, boxer, 1990
Larry Jackson, baseball pitcher, 1990
Charlie Keller, baseball outfielder, 1990

Martina Navratilova Dominates Women's Tennis

▲ Martina Navratilova (left) and Chris Evert talk after a 1987 match at the French Open.

In 1978 many people said that the only reason Martina Navratilova was dominating women's tennis was because reigning star Chris Evert was away on vacation. When Navratilova faced Evert at Wimbledon in July, they said, now we will see how good she really is. And did they ever. Navratilova defeated Evert in straight sets and went on to end the season by winning 78 of her 86 matches.

As a result, Navratilova was ranked first by the Women's Tennis Association in 1979, a distinction she repeated from 1982 through 1986. With her powerful forehand and superb serve-and-volley game, Navratilova reigned as queen of the courts.

Born and raised in Czechoslovakia, Navratilova led her nation to victory in the Federation Cup before moving to the United States in 1975. Even before her impressive performance in 1978, Navratilova distinguished herself in doubles playing. Teamed with Evert, she won the French and Italian doubles titles in 1975 and the Wimbledon crown in 1976.

Her rapid rise in singles play made her a favorite of tennis fans around the world. In 1984, at the height of her career, Navratilova won an all-time record 74 straight matches.

Wimbledon and four times at the U.S. Open. Other dominant players of the era included Sweden's Bjorn Borg, who won five straight Wimbledon and four straight French Open championships before retiring, and American John McEnroe, who won four U.S. Open and three Wimbledon competitions. Germany's Boris Becker took top honors at one U.S. Open and two Wimbledon championships.

Boxing

Two fighters dominated boxing. Larry Holmes, called the "Easton Assassin" because he was raised in Easton, Pennsylvania, gained the heavyweight title in 1978. He defeated then-champion Ken Norton in a grueling 15-round decision. Holmes went on to win 47 consecutive professional fights over the next seven years, one short of the record set by Rocky Marciano, who won all of his 49 professional fights before retiring undefeated.

When Holmes squared off against light heavyweight champion Michael Spinks in 1985, he was heavily favored to win his forty-ninth fight and tie Marciano's record. In a stunning upset, however, Spinks beat the champion, becoming the first light heavyweight ever to defeat a heavyweight champion. Holmes lost both of his attempts to regain his crown and finished his professional career in 1988 with an overall record of 49 wins and three losses.

In 1986 20-year-old Mike Tyson became the youngest heavyweight boxing champion in history. He dispatched Trevor Berbick, holder of the World Boxing Council crown, in just two rounds.

It took the aggressive Tyson only 91 seconds to knock out challenger Michael Spinks two years later. Tyson's continuous bobbing in the ring made him almost impossible to reach. He successfully defended his title ten times between 1986 and 1990, compiling a record of 37 wins—33 by knockout—with no losses.

In 1990, however, the seemingly unbeatable Tyson was decisively outpunched and outboxed by an underdog American, James "Buster" Douglas, before an astonished worldwide television audience. Later that year a flabby and overweight Douglas lost a pathetic match—and the world championship—to Evander Holyfield, the former world champion in a lower weight class. The fight, which paid Douglas a reported $24 million, exploited the growing market for high-priced, pay-per-view television sports events.

▲ Mike Tyson prepares for his heavyweight championship fight against former champ Larry Holmes in 1988.

Golf

On tournament fairways and putting greens, competition took on an international flavor. No individual golfers dominated the game as Arnold Palmer and Jack Nicklaus had in the 1960s and early

The Great Gretzky: A Hockey Superstar

Wayne "The Great" Gretzky is not an obvious hockey superstar, especially not playing center. At only 5 feet 11 inches and 165 pounds, Gretzky was thought too small to take the brutal pounding of National Hockey League (NHL) defensemen. But Gretzky rewrote the book on playing center, as he would eventually rewrite the record books. Instead of trying to outdo his larger opponents with the violent blocking of a body check, Gretzky simply evaded them.

Gretzky's unusual strategy worked. In 1980–1981, as the NHL's youngest player, he set league records for scoring and assists and won the league's Most Valuable Player (MVP) award.

If possible, the young Gretzky became even better as the 1980s progressed. Playing for the Edmonton Oilers (1979–1988) and the Los Angeles Kings (since 1988), he won the MVP trophy nine times in ten years. He set new NHL single-season records for goals, assists, and points.

By the 1990–1991 season he had become only the fourth player in NHL history to score a total of 700 goals. In all, Gretzky holds almost 50 NHL records. He is the dominant athletic figure of the decade.

FIRST WOMAN TO RACE IN THE INDY 500

In 1977 Janet Guthrie made automotive history as the first woman to compete in the Indianapolis 500. Although mechanical trouble forced Guthrie to drop out of the race before the end, she finished in ninth place in 1978. She raced again in 1979, but again dropped out because of car troubles.

Guthrie was born in Iowa City, Iowa, on March 4, 1938. She was an aerospace engineer before she began auto racing. Two of her major victories included the under-2-liter prototype class in 1970 and the North Atlantic Road Racing Championship B sedan class in 1973.

1970s. Nevertheless, several golfers consistently finished at or near the top: Nicklaus, American Tom Watson, Spain's Seve Ballesteros, and Nick Faldo of the United Kingdom. In fact, Watson was the leading money winner on the Professional Golfers' Association (PGA) tour for five years.

Yachting

The America's Cup, competitive yachting's most prestigious prize, had been held exclusively by the New York Yacht Club from the competition's start in the 1850s until 1983. In that year the Australian sailboat *Australia II* defeated the *Liberty*, the U.S. entry skippered by Dennis Connor. Connor retook the Cup for the United States in 1987 with a twin-hulled sailboat called a "catamaran." Australia mounted a legal challenge, but the victory was confirmed two years later by the New York Court of Appeals.

Bicycle Racing

In 1986 American cyclist Greg LeMond became the first non-European ever to win the Tour de France, a grueling 2,500-mile bicycle race. Following serious injury in a near-fatal hunting accident in 1987, the courageous LeMond repeated his triumphant feat in 1989 and 1990.

► Greg LeMond speeds to victory in the 1989 Tour de France.

Leisure

AMERICANS PURSUE FUN WITH INTENSITY

In both work and leisure Americans focused on individual comfort, appearance, and pleasure. Americans wanted to have fun, and those who could afford to do so approached the task with the intensity of a military invasion.

Of course, the nation's consumer-goods manufacturers actively supported and encouraged Americans' efforts. As the number of two-income households increased, families had more money to spend on leisure pursuits. Businesses responded with an increasing range of recreational choices.

High-Tech Consumer Products

High-tech audio and video gear fascinated consumers during the 1980s. People jogged to the sound of the "walkabout stereo," as the Walkman introduced by Sony came to be called. "Boom boxes," large portable radio and cassette players, also became popular, as did VCRs, compact disk (CD) players, home video games, and high-tech video cameras. Expensive home theaters, furnished with laser disk players, large-screen televisions, and multichannel digital sound, graced upscale family rooms of the early 1990s.

High-tech advances transformed other leisure products as well, from skateboards and roller blades to lightweight all-terrain bicycles and camping gear. Technology also created new forms of enjoyment at America's amusement parks and video arcades. Multiloop roller coasters and computer-driven video games offered unexpected thrills and challenges. All-terrain vehicles, whale-watching cruises, and white-water rafting expeditions were just a few of the unconventional pursuits that excited Americans who were tired of ordinary outdoor activities.

Other Forms of Entertainment

Not all forms of 1980s entertainment were high-tech. The board game *Trivial Pursuit,* in which players displayed their knowledge of little-known facts and figures, became a brief national craze and spawned a variety of similar trivia games. Americans also continued to enjoy their all-time favorite leisure-time activity: eating out.

Fast-food restaurants continued to spread across the landscape. Americans could grab a quick burger or a fried chicken drumstick anywhere. People with even less time could pick up soda, coffee, and a bag of chips at a convenience store. Ethnic restaurants—Chinese, Mexican, Japanese, Thai, Vietnamese, to name just a few—also became increasingly popular, as did home-delivered pizza in "30 minutes or less, guaranteed."

▲ Punk style became popular in England before spreading to the United States.

Fashion Trends

In the image-conscious 1980s, labels and brand names, once hidden inside garments along with size information and care instructions, were displayed out front or out back. Many people gladly paid more money for designer-label and celebrity-endorsed goods, as long as the brand name was displayed and recognizable for all to see.

The T-shirt, more so than any other single garment, underwent a dramatic transformation during the period, becoming the message center of the "Me Decade." This immensely popular garment carried everything from political messages and advertising slogans to sports-team symbols, cartoon characters, and the wearer's favorite rock stars. Americans who could afford the fun and games of the 1980s enjoyed themselves. But the 1990s promised to be less freewheeling. The roller coaster ride was beginning to slow down.

SOME FACTS ABOUT EPCOT

EPCOT Center, or the Experimental Prototype Community of Tomorrow, was built in Orlando, Florida, and completed in 1982. As with other Disney theme parks, the building of EPCOT required immense planning.

Fifty-four million tons of earth were moved to build the park, which stands on 240 acres. Sixteen thousand tons of steel were needed, and 500,000 feet of wood were used to build the sets alone. A 40-acre artificial lagoon was surrounded by 70 acres of sod, 12,500 trees, and 10,000 shrubs. An erupting volcano, which spews forth 7,000 gallons of fake lava, was designed for the Universe of Energy pavilion.

VOICES OF THE ERA

***E.T.* phone home.**

—From the film *E.T.—The Extra-Terrestrial,* 1982

J.R.—The man you love to hate.

—Ad for TV show *Dallas,* 1980

POSSIBLE 'MELT-DOWN' FEARED AS ATOMIC PLANT COOLS SLOWLY

Bubble Imperils Reactor

—*Philadelphia Inquirer,* March 31, 1979

SADAT ACCEPTS ISRAEL AS A NATION

Begin Opens Borders to Egypt; But Deadlock Remains

—*Los Angeles Times,* November 21, 1977

400 IN SECT LINED UP TO DIE

Guyana Poison Rite Described

—*Chicago Tribune,* November 21, 1978

"Who's minding the store?"

—Ronald Reagan, after being shot, to Edwin Meese, March 30, 1981

We start with the simple premise—human rights for human beings. No longer will we accept superior rights for some and inferior rights for others, but equal rights for all. Justice must be measured by one yardstick. We must demand sameness of respect though we may not have oneness of roles. Roles may differ by culture and choice, but equal protection is a matter of law. This is called simple justice. Our judicial system, which enunciates our society's laws, must catch up with natural law. Simple justice is a threat to the hardened arteries of the status quo which cling to the past by habit, culture, ignorance, superstition, economic exploitation, or a combination of them.

We as a people must affirm the personhood of our mothers and sisters, our aunts and daughters. Any man who would condemn his mother or wife or sister to the eternal damnation of second-class status must examine himself. And any woman who would volunteer for such a status likewise needs examination.

We in America are just 4 percent of the world. We need everybody in the race for productivity. All minds must be used at optimum speed for us to survive. We must be concerned about foreign policy. We came here on a foreign policy. Foreign policy is domestic policy.

—Jesse Jackson, May 17, 1980

May the Force be with you.

—From the film *Star Wars,* 1977

HOSTAGES FREED!

Reagan Sworn In, Urges 'National Renewal'

—*Los Angeles Times,* January 20, 1981

"He knows that if he dies there will be so much anger stored up in the Irish people that it will fuel the struggle for the next ten years."

—A friend of IRA hunger striker Bobby Sands, before Sands's death in 1981

VOICES OF THE ERA

Now Main Street's whitewashed
and vacant stores
Seems like there ain't nobody wants to
come down here no more
They're closing down the textile mill
across the railroad tracks
Foreman says these jobs are going boys
and they ain't coming back
to your hometown

—Bruce Springsteen, "My Hometown," 1984

SOVIETS SHOOT DOWN JETLINER

30 Yanks among 269 Victims

—*New York Daily News*, September 2, 1983

It's morning again in America.

—Ronald Reagan's campaign slogan, 1984

"You can take a bunch of young people and you can make them into the Boy Scouts or into Hitler Youth, depending on what you teach them, and MTV's definitely a bad influence."

—Ted Turner, 1984

Go ahead—make my day.

—Clint Eastwood in the film *Sudden Impact*, 1983

"Being really caught up in rock 'n' roll . . . that's something you do when you're a teenager. It'd be stupid to do that all the time."

—Mick Jagger, 1984

Now you can get a smarter kid than Mom did.

—Computers for Kids ad, Mattel, 1982

"People used to throw rocks at me for my clothes. Now they wanna know where I buy them."

—Cyndi Lauper, 1984

"Prince is me in this generation."

—Little Richard, 1984

As a boy, Ramius sensed more than thought that Soviet Communism ignored a basic human need. In his teens, his misgivings began to take a coherent shape. The Good of the People was a laudable enough goal, but in denying a man's soul, an enduring part of his being, Marxism stripped away the foundation of human dignity and individual value. It also cast aside the objective measure of justice and ethics which, he decided, was the principal legacy of religion to civilized life. From earliest adulthood on, Marko [Ramius] had his own idea about right and wrong, an idea he did not share with the State. It gave him a means of gauging his actions and those of others. It was something he was careful to conceal. It served as an anchor for his soul and, like an anchor, it was hidden far below the visible surface.

—Tom Clancy, *The Hunt for Red October*, 1984

VOICES OF THE ERA

You can never be too powerful. Or too well connected.

—Apple Macintosh ad, 1986

STOCKS, RECORDS KEEP FALLING

108-Point Dive Ends Dow's Worst Week

—*Chicago Tribune*, October 17, 1987

"The crew of the space shuttle Challenger *honored us by the manner in which they lived their lives. We will never forget them, nor the last time we saw them—this morning, as they prepared for their journey, and waved good-bye, and 'slipped the surly bonds of earth' to 'touch the face of God.'"*

—Ronald Reagan, 1986

The pride is back. Born in America.

—Chrysler ad, 1980s

We are living in a material world
And I am a material girl.

—Madonna, "Material Girl," 1985

You get a fast car
I got a plan to get us out of here
Been workin' at a convenience store
Managed to save just a little bit of money
Won't have to drive too far
Just 'cross the border and into the city
You and I can both get jobs
And finally see what it means to be living

See my old man's got a problem
With the bottle that's the way it is
He says his body's too old for workin'
His body's too young to look like his
My mama went off and left him
She wanted more from life than he could give
I said somebody's got to take care of him
So I quit school and that's what I did

You get a fast car
Is it fast enough so we can fly away
We've got to make a decision
Leave tonight or live and die this way

—Tracy Chapman, "Fast Car," 1988

FIERY BLAST DESTROYS SPACE SHUTTLE; MC AULIFFE, SIX ASTRONAUTS ARE KILLED

Searchers find debris, no bodies

—*Boston Globe*, January 29, 1986

Where's the beef?

—Wendy's ad, 1984

Just say no.

—Slogan coined by Nancy Reagan as part of war on drugs, 1980s

"As long as some of God's children are not free, none of God's children will be free."

—Desmond Tutu, 1984

VOICES OF THE ERA

"*This spill is America's Chernobyl.*"

—A naturalist on the *Exxon Valdez* oil spill, 1989

Isn't that special?

—Dana Carvey as the Church Lady on *Saturday Night Live*, 1980s

Cowabunga, dude!

—Teenage Mutant Ninja Turtles, 1980s

Why didn't he and Judy and Campbell get out of the madness of New York . . . and the megalomania of Wall Street? Who but an arrogant fool would want to be a Master of the Universe—and take the insane chances he had been taking? . . . Why didn't they sell the apartment and move out here to Southampton year round—or to Tennessee. . . . His grandfather William Sherman McCoy had come to New York from Knoxville when he was thirty-one. . . . He had seen the perfectly adequate house where his grandfather had grown up. . . . A lovely little city, a sober, reasonable little city, Knoxville. . . . Why didn't he go there and get a job in a brokerage house, a regular job, a sane, responsible job, not trying to spin the world on its head, a nine-to-five job, or whenever it is they work in places like Knoxville; $90,000 or $100,000 a year, a tenth or less of what he so foolishly thought he needed now, and it would be plenty.

—Tom Wolfe, *The Bonfire of the Vanities*, 1987

We're now living in a new world. An end has been put to the cold war and to the arms race, as well as to the mad militarization of the country, which has crippled our economy, public attitudes, and morals. The threat of nuclear war has been removed.

Once again, I would like to stress that during this transitional period, I did everything that needed to be done to insure that there was reliable control of nuclear weapons. We opened up ourselves to the rest of the world, abandoned the practices of interfering in others' internal affairs and using troops outside this country, and we were reciprocated with trust, solidarity, and respect.

We have become one of the key strongholds in terms of restructuring modern civilization on a peaceful democratic basis. The nations and peoples of this country have acquired the right to freely choose their format for self-determination.

—Mikhail S. Gorbachev, upon resigning as president of the USSR, December 25, 1991

Silence = Death

—Slogan coined by the group ACT UP to encourage education about AIDS, 1980s

"*No, wait, I want to breathe the air of freedom in Moscow.*"

—Mikhail Gorbachev, after aides tried to get him into a car upon his return to Moscow after the attempted coup, 1991

Just Do It.

—Nike ad campaign, 1980s

Glossary

acid rain: rain that is high in sulfuric and nitric acid content as a result of industrial pollution

acquisition: in business, the act of obtaining ownership

affirmative action: a governmental effort to improve educational and employment opportunities for minority groups

AIDS (acquired immunodeficiency syndrome): a fatal condition in which the body's immune system is attacked and disabled by the HIV virus

Allies: during World War II, the countries that fought against Germany, Italy, and Japan, including the United Kingdom, the USSR, and the United States

annex: to incorporate new territory into an existing state or country

annexation: the process of incorporating new territory into an existing state or country

apartheid: a government policy of racial segregation in South Africa

arbitration: settlement of a dispute between parties by an impartial person or group

artificial intelligence: the capability of a computer to mimic human thought processes

bilingual education: education in an English-language school system in which minority students are taught in their native language

biotechnology: the use of biological materials and methods to produce useful substances

boycott: to refuse to use, buy, or deal with something in order to express disapproval

chlorofluorocarbon: a synthetic chemical used primarily as a coolant, which, when released into the atmosphere, deteriorates the earth's protective ozone layer

coalition: a working union of parties, persons, or governments, which usually has a specific goal or purpose

coup: a sudden, often violent, action taken to obtain power over a government

deficit: having more expenses than income

deficit spending: a government policy that involves spending public funds obtained from borrowing rather than from taxation

deregulation: the process of removing restrictions

détente: the easing of tension between countries

entrepreneur: an individual who organizes, manages, and assumes the risk for a business venture

epidemic: the rapid spread of a contagious disease

free agency: the state of a professional player who is free to sign a contract with any team

genetic engineering: the deliberate alteration of genetic material to prevent hereditary defects

gentrification: the movement of middle-class families into a deteriorating or recently renewed urban area

ghetto: a poor section of a city occupied by a specific racial or ethnic group

greenhouse effect: a gradual warming of the earth's surface caused by increased carbon dioxide in the atmosphere

gross national product: the total dollar value of all the goods and services produced in a country in one year

guerrillas: a small, independent band of people who fight as part of a patriotic or revolutionary movement

HIV (human immunodeficiency virus): the organism that causes AIDS; it destroys T cells, a major component of the immune system, leaving the body vulnerable to disease

immigrant: a person who leaves his or her native country to live in another country

indict: to charge with a crime

inflation: a general increase in prices and fall in the purchasing value of money in an economy

leveraged buyout: acquisition of an existing company by a new company, usually funded by substantial borrowing rather than by using existing assets

meltdown: the melting of a nuclear reactor core

merger: the union of two or more businesses into one

microprocessor: a semiconductor central processing unit usually contained on a single circuit chip

nationalism: loyalty and devotion to a nation

Nielsen ratings: ratings of television program audience size used by the A. O. Nielsen Company

recession: a temporary decline in economic activity

referendum: the referring of a proposed public measure to a direct public vote

sequel: a creative work that continues a story begun in an earlier work

serial: a story presented in a series of installments

socialism: an economic theory that promotes governmental control of factories and other businesses

steroids: drugs that have muscle-building effects similar to testosterone and other male sex hormones; they are widely abused by athletes despite serious health risks

subsidy: a grant or gift of money

summit: a meeting between the heads of two or more governments

supply-side economics: an economic policy that recommends the reduction of tax rates to encourage more earning, saving, and investment

tariff: a charge imposed by a government on imports and exports

Third World: the underdeveloped countries of Asia, Africa, and Latin America

trade deficit: an excess of imports over exports

urbanization: the process of changing a place into a citylike area

welfare state: a social system in which the state assumes responsibility for the social welfare of its citizens

Suggested Readings

General

Abbott, Carl. *Urban America in the Modern Age, 1920 to Present.* H. Davidson, 1987.

Allen, Frederick Lewis. *The Big Change, 1900–1950.* Bantam, 1965.

Blum, Daniel. *A Pictorial History of the Silent Screen.* Grosset & Dunlap, 1953.

Cairns, Trevor. *The Twentieth Century.* Cambridge University Press, 1984.

Cantor, Norman F., and Michael S. Werthman, eds. *The History of Popular Culture.* Macmillan, 1968.

Churchill, Allen. *The Great White Way.* E. P. Dutton, 1962.

Daniels, Roger. *Coming to America: A History of Immigration and Ethnicity in American Life.* HarperCollins, 1990.

Davids, Jules. *America and the World of Our Time.* Random House, 1960.

Ewing, Elizabeth. *History of Twentieth Century Fashion.* Barnes & Noble, 1986.

Filene, Peter G. *Him/Her/Self: Sex Roles in Modern America.* Johns Hopkins University Press, 1986.

Flink, James J. *The Automobile Age.* MIT, 1988.

Freidel, Frank. *America in the Twentieth Century.* Knopf, 1960.

Goff, Richard. *The Twentieth Century: A Brief Global History.* John Wiley, 1983.

Hine, Darlene Clark, ed. *Black Women in American History.* Carlson Publishing, 1990.

Manchester, William. *The Glory and the Dream: A Narrative History of America, 1932–1972.* Little, Brown, 1974.

May, George S., ed. *The Automobile Industry, 1920–1980.* Facts on File, 1989.

Morgan, Robert P. *Twentieth-Century Music: A History of Musical Style in Modern Europe and America.* Norton, 1991.

Noble, David W., David A. Horowitz, and Peter N. Carroll. *Twentieth Century Limited: A History of Recent America.* Houghton Mifflin, 1980.

Norman, Philip. *The Road Goes On Forever: Portraits from a Journey Through Contemporary Music.* Simon & Schuster, 1982.

Olderman, Murray. *Nelson's Twentieth Century Encyclopedia of Baseball.* Nelson, 1963.

Oliver, John W. *History of American Technology.* Books on Demand UMI, 1956.

Ritter, Lawrence S. *The Story of Baseball.* Morrow, 1983.

Sklar, Robert. *Movie-Made America: A Cultural History of American Movies.* Random House, 1976.

Spaeth, Sigmund. *A History of Popular Music in America.* Random House, 1948.

Susman, Warren I. *Culture as History: The Transformation of American Society in the Twentieth Century.* Pantheon, 1984.

Taft, Philip. *Organized Labor in American History.* Harper & Row, 1964.

Vecsey, George, ed. *The Way It Was: Great Sports Events from the Past.* McGraw-Hill, 1974.

Zinn, Howard. *The Twentieth Century: A People's History.* Harper & Row, 1984.

About the Era

Altman, Dennis. *AIDS in the Mind of America: The Social, Political, and Psychological Impact of a New Epidemic.* Doubleday, 1986.

Baker, Howard Henry. *No Margin for Error: America in the Eighties.* Times Books, 1980.

Booker, Christopher. *The Seventies: The Decade That Changed the Future.* Stein and Day, 1980.

Carroll, Peter. *It Seemed Like Nothing Happened: The Tragedy and Promise of America in the 1970s.* Rutgers University Press, 1990.

Carter, Jimmy. *Keeping Faith: Memoirs of a President.* Bantam, 1982.

Fox, Mary Virginia. *Mr. President: The Story of Ronald Reagan.* Enslow, 1982.

Hoobler, Dorothy, and Thomas Hoobler. *An Album of the Seventies.* Franklin Watts, 1981.

Johnson, Hayes Bonner. *Sleepwalking Through History: America in the Reagan Years.* Norton, 1991.

Krauthammer, Charles. *Cutting Edge: Making Sense of the Eighties.* Random House, 1985.

Miller, Judith, and Laurie Mylroie. *Saddam Hussein and the Crisis in the Gulf.* Random House, 1990.

Phillips, Kevin. *The Politics of Rich and Poor: Wealth and the American Electorate in the Reagan Aftermath.* Random House, 1990.

Pick, Christopher. *What's What in the Nineteen Eighties.* Gale, 1982.

Ramazani, R. K. *The United States and Iran: The Patterns of Influence.* Greenwood, 1982.

Reagan, Ronald. *An American Life.* Simon & Schuster, 1990.

Smith, Geoffrey. *Reagan and Thatcher.* Bodley Head, 1990.

Smith, Hendrick. *The New Russians.* Random House, 1990.

Wells, Tim. *444 Days: The Hostages Remember.* Harcourt Brace Jovanovich, 1985.

Wright, Lawrence. *In the New World: Growing Up with America from the Sixties to the Eighties.* Random House, 1989.

Index

Note: A page number in italic indicates a table, map, graph, or illustration.

ABC, 91, 100
Abortion, 26, 27
Abscam, 13
Academy Award winners, 95
Acid rain, 40, 61, 80
Advertising, 66, 92, 101
Afghanistan, 14, 39, 41, 106
Africa, 14, 22, 38, 49, 53–56, 99
African-Americans, 18, 24, 27, 33, 97. *See also* Race relations
  in politics, 25–26, 28
African National Congress (ANC), 54, 55, 56
Agent Orange, 29
Agnew, Spiro, 13
AIDS (acquired immune deficiency syndrome), 24, 29, 38, 53, 82–83, *83*, 111
Airline industry, 74–75
Airlines Deregulation Act (1978), 74
Alcohol, 34
Alien, 95
Allen, Robert G., 102
Allen, Woody, 96
Alliance for Germany, 46
All I Really Need to Know I Learned in Kindergarten, 103
All Things Considered, 100
AMC, 73
American Airlines, 75
American Association for Retired People (AARP), 28
American Cancer Society, 84
Amnesty International, 99
Amritsar, 58
Andropov, Yuri, 30, 41, 61
Annie Hall, 96
Aoun, Michel, 52
Apartheid, 54–56, 76, 107
Apocalypse Now, 95
Apollo program, 92
Apple Computer, 70, 85
Aquino, Corazon, 57
Arabs, Jews and, 21, 49–50, 51
Argentina, 47, 48, 59, 60
Armenia, 43, 51
Arms race, 29, 30
Arsenio Hall Show, The, 94
Art, 102
Artificial heart, 84
Astaire, Fred, 100
Atlanta, 23
Australia II, 116
Automobile industry, 15, 70–71, 72, 73–74
Aylwin, Patricio, 60

Baby Boom, 19, 33–35, 93, 97
Baker, James, 50
Baker, Kristin, 26
Bakke, Alan, 24
Balanchine, George, 100
Baldwin, James, 100
Ballesteros, Seve, 116
Banking, 67, *67*, 71
Bart Simpson, 93
Baseball, *105*, 108–110
Basketball, 107, 110–111, 113
Batman, 95
Becker, Boris, 114
Begin, Menachem, 14–15, 49–50, 51
Belgium, 47, 81
Bellow, Saul, 103
Berbick, Trevor, 114
Beresford, Bruce, 97
Berlin, Irving, 100
Berlin Wall, 44, 45
Berri, Claude, 97
Bhutto, Benazir, 49
Bhutto, Zulfikar Ali, 49
Bias, Len, 112
Bicycling, 116
Bidwell, Ben, 75
Biko, Stephen, 54
Biotechnology, 87
Bird, Larry, 111, 113
Black Monday, 20
Black Muslims, 33
Blues, 97
Boat people, 22, 57
Boesky, Ivan, 69
Boggs, Wade, 110
Bonilla, Bobby, 109
Books, 33, 102–103, 105
Borg, Bjorn, 114
Bork, Robert, 27
Born in the U.S.A., 98
Born on the Fourth of July, 95
Botha, P. W., 54
Bowie, David, 98
Boxing, 114–115
Brady, James, 16
Branch, Taylor, 103
Braniff International, 75
Brazil, 59, 60
Breakfast Club, The, 96
Brezhnev, Leonid, 41, 61
Bright Lights, Big City, 103
Britain, 47–48, 56, 81
Broadway, 101
Brock, Lou, 110
Bryant, Paul "Bear," 113
Budapest, 40, 44
Budd, Zola, 108
Bulgaria, 40, 45
Burger, Warren, 27
Bush, George, 20–21, 26, 27, 29, 34, 48, 53, 61, 75
  economy and, 64, 66
  foreign policy of, 21, 32
Business, 16, 17, 20, 24, 38, 65, 72, 94
  corporations and, 67–70, 75, 77, 106
Buthelezi, Gatsha, 56

Cable News Network (CNN), 91, 92, 100
Cable television, 91–92
Cagney, James, 100
California, 16, 23
Cambodia, 22, 57
Camp David Accords, 14–15, 49–50, 51
Canada, 38, 40, 61, 80
Cancer, 83–84
Caribbean, 22
Carter, Jimmy, 12–15, 16, 17, 50–51, 59, 100
  economy and, 13–14, 15, 64
  foreign policy of, 14–15, 30
Carter, Rosalyn, 13
Casey, William, 17
Castro, Fidel, 22
Cats, 101
CBS, 91
Ceausescu, Nicolae, 45
Central America, 22
Central Intelligence Agency (CIA), 11, 60
Chad, 54
Challenger, 88–89
Chamorro, Violeta, 60
Chaplin, Charlie, 100
Chapman, Mark David, 98
Chernenko, Konstantin, 41, 61
Chernobyl, 81
Chile, 60
China, 14, 22, 56, 57–58
Chlorofluorocarbons (CFCs), 79
Chorus Line, A, 101
Christo, 102
Chrysler Corporation, 73
Cimino, Michael, 95
Cinemax, 92
Cities, 22, 23–24
Clancy, Tom, 103
Clapton, Eric, 97
Clark, Dr. Barney, 84
Class divisions
  in Japan, 56
  in U.S., *19*, *20*, 20, 25, 33, 35, 66, 77
Clear and Present Danger, 103
Clemens, Roger, 110
Close Encounters of the Third Kind, 94
CNN Headline News, 91
COBE, 86
College sports, 112–113
Collins, Phil, 98
Colombia, 34, 39, 59
Columbia, 88
Columbia Pictures, 72, 94
Comaneci, Nadia, 107
Common Market, 38, 46–49, *47*
Commonwealth of Independent States, 43–44
Communism, 57
  collapse of, 40–46
Communist party, 42, 43, 45
Compact disks (CDs), 97
Complete Book of Running, The, 105
CompuServe, 72
Computers, 71–72, *79*, 85–86
Congress, U.S., 13
Congress of Racial Equality (CORE), 25
Connor, Dennis, 116
Connors, Jimmy, 113–114
Conservatism, 16, 27, 59, 61
Conservative party
  Canadian, 61
  Colombian, 59
Consolidated Rail Corporation (Conrail), 74
Constitution, U.S., Equal Rights Amendment and, 26
Consumerism, 76
Consumer Product Safety Commission, 76
Contras, 20, 31–32, 59–60
Coppola, Francis Ford, 95
Corporations, 65, 67–70, 75, 77, 106
Corsica, 49
Cosby, Bill, 102
Cosby Show, The, 93
Costa Rica, 59, 60
C-SPAN, 91
Cuba, 22, 23
Cultural Revolution, 57
Czechoslovakia, 40, 44, 45

Daley, Richard, 13
Dallas, 92–93
Davies, Bobby, 113
Davis, Bette, 100
Davis, Victor, 113
Dean's December, The, 103
Debt crisis, 59–60
Decker, Mary (Slaney), 108
Deer Hunter, The, 95
De Klerk, F. W., 54–55
Demokratiztsiya, 41
Dempsey, Jack, 113
Deng Xiaoping, 57, 58
Denmark, 47
Department of Veterans Affairs, 29
Deregulation, 17, 19, 67, 73, 74
Détente, 14, 30
DeVries, Dr. William C., 84
Dire Straits, 97
Dirty Harry series, 95
Donahue, Phil, 93

Do the Right Thing, 96
Douglas, James "Buster," 115
Douglas, William O., 17
Dow-Jones industrial average, *68*
Drexel Burnham Lambert, 69
Drugs
illegal, 21, 24, 33, 34, 39, 59, 112
sports and, 107, 112
Dukakis, Michael, 20, 25
Duran, Duran, 92
Dynasty, 92

Earthquakes, 32, 51
East Germany, 40, 44, 45–46
Eastwood, Clint, 95
Economic Recovery Tax Act, 17
Economy, 13–17, 19–21, 24, 63–66
Canadian, 61
Chinese, 57
German, 46
global, 38–39, 72
information, 71–72
Iranian, 50–51
Japanese, 56
Mexican, 60
Soviet, 41
Ecosystem, global, 39–40
Education, 21, 22, 35
Egypt, 14, 49–50
Eight Week Cholesterol Cure, The, 102
Elderly, 28
Elections
Eastern European, 44, 45
Pakistani, 49
presidential, 12–13, 16, 17, 18, 19, 20–21, 23, 25, 31, 64, 100
Ellis Island, 21–22
El Salvador, 31, 60
Empire Strikes Back, The, 94
Employment, 19, 24, 28, 69, 70, 72, 75, 77
of women, 24, 26, 28, 75
Energy, 13, 15
England. *See* Britain
English Channel Tunnel, 89
Entrepreneurs, 70
Environmentalism, 76
Environmental Protection Agency (EPA), 80
EPCOT center, 117
Equal Rights Amendment (ERA), 26
Eritrea, 54
Ervin, Sam, 17
ESPN, 92, 106
Esquire magazine, 101
Estonia, 43
E.T.—The Extra-Terrestrial, 94
Ethiopia, 39, 51, 53, 54
Europe '92, 46–49
European Assembly, 47
European Community (EC), 38, 46–49, *47*
European Monetary System, 47
European Space Agency, 88

Evert, Chris, 114
Executioner's Song, The, 103
Exxon Valdez, 81

Faldo, Nick, 116
Falkland Islands War, 47, 48
Falwell, Jerry, 16
"Farm Aid," 99
Farmer, James, 25
Farming, 19, 22–23, 76, 77
Fassbinder, Rainer Werner, 97
Fatherhood, 102
Federal budget deficit, 19, 20, 21, 64, *65*, 65–66, 72
Federal Bureau of Investigation (FBI), 11, 13
Federal Deposit Insurance Corporation (FDIC), 67
Ferraro, Geraldine, 18
Fielder, Cecil, 110
Fit for Life, 105
Fitness, 33, 105, 106
Flashdance, 92, 96
Flutie, Doug, 111
Follett, Ken, 102
Football, 109, 111–112, 113
Ford, Gerald, 12, 13
Ford, Harrison, 95
Ford Motor Company, 72, 73, 74
Fort Worth, 23
France, 47, 48, 81
Free-Trade Agreement, 38, 60, 61
French Canadians, 61
Friday the 13th, 95
Frugal Gourmet Cooks with Wine, The, 105
Fulghum, Robert, 103
Full Metal Jacket, 95

Gandhi, Indira, 58
Gandhi, Rajiv, 58
Garcia, Alan, 59
García Márquez, Gabriel, 103
Gates, William, III, 70, 85
Gathers, Hank, 113
Gay rights, 29
Geisel, Theodor (Dr. Seuss), 100
Gekko, Gordon, 69
Geldof, Bob, 99
Gemayel, Bashir, 52
General Motors (GM), 73, 74, 75
Genetic engineering, 87
Germany, 40, 44, 45–46, 47, 48–49, 81
Ghostbusters, 95
Giamatti, A. Bartlett, 110
Ginsburg, Douglas, 27
Glasnost, 41, 43
Global politics, 39
Global village, 37–38, 72
Golf, 115–116
Goodman, Benny, 100
Gorbachev, Mikhail, 21, 32, 38, 43, 45, 48, 49, 51, 58
collapse of communism and, 41–44
Gorbachev, Raisa, 42

Government bureaucracy, 16–17
Government spending, 17, 19–20, 35, 64, 66
Graf, Steffi, 113
Grant, Cary, 100
Gray Panthers, 28
Graziano, Rocky, 113
Great Britain. *See* Britain
Greece, 47
Greenhouse effect, 40, 80
Greenpeace, 40
Grenada, 30
Gretzky, Wayne, 115
Gross national product (GNP), *37*, 65
Gulf War, 26, 35, 38, 52–53, 92, 100
Guthrie, Janet, 116

Halas, George, 113
Haley, Alex, 92
Hammer, 98
Handicapped people, 29
Harvey, Doug, 113
HBO, 92
Heiden, Eric, 107
Henderson, Rickey, 110
Henson, Jim, 100
Hijuelos, Oscar, 103
Hill Street Blues, 93
Hinckley, John W., Jr., 16
Hirohito, emperor of Japan, 61
Hispanics, 18, 22, 24, 26
HIV (human immunodeficiency virus), 82, 83
Hmong people, 21
Hockey, 107, 115
Hoffman, Abbie, 17
Hoffman, Dustin, 95–96
Holmes, Larry, 114
Holyfield, Evander, 115
Homelessness, 35
Honecker, Erich, 45
Hong Kong, 56
Horton, Willie, 20
Hostages, 15, 39, 50–51
Hubbell, Carl, 113
Hubble Space Telescope, 88
Hudson, Rock, 100
"Human Rights Now!" 99
Humphrey, Hubert H., 17
Hungary, 44, 45
Hunter, Jim "Catfish," 108
Hunt for Red October, The, 103
Hussein, Saddam, 50–51, 52–53

Iacocca: An Autobiography, 103
Iacocca, Lee, 73
Icahn, Carl, 67, 68
Ice hockey, 107, 115
Immigration, 21, 22–23
Immigration Act (1965), 22
Immigration Control and Reform Act (1985), 23
Income taxes, 64–65
India, 22, 56, 58
Indiana Jones, 94–95
Indiana Jones films, 95

Indianapolis 500, 116
Indochina, 22
Indonesia, 56
Industrial Light and Magic, 95
Industry, 70–72
Inflation, 13, 19, 20, 63, 64, 65
Information economy, 71–72
Inkatha movement, 55, 56
Institutional Revolutionary Party (PRI), (Mexican), 60
Interest rates, 15, 65, 67
International Business Machines (IBM), 85
International trade, 15, 38–39, 56, 59, 66, 72, 73, 74, 77
Intifada, 51
Iran, 15, 49, 50
Iran-Contra scandal, 20, 31–32, 60
Iran-Iraq War, 53
Iraq, 21, 32, 49, 50–51, 52–53, 53. *See also* Gulf War
Ireland, 47, 49
Ironweed, 103
Israel, 21, 49–50, 51–52
Italy, 47, 81

Jackson, Jesse, 18, 25
Jackson, Leroy, 113
Jackson, Michael, 98
Jackson, Reggie, 108
Jane Fonda's Workout Book, 105
Japan, 22, 56, 71, 72, 74
Jarvis, Gregory, 89
Jenner, Bruce, 107
Jerusalem, 49, 51
Jews, 49
Jobs, Steven, 70, 85
Joe's Bed-Stuy Barbershop: We Cut Heads, 96
John Paul II, pope, 46
Johnson, Andrew, 13
Johnson, Ben, 107, 112
Johnson, Earvin "Magic," 83, 111, 113
Johnson, Lyndon, 11, 18, 63
Johnson, Robert, 97
Jordan, 51
Jordan, Michael, 111, 113
Joshua Tree, The, 98

Karami, Omar, 52
Keller, Charlie, 113
Kelly, Judge Patrick, 26
Kennedy, Anthony M., 27
Kennedy, John F., assassination of, 92
Kennedy, William P., 103
Keynes, John Maynard, 64
Key to Rebecca, The, 102
Khmer Rouge, 57
Khomeini, Ayatollah Ruhollah, 15, 50–51, 51, 53, 61, 103
Khrushchev, Nikita, 42
King, Martin Luther, Jr., 18, 103
King, Rodney, 24
King, Stephen, 103
Knight-Ridder, 100

Kohl, Helmut, 46, 48–49
Koppel, Ted, 100
Korea, 22
Kowalski, Robert E., 102
Kramer vs. Kramer, 95
Krantz, Judith, 102
Krenz, Egon, 45
Kubrick, Stanley, 95
Kundera, Milan, 103
Kuwait, 21, 32, 52–53, 81. *See also* Gulf War

L.A. Law, 93
Labor movement, 77
LA Gear, 66
Laker Airways, 74
Laos, 21, 22
Late Night with David Letterman, 94
Latin America, 14, 22, 59–60, 72
Latvia, 43
Lauper, Cyndi, 92
Leavitt, David, 103
Lebanese Front, 51
Lebanon, 31, 39, 49, 51–52
Le Carré, John, 103
Lee, Spike, 96, 97
Leipzig, 44
Leisure, 116–117
LeMond, Greg, 116
Lennon, John, 98
Les Miserables, 101
Liberal-Democratic party (Japanese), 56
Liberty, 116
Libya, 30
Lifestyles of the Rich and Famous, 93
"Like a Virgin," 98
Lin, Maya Yang, 99
Lincoln, 103
Lithuania, 43
"Live Aid," 99
Living standard, 75
Lorenzo, Frank, 68
Lost Language of Cranes, The, 103
Louganis, Greg, 108
Louis, Joe, 113
Love Canal, New York, 15, 80
LSD, 34
Lucas, George, 94, 95
Lupica, Mike, 112
Luxembourg, 47
Lyme disease, 82
Lynch, David, 93

McAuliffe, Christa, 88, 89
McEnroe, John, 114
McInerney, Jay, 103
McNair, Ronald, 89
MacNeil-Lehrer News Hour, The, 100
Madison Square Garden network, 106
Madonna, 92, 98
Magazines, 33, 100–101
Mailer, Norman, 103
Major, John, 48
Malaysia, 56
Mandela, Nelson, 55, 99
Mao Ze-dong (Mao Tse-tung), 57, 61
Mapplethorpe, Robert, 102
Marciano, Rocky, 114
Marcos, Ferdinand, 57, 61
Mariam, Mengistu Haile, 53
Maris, Roger, 113
Married with Children, 93
Marshall, Thurgood, 27
Martin, Billy, 113
"Material Girl," 98
Matsushita Electric Industrial Company Limited, 94
MCA, 94
Medical insurance, 28, 77, 84
Medicine, *82*, 82–84
Meech Lake Accord, 61
Meir, Golda, 61
Mergers, 65
Mexico, 22, 40, 59, 60
Miami Vice, 92
Michael, George, 98
Michaels, Al, 107
Microprocessors, 85–86
Microsoft Corporation, 70, 85
Middle class, 23
Middle East, 49–53
Midnight's Children, 103
Migration, 21–22, 77
Military, 26, 46
Milken, Michael, 69
Miller, Marvin, 109
Miss Saigon, 101
Mitterrand, François, 48
M-19 movement, 59
Moawad, Rene, 52
Monk, Thelonious, 100
Montana, Joe, 111–112
Moon landing, 92
Moral Majority, 16
Morita, Akio, 98
Morning Edition, 100
Morrison, Toni, 103
Mothers Against Drunk Driving (MADD), 34
Mount Saint Helens, 87
Movie Channel, The, 92
Movies, 94–96
Mozambique, 54
Mulroney, Brian, 61
Music, 92, 97–99
Music Television (MTV), 92
Muslims, 103
  Black, 33

Nashville Network, The, 92
National Aeronautics and Space Administration (NASA), 88–89
National AIDS Memorial Quilt, 83
National Basketball Association (NBA), 107, 110–111
National Collegiate Athletic Association (NCAA), 113
National Football League (NFL), 111
Nationalism, 57
Nationalist Movement, 51
National party, 55
National Public Radio, 100
National Rifle Association (NRA), 16
National Security Council (NSC), 31
Nation at Risk, A, 35
Navratilova, Martina, 113, 413
NBC, 91
Neptune, 89
Netherlands, 47, 81
New Kids on the Block, 97
News broadcasting, 38, 91, 92, 99–101
Newspapers, 100
New York City, 12, 22, 24, 25, 29
New York Shakespeare Festival, 101
New York Yacht Club, 116
New York Yankees, 106, 108–109
Nicaragua, 31, 59–60
Nicklaus, Jack, 115, 116
Nigeria, 81
Nightline, 100
Nike, 66
Nixon, Richard M., 11, 13, 18, 57, 61
Nobel Prize winners, 15, 44
Noriega, Manuel, 21, 60
North, Lieutenant Colonel Oliver, 31
Northeast Rail Service Act, 74
Northern Ireland, 49
Norton, Ken, 114
Nothing Down: How to Buy Real Estate with Little or No Money Down, 102
Novello, Dr. Antonia, 26
Nuclear accidents, 15, 81
Nuclear arms control, 21, 29, 32, 39
Nuclear power, 13, 15

O'Connor, Sandra Day, 27
Oil spills, 81
O'Keeffe, Georgia, 100
Olympics, 14, 30, 106–108
O'Neill, Thomas P. "Tip," Jr., 42
Onizuka, Ellison, 89
Operation Desert Storm, 53
Ordinary People, 95
Organization of Petroleum Exporting Countries (OPEC), 63
Ortega, Daniel, 31
Owens, Jesse, 113
Ozone layer, 79

Pacific Rim nations, 72
Paige, Leroy "Satchel," 113
Pakistan, 49
Palestine, 49
Palestine Liberation Organization (PLO), 49, 51, 52
Palmer, Arnold, 115
Panama, 21
Panama Canal, 14, 59
Pan Am flight 103, 39
Papp, Joseph, 101
Particle accelerators, 86
Parting the Waters, 103
Parti Quebecois, 61
People Express, 74
Perestroika, 41
Perez, Moreno, 23
Pérez de Cuéllar, Javier, 39
Persian Gulf, 30, 49. *See also* Gulf War
Peru, 59
Petroleum industry, 13–14
Phantom of the Opera, 101
Philippines, 56–57
Phnom Penh, 57
Pinochet, General Augusto, 60
Pioneer missions, 89
Platoon, 95
Poland, 30, 40, 44, 45
Pollution, 39, 40
Pol Pot, 57
Poltergeist, 95
Pop music, 97–98
Population growth, *11*
Portugal, 47
Powell, Lewis F., Jr., 27
President, U.S., power of, 11
Presidential elections, 12–13, 16, 17, 18, 19, 20–21, 23, 25, 31, 64, 100
President's Commission on Education, 35
Presley, Elvis, 100
Prices, *63*, 75
Prince, 98
Prodigy, 72
Proposition 13, 16
Public Enemy, 98
Pulitzer Prize winners, 103
Purple Rain, 92, 98

Quebec, 61
Quinlan, Karen Ann, 84

Rabbit at Rest, 103
Rabbit Is Rich, 103
Race relations, 22, 96
  riots and, 24
  in South Africa, 54–56, 76, 107
Radio, 38, 100
Raiders of the Lost Ark, 95
Rain Man, 96
Rap music, 98
Rattle and Hum, 98
Reagan, Ronald, 15, 16, 26, 27, 29, 34, 48, 50–51, 60, 61, 67, 76, 77, 89
  economy and, 16–17, 19–20, 64–65, 74
  foreign policy of, 30–32
  Iran-Contra scandal and, 31–32
Recession, 19, 21, 23, 25, 39, 63, 65, 66, 70, 71
Recycling, 76
Reebok International Ltd., 66
Rehnquist, William H., 27
Religion, 16, 33, 49
Resnik, Judith, 89
Return of the Jedi, 94
Reza Shah Pahlavi, 50–51
Rich, Matty, 97

Ride, Sally K., 88
Risky Business, 96
Rivera, Geraldo, 93
Roads, 75
Robeson, Paul, 100
Robinson, Sugar Ray, 113
Rockefeller Center, 72
Rocky films, 95
Roe v. Wade, 27
Rogers, Roy, 16
Rolling Stones, 97
Romania, 40, 45
Roosevelt, Franklin Delano, 18
Roots, 92
Rose, Pete, 109–110
Ross Ice Shelf, 80
Roth, Philip, 103
Rushdie, Salman, 103
Russian Republic, 43
Ryan, Nolan, 110

Sadat, Anwar, 14–15, 49–50
Saigon, 57
St. Elsewhere, 93
Sakharov, Andrey, 61
Sandinistas, 31, 59–60
San Francisco earthquake, 32
Satanic Verses, The, 103
Satellite dish, 99–100
Saturday Night Fever, 96
Saturday Night Live, 94
Saudi Arabia, 52
Scalia, Antonin, 27
Schmidt, Mike, 110
School Daze, 96
Schwarzenegger, Arnold, 95
Scientific American magazine, 101
Scobee, Dick, 89
Selassie, Haile, 53
Service industries, 33, 66, 77
Shame, 103
Shaw, Bernard, 92
She's Gotta Have It, 96, 97
Shining Path movement, 59
Showtime, 92
Sihanouk, Prince Norodom, 57
Silicon Valley, 71
Simon, Paul, 98
Singapore, 56
Single European Act (1986), 47
Singleton, John, 97
Slaney, Mary Decker, 108
Smith, Michael, 89
Smith, Roger, 73
Smith, Samantha, 30
Smoking, 83–84
Social Security, 28
Social welfare programs, 17, 19–20, 24, 35, 65
Solidarity trade union, 30, 44, 45
Somoza family, 31
Sony Corporation, 94
Sony Walkman, 98, 116
Souter, David, 27
South Africa, 54–56, 76, 106, 107
Southeast Asia, 22, 72
Southern Methodist University, 113
South Korea, 56, 71, 72
Soviet Union, 14, 21, 29, 32, 38, 49, 51, 57, 80, 88, 106–107
  arms control and, 21, 29, 32, 39
  collapse of communism in, 40, 41–44
Space flight, 88–89
Spain, 47, 49, 81
Spielberg, Steven, 94, 95
Spinks, Michael, 114, 115
Sports, 92, 105–116
  professional, 106. *See also specific sports*
  women in, 113, 116
SportsChannel, 106
Sports shoe market, 66
Springsteen, Bruce, 98
Sri Lanka, 39
Stagflation, 13
Stalin, Joseph, 43
Stallone, Sylvester, 95
START talks, 32
Star Wars (defense program), 30, 32
Star Wars (film), 94
Steel, Danielle, 103
Steel industry, 15, 70–71
Steinbrenner, George, 108–109
Sting, 98
Stock market, 20, 65, *68,* 69
Stone, Oliver, 95
Strategic Defense Initiative, 30, 32
Streep, Meryl, 95
Strikes, 77, 109, 111
Students Against Drunk Driving (SADD), 34
Suburbs, 23
Sudan, 54
Sudden Unexplained Death Syndrome (SUDS), 21
Suez Canal, 49
Summit meetings, 32
Sun Belt, 23, 77
Super Bowl, 92, 111
Superconductors, 87
Supply-side economics, 17, 19, 64–65
Supreme Court, U.S., 18, 26, 27
Switzer, Barry, 113
Syria, 51, 52

Taiwan, 56
Talking Heads, 98
Tan, Amy, 103
Tarkanian, Jerry, 113
Tarpley, Roy, 112
Taylor, Lawrence, 112
Technology, 75, 85–86
Television, 91–94, 99–100, 106
Tennis, 113–114
Terminator, 95
Terms of Endearment, 95
Terrorism, 39, 49, 51, 52
Texas Air Corporation, 68
Thailand, 56
Thatcher, Margaret, 40, 47–48
Theater, 101
Third World nations, 38, 39, 81
thirtysomething, 93
Thomas, Clarence, 27, 92
Three Mile Island, 15, 81
Thriller, 98
Tiananmen Square, 58
Titanic, 85
Tito, Marshall, 61
Tokyo, 40
Tonight Show, The, 94
Tour de France, 116
Tower, John, 31
Tower committee, 31–32
Trade, international, 15, 38–39, 56, 59, 66, 72, 73, 74, 77
Trade deficit, 66, 72
Trans World Airlines (TWA), 67, 68
Triple, 102
Trivial Pursuit, 117
Trudeau, Pierre Elliott, 61
Trump, Donald, 70
Trump Shuttle airline, 70
T-shirts, 117
Tunisia, 51
Tunnel of Love, 98
Twin Peaks, 93
Tyson, Mike, 114–115

U2, 98
Unemployment, 15, 19, 20, 63, 64, 65, 69
United Nations, 41, 52
United States Football League (USFL), 111
Updike, John, 103
Uranus, 89
Uruguay, 60
USAir, 75
USA Today, 100

Van Gogh, Vincent, 102
Van Peebles, Mario, 97
Vargas Llosa, Mario, 103
Venezuela, 59
Veterans, 28–29
VH-1, 92
Vidal, Gore, 103
Videocassette recorders (VCRs), *91,* 94
"Video Killed the Radio Star," 92
Vietnam, 22, 57
Vietnam Veterans Memorial, 28, 99
Vietnam War, 11, 14, 57, 63
Viking Penguin, 103
Viking probes, 89
Volcanic events, 87
Volkswagen, 72
Voyager probes, 89

Wages, 26, 33, 77, *105,* 106, 109
Waikiki Beach, 72
Walesa, Lech, 44
Walker, Alice, 103
Walker, Herschel, 111
Wallace, George, 18
Wall Street, 69
Warhol, Andy, 100
War on Drugs, 34
Warren, Earl, 27
Washington, D.C., 23, 25
Waste disposal, 80, 81
Watergate scandal, 113
Watson, Tom, 116
Wayne, John, 100
Webber, Andrew Lloyd, 101
Weissmuller, Johnny, 113
Welfare state, 16
Welles, Orson, 100
West Point, 26
White-collar workers, 19
Wilder, Douglas, 25
Williams, Tennessee, 100
Winfrey, Oprah, 93
Witt, Katarina, 108
Wojtyla, Karol (Pope John Paul II), 46
Wolfe, Tom, 33
Woman's Day magazine, 101
Women, 18, 26, 27
  employment of, 24, 26, 28, 75
  in military, 26
  in politics, 18
  in sports, 113, 116
Wonder Years, 93
World Health Organization (WHO), 82
World League of American Football (WLAF), 111
World Series, 92, 108, 109
Worthy, James, 113

Yachting, 116
Yeltsin, Boris, 43, 44
Yugoslavia, 39, 45
Yuppies, 19, 23, 33, 34

Zen Buddhism, 33
Zhivkov, Todor, 45
Zia al-Haq, General Mohammed, 49
Zuckerman Unbound, 103

Cumulative Index

Note: Volume numbers are in bold. A page number in italic indicates a table, map, graph, or illustration.

Aaron, Hank, **II:**108; **III:**110; **V:**109
ABC, **IV:**93; **V:**98; **VI:**91, 100
Abdul-Jabbar, Kareem, **IV:**110; **V:**106, 114
Abie's Irish Rose, **II:**95
Abortion, **VI:**26, 27
Abscam, **VI:**13
Abzug, Bella, **II:**24
Academy Award winners, **V:**100, 101; **VI:**95
Academy of Motion Picture Arts and Sciences, **II:**99–100
Acheson, Dean, **IV:**21
Acid rain, **VI:**40, 61, 80
Addams, Jane, **I:**15, 86; **III:**32
Adenauer, Konrad, **V:**43
Adirondack Park, **I:**116
Adventures of Augie March, The, **IV:**104
Advertising, **I:**61; **II:**19–20, 28, 33, 66–67, 80–81, 98; **IV:**67–68, 93, 116; **VI:**66, 92, 101
Affluent Society, The, **IV:**68
Afghanistan, **VI:**14, 39, 41, 106
AFL-CIO, **II:**61; **IV:**73
Africa, **II:**55–56; **IV:**55–58, *56;* **V:**55–57; **VI:**14, 22, 38, 49, 53–56, 99
colonization of, **I:**36, 38, 40–41
African-Americans, **IV:**65–66, 98, 100, 104; **V:**70, 96–97, 98; **VI:**18, 24, 27, 33, 97. *See also* Race relations
Harlem Renaissance and, **II:**89–91
labor movement and, **II:**61
migration of, **II:**17–19; **IV:**15–16, 74
music and, **II:**87–89
in politics, **VI:**25–26, 28
in sports, **II:**110, 112; **IV:**107–108, 110, 112; **V:**106–116
vote and, **II:**22; **IV:**30, 32; **V:**20–21
African National Congress (ANC), **IV:**57–58; **VI:**54, 55, 56
Afrikaners, **IV:**56
Afrika Korps, **III:**50
Against Our Will: Men, Women, and Rape, **V:**97
Agent Orange, **VI:**29
Age of Innocence, The, **II:**93
Agnew, Spiro, **V:**29, 98; **VI:**13
Agricultural Adjustment Act (1938), **III:**68, 81
Agricultural Adjustment Administration (AAA), **III:**21, 67–68, 69
Agricultural Marketing Act, **II:**71
Aguinaldo, Emilio, **I:**13
AIDS (acquired immune deficiency syndrome), **VI:**24, 29, 38, 53, 82–83, *83,* 111
Air-conditioning, of factories, **I:**71
Aircraft, **I:**87–88; **II:***75,* 77–79; **III:**77, 83–84, 87–88, 89; **V:**47, 71–72
production during 1913–1919, **I:***88*
in World War I, **I:**55, 57
Aircraft carriers, **III:**87–88
Airline industry, **VI:**74–75
Airlines Deregulation Act (1978), **VI:**74
Airships, **III:**84
Akhmatova, Anna, **II:**41
Alaska, **IV:**19
Albee, Edward, **IV:**99; **V:**102
Alcatraz island, **V:**18
Alcindor, Lew. *See* Abdul-Jabbar, Kareem
Alcohol, **VI:**34
Aldrin, Edwin "Buzz," Jr., **V:**77
Alexander, Grover Cleveland, **I:**112
Al Fatah, **V:**36
Alger, Horatio, Jr., **I:**95
Algeria, **I:**36; **IV:**48; **V:**45
Ali, Muhammad, **III:**110; **IV:**116; **V:**106–107, 112
Alien, **VI:**95
All-American Football Conference (AAFC), **IV:**111, 112
Allen, Dick, **V:**106
Allen, Gracie, **I:**92; **III:**96, 98
Allen, Robert G., **VI:**102
Allen, Woody, **III:**98; **IV:**92; **VI:**96
Allende, Salvador, **V:**42, 43
Alliance for Germany, **VI:**46
Alliance for Progress, **IV:**34
Allies, **I:**31, 33, 43, 54, 55; **II:**12, 40, 45; **III:**31, 49–50, 56–58; **IV:**37. *See also* World War I; World War II
All in the Family, **V:**100
All I Really Need to Know I Learned in Kindergarten, **VI:**103
"All Shook Up," **IV:**101
All Things Considered, **VI:**100
Alsop, Stewart, **V:**97
Altair 8800, **V:**85
AMC, **VI:**73
America First Committee, **III:**27
American Airlines, **VI:**75
American Association for Retired People (AARP), **VI:**28
American Association of Medical Colleges, **I:**81
American Ballet Theatre, **V:**95
American Birth Control League, **I:**82
American Cancer Society, **VI:**84
American Civil Liberties Union (ACLU), **II:**85
American Expeditionary Force, **I:**32
American Farm Bureau Federation, **II:**71
American Federation of Labor (AFL), **I:**72, 74; **II:**61; **III:**71–72, 73; **IV:**73, 74
American Football League (AFL), **IV:**113
American Indian Movement (AIM), **V:**18
American League, **IV:**109
American Medical Association (AMA), **IV:**66
American Mercury magazine, **II:**94
American Motors, **IV:**69
American Professional Football Association (APFL), **II:**111
American Temperance Society, **II:**25
American Tobacco Company, **I:**64, 67
American Wright Company, **I:**87
Amin Dada, Idi, **V:**57
Amnesty International, **VI:**99
Amniocentesis, **V:**83
Amos 'n' Andy, **II:**80, 101; **III:**96
Amritsar, **VI:**58
Amtrak, **V:**72
Amundsen, Roald, **I:**89; **II:**79
Amusement parks, **I:**91–92
Anderson, Carl, **III:**77
Anderson, Marian, **III:**102
Anderson, Maxwell, **III:**98
Anderson, Sherwood, **II:**85
Andropov, Yuri, **VI:**30, 41, 61
Andy Griffith Show, The, **V:**100
Angel Island, **I:**24
Angelou, Maya, **V:**97
Angelus Temple, **II:**97
Angola, **IV:**56
Anna Christie, **II:**96
Anna Karenina, **II:**99
Annapolis, **V:**31
Anne Frank: The Diary of a Young Girl, **IV:**103
Anne of Green Gables, **I:**96
Annie Hall, **VI:**96
Antarctica, **I:**89
Anthony, Susan B., **I:**18; **II:**22
Antibiotics, **II:**82–83; **III:**85; **IV:**88
Anti-Comintern Pact, **III:**39–40
Antievolution bills, **II:**84–85
Antihistamines, **III:**85; **IV:**88
Anti-Saloon League, **II:**25, 26
Anti-Semitism. *See* Jews
Antitrust laws, **I:**27, 30–31, 66, 67, 73
Antiwar movement, **V:**16, 18, 96, 107
Anuszkiewicz, Richard, **V:**103
Aoun, Michel, **VI:**52
Apartheid, **IV:**56–58; **VI:**54–56, 76, 107
Apocalypse Now, **VI:**95
Apollo program, **V:**76–79, 84, 98; **VI:**92
Appalachian Spring, **IV:**105
Appeasement policy, **III:**43, 45
Apple Computer, **VI:**70, 85
"Aquarius," **V:**102
Aquino, Corazon, **VI:**57
Arab League, **V:**36, 49
Arab oil embargo, **V:**29, 38–39, 60–61, 64, 65
Arabs, Israel and, **II:**49–53; **IV:**53, 54; **V:**35, 36
Arabs, Jews and, **VI:**21, 49–50, 51
Arafat, Yasser, **V:**36
Arantes do Nascimento, Edson. *See* Pelé
Architecture, **I:**79, 100; **II:**103; **III:**105; **IV:**105
Argentina, **II:**56; **VI:**47, 48, 59, 60
Arizona, **I:**27
Arizona, **III:**30
Armat, Thomas, **I:**103
Armenia, **II:**39, 51; **VI:**43, 51
Armory show, **I:**102
Arms race, **IV:**23, 34, 40, 79–81; **VI:**29, 30
Armstrong, Edwin, **III:**83
Armstrong, Henry, **III:**112
Armstrong, Jack, **III:**92
Armstrong, Louis "Satchmo," **II:**88, 89
Armstrong, Neil, **III:**32; **IV:**86; **V:**75, 77, 78
Army (football team), **II:**110
Arnold, Roseanne Barr, **IV:**94; **V:**99
Arsenio Hall Show, The, **VI:**94
Art, **II:**90, 102–103; **III:**105; **IV:**105; **V:**14, 102–103; **VI:**102
Art Deco movement, **II:**103; **III:**105
Artificial heart, **VI:**84
Ashcan School, **I:**103
Ashe, Arthur, **V:**113
Asia Minor, **II:**51
Asians, **II:**32
Asimov, Isaac, **IV:**103
Assembly line, **I:**69, 71, **II:**63, 75–76
Astaire, Adele, **II:**95
Astaire, Fred, **I:**92; **II:**95; **III:**92, 94, 95; **VI:**100
Aswan High Dam project, **IV:**55; **V:**37
Atanasoff, John, **III:**83
Atatürk, Kemal, **II:**51; **III:**37
Athletics. *See* Sports
Atlanta, **VI:**23
Atlantic Charter, **III:**30
Atomic bomb, **III:**59, 78–80; **IV:**17, 22, 25–26, 40, 79–81
Atomic Energy Act (1954), **IV:**81
Atomic Energy Commission, **IV:**22, 81
Atomic physics, **III:**77–80
Atoms for Peace, **IV:**81
Attlee, Clement, **IV:**39
Auden, W. H., **III:**104
Australia, **I:**39
Australia II, **VI:**116
Austria, **IV:**46, 49
Austria-Hungary, **I:**31, 45; **II:**37
dual monarchy of, **I:**47
U.S. trade with, **I:**54
World War I and, **I:**47, 48, 49, 50, 51
Automation, **IV:**65, 66, 72, 82
Automobile industry, **I:**67–71; **II:**63, 68–69, 76, *76;* **III:**70, 72, 73–74; **IV:**69, *69;* **V:***62,* 67, 71; **VI:**15, 70–71, 72, 73–74
Automobiles, **II:**67–70; **IV:**13, 67, 69, 117; **V:**14, 61
Auto racing, **I:**114
Axis, **IV:**37
Axis powers, **III:**28, 42. *See also* World War II
Aylwin, Patricio, **VI:**60

Baader-Meinhof gang, **V:**49
Babbitt, **II:**92
Babbitt, Milton, **IV:**105; **V:**95
Babcock, Joseph, **II:**107
Babi Yar, **III:**48
Baby Boom, **IV:***11, 13,* 13–15, 88, 92, 101–102, 103; **VI:**19, 33–35, 93, 97

Bacall, Lauren, **IV:**95
Bach, Richard, **V:**95
Baez, Joan, **III:**98; **V:**93
Baker, James, **VI:**50
Baker, Kristin, **VI:**26
Bakke, Alan, **VI:**24
Balanchine, George, **VI:**100
Baldwin, James, **IV:**104; **V:**97; **VI:**100
Balfour, Lord Arthur James, **II:**50–51
Balfour Declaration, **II:**51–52, 53; **IV:**54
Balkan Entente, **III:**38
Balkans, **I:**43
World War I and, **I:**48–49
Ball, Lucille, **I:**105; **IV:**92
"Ball and Chain," **V:**92
Ballesteros, Seve, **VI:**116
Balloons, **II:**79; **III:**83–84
Bangladesh, **V:**53, 55
Banking, **I:**30, 65, 73; **II:**45–46, 64, 72; **III:**20, 63, 68–69; **V:**63, 70; **VI:**67, *67*, 71
Bank of England, **V:**46
Bank of Manhattan, **II:**19
Bannister, Roger, **IV:**115
Banting, Frederick, **II:**82
Baptism in Kansas, **II:**102
Barber, Samuel, **III:**102
Bardeen, John, **IV:**81
Barker, Kate "Ma," **III:**16
Barnard, Dr. Christiaan, **V:**81–82
Barnstorming, **II:**77
Barrow, Clyde, **III:**16
Barrow gang, **III:**16
Barry, Philip, **III:**99
Barrymore, John, **II:**100
Barton, Bruce, **II:**66–67
Bart Simpson, **VI:**93
Baruch, Bernard, **I:**33, 74
Baryshnikov, Mikhail, **IV:**94; **V:**95
Baseball, **I:***107*, 107–108, 110–112; **II:**107–110; **III:**107–109, 115; **IV:**14, 107–110; **V:**105, 106, 108–109; **VI:***105*, 108–110
Basie, William "Count," **III:**100, 101
Basketball, **IV:**110–111; **V:**105, 106, 114, 116; **VI:**107, 110–111, 113
Basketball Association of America (BAA), **IV:**110
Basque separatists, **V:**49
Bataan, **III:**95
Batista, Fulgencio, **IV:**60, 61; **V:**43
Batman, **VI:**95
Battle Creek Corn Flake Company, **I:**63
Battle Creek Sanitarium, **I:**63
Baugh, "Slingin'" Sammy, **III:**110
Bauhaus style, **II:**103
Bay Area Rapid Transit (BART), **V:**72
Bay of Pigs invasion, **IV:**34, 61
Beach Boys, **V:**92
Beamon, Bob, **V:**116
Beatles, **V:***89*, 89–91, 92, 93
Beatty, Warren, **V:**100
Beau Brummel, **II:**100
Bebop, **III:**101
Becker, Boris, **VI:**114
Beckett, Samuel, **IV:**99
Becquerel, Henri, **I:**83–84
Begin, Menachem, **VI:**14–15, 49–50, 51
Beiderbecke, Bix, **II:**89
Belgium, **IV:**40, 48, 56; **V:**56; **VI:**47, 81
colonization by, **I:**36, 38
World War I and, **I:**50
Bell, Alexander Graham, **II:**32
Bella Donna, **II:**100
Bellamy, Francis, **IV:**14
Bell Laboratories, **IV:**81, 82
Bellow, Saul, **IV:**104, **V:**96, **VI:**103
Bell X-1, **IV:**86
Belorussia, **II:**42
Benchley, Peter, **V:**96
Ben-Gurion, David, **IV:**54, **V:**54
Ben-Hur, **I:**93, **IV:**97
Benny, Jack, **III:**96, **V:**102
Benton, Thomas Hart, **III:**105
Berbick, Trevor, **VI:**114
Beresford, Bruce, **VI:**97
Bergen, Edgar, **III:**96
Bergman, Ingmar, **V:**101
Bergman, Ingrid, **I:**105
Berkeley, Busby, **III:**94
Berle, Milton, **IV:**92
Berlin, **IV:**34–35
occupation of, **III:**55
partitioning of, **IV:**38, *39*, 40, 42
Berlin, Irving, **I:**93; **III:**99, 102; **VI:**100
Berliner, Emile, **I:**94
Berlin Wall, **IV:**35, 42; **VI:**44, 45
Bernstein, Carl, **V:**28
Bernstein, Leonard, **IV:**99, 105; **V:**94, 101
Berra, Lawrence "Yogi," **IV:**109, 110
Berri, Claude, **VI:**97
Best, Charles, **II:**82
Bethune, Mary MacLeod, **III:**26
Bhutto, Benazir, **VI:**49
Bhutto, Zulfikar Ali, **VI:**49
Biafra, **V:**56
Bias, Len, **VI:**112
Bible, **IV:**104
Bicycling, **I:**70, 108–109; **VI:**116
Bidwell, Ben, **VI:**75
Big Band era, **III:**100–102
Big Four (Paris Peace Conference), **II:**12
Big Labor, **IV:**74
Big Three automakers, **II:**68, **IV:**69
Big Three leaders, **IV:**38, 39
Bikini Atoll, **IV:**22, 80
Biko, Stephen, **VI:**54
Binding arbitration, **I:**73
Bingo, **III:**115
Biograph, **I:**104, 105
Biograph Girl, **I:**104
Biotechnology, **VI:**87
Bird, Larry, **VI:**111, 113
Birdseye, Clarence, **III:**82
Birth control, **I:**82
Birth-control pill, **IV:**88–89
Birth Control Review, **I:**82
Birth of a Nation, The, **I:**105
Bishop, Billy, **I:**50
Bismarck, Chancellor Otto von, **I:**38, 46
Bismarck Sea, Battle of the, **III:**58
Black, Hugo L., **III:**22
Blackboard Jungle, **IV:**97
Black Monday, **VI:**20
Black Muslims, **IV:**33; **V:**21, 107; **VI:**33
Black Pride movement, **V:**22
Black September group, **V:**49
Black Sox scandal, **II:**107
Black Star Line, **II:**18
Black Thursday, **II:**73
Blatty, William Peter, **V:**96
Blitz, **III:**47, 97
Blitzkrieg, **III:**44, 45
Blob, The, **IV:**97
Bloody Sunday (St. Petersburg), **I:**52
"Blowin' in the Wind," **V:**91
Blue, Vida, **V:**108
Blue-collar workers, **II:**19–20, 60–61; **IV:**66, 71–74
Blue Cross, **II:**62
Blues, **I:**94; **II:**89; **V:**89; **VI:**97
Blue Shield, **II:**62
Boat people, **VI:**22, 57
Bob's Party Number One, **II:**103
Boer War, **I:**40–41
Boesky, Ivan, **VI:**69
Bogart, Humphrey, **III:**94; **IV:**94, 95
Boggs, Wade, **VI:**110
Bohr, Niels, **I:**85; **II:**83
Bolden, Buddy, **II:**88
Bolshevik Revolution, **I:**52; **II:**41, 42, 44
Bolshoi Ballet, **V:**95
Bombs, **III:**59, 78–80, 88–89; **IV:**17, 22, 25–26, 79–81
Bonanza, **V:**99–100
Bonilla, Bobby, **VI:**109
Bonnie and Clyde, **V:**100
Book-of-the-Month Club (BOMC), **II:**93
Books, **I:**14–15, *95*, 95–97, 101; **II:**49, 90, 92–93, 94, 106; **III:**103–104; **IV:**28, 66, 103–104; **V:**95–97; **VI:**33, 102–103, 105
Boone, Pat, **IV:**103
Bootlegging, **II:**26–27, 29
Borg, Bjorn, **VI:**114
Bork, Robert, **VI:**27
Born in the U.S.A., **VI:**98
Born on the Fourth of July, **VI:**95
Bosnia, World War I and, **I:**47, 48, 49
Boston, **I:**79, 102; **II:**113
Botha, P. W., **VI:**54
Bovet, Daniel, **III:**85
Bow, Clara, **II:**99
Bowie, David, **VI:**98
Boxer Rebellion, **I:**43
Boxing, **I:**113–114; **II:**111–113; **III:**112; **IV:**116; **V:**106–107; **VI:**114–115
Braddock, James, **III:**112
Brady, James, **VI:**16
Bragg, Don, **IV:**115
Brain Trust, **III:**19
Branch, Taylor, **VI:**103
Brando, Marlon, **IV:**97, 116
Brandt, Willy, **V:**44
Braniff International, **VI:**75
Brattain, Walter, **IV:**81
Brave New World, **III:**103–104
Bravo, **IV:**80
Brazil, **II:**56; **IV:**67; **VI:**59, 60
Breakfast Club, The, **VI:**96
Breslin, Jimmy, **II:**116
Brest-Litovsk, Treaty of, **II:**42, 43
Brezhnev, Leonid, **V:**48, 50; **VI:**41, 61
Brezhnev doctrine, **V:**48
Brice, Fanny, **I:**92
Brigadoon, **IV:**99
Bright Lights, Big City, **VI:**103
Brink's, Inc., **IV:**70
Britain, **I:**31, 45; **II:**32, 40; **IV:**38, 40, 47–48, 49; **V:**40, 46–47, 56–57; **VI:**47–48, 56, 81. *See also* Churchill, Winston
appeasement policy of, **III:**45
Battle of, **III:**45, 47, 88
colonies of, **I:**37, 39–40; **III:**35–37; **IV:**48, 51–52
economy of, **II:**45, **IV:**47–48
Egypt and, **II:**52
India and, **II:**54–55
Industrial Revolution in, **I:**35, 59
Palestine and, **II:**52–53; **IV:**54
test ban treaty with, **IV:**34, 80
World War I and, **I:**47, 50, 55; **II:**12, 36, 37, 45, 46, 50, 55
World War II and, **III:**27, 43, 44, 45, 47, 54, 88, 89
British East India Company, **I:**36
Broadway, **I:**93; **II:**89, 95–96; **III:**99; **IV:**99; **V:**101; **VI:**101
Brock, Lou, **II:**109; **V:**110; **VI:**110
Brooks, Gwendolyn, **IV:**104
Brooks, Mel, **IV:**92
Brotherhood of Sleeping Car Porters, **II:**61
Brown, James, **V:**22, 92
Brown, Jim, **IV:**113; **V:**111
Brown, Warren, **III:**115
Brownmiller, Susan, **V:**97
Bryan, William Jennings, **II:**85
Bryant, Paul "Bear," **V:**112; **VI:**113
Buck, Pearl S., **III:**104
Buck Rogers, **III:**91
Budapest, **VI:**40, 44
Budd, Zola, **VI:**108
Budge, Donald, **III:**113
Buganda, **V:**57
Buick Motor Car Company, **I:**68
Bulgaria, **II:**38; **VI:**40, 45
World War I and, **I:**48, 50, 51
Bulge, Battle of the, **III:**53–54
Bull Moose party, **I:**30
Bunau-Varilla, Philippe, **I:**28
Bunche, Ralph, **I:**19
Bunford, **II:**31
Bunyan, John, **I:**14
Burchfield, Charles, **III:**105
Burdick, Eugene, **IV:**103
Burger, Warren, **VI:**27
Burma, **IV:**52
Burns, George, **I:**92; **III:**96, 98
Burns, Tommy, **I:**113
Burroughs, Edgar Rice, **I:**96, 97; **III:**91
Bush, George, **II:**32; **VI:**20–21, 26, 27, 29, 34, 48, 53, 61, 75
economy and, **VI:**64, 66
foreign policy of, **VI:**21, 32
Business, **II:**13, 16, 60, 72; **IV:**16–17, 46, 58, 63, 64, 65, 67–68, 70, 75, 82; **V:**61, 62, 66–68, 70, 93; **VI:**16, 17, 20, 24, 38, 65, 72, 94. *See also* Advertising; Commerce; Trade
assembly line and, **II:**75–76
automobile industry and, **I:**67–71; **II:**63, 68–69, 76, *76*
black, **II:**18
corporations and, **I:**64–67; **II:**62–63; **IV:**68, 70–71, 74; **VI:**67–70, 75, 77, 106
during Depression, **III:**19, 63–64
industrialization and, **I:**59–60
labor and, **II:**19–20
mail-order, **I:**61
marketing and, **I:**61
New Deal and, **III:**24, 64
railroads and, **I:**60–61
stores and, **I:**61, 62
unions and, **II:**61–62
after World War I, **II:**45, 46
during World War II, **III:**31
Business cycle, **II:**59
Buthelezi, Gatsha, **VI:**56
Butler Act, **II:**84–85
Byrd, Richard E., **II:**78–79
Byrnes, James F., **III:**22

Cable News Network (CNN), **VI:**91, 92, 100
Cable television, **VI:**91–92
Caesar, Sid, **IV:**92
Caetano, Marcello, **V:**46
Cafe society, **III:**115–116
Cage, John, **IV:**105; **V:**95
Cagney, James, **III:**92, 95; **VI:**100
Caine Mutiny, The, **IV:**103
California, **I:**25; **V:**68; **VI:**16, 23
Camacho, Manuel Avila, **IV:**60
Cambodia, **IV:**48, 52–53; **V:**27, 55; **VI:**22, 57
Camelot, **IV:**99
Camera Work, **I:**103
Camille, **II:**99
Camp, Walter, **I:**113; **II:**111
Campanella, Roy, **III:**108
Campbell, Malcolm, **III:**117
Camp David Accords, **VI:**14–15, 49–50, 51
Camus, Albert, **IV:**104
Canada, **I:**39; **II:**32; **IV:**40; **V:**40–41, 68; **VI:**38, 40, 61, 80
Cancer, **V:***83;* **VI:**83–84
Candide, **IV:**105
Cantos, **II:**93–94
Capone, Al, **II:**26
Capp, Al, **III:**91
Capra, Frank, **III:**93, 94–95
Captain Kangaroo, **IV:**92
Carbon-14 dating, **IV:**86
Caribbean, **I:***31,* 46; **VI:**22
Carlos, John, **V:**17, 116
Carlos, Juan, **V:**46
Carmichael, Stokely, **V:**21, 22
Carnarvon, Lord (George Edward Stanhope Molyneux), **II:**81
Carnegie, Andrew, **I:**12, 60, 65, 67, 95
Carnegie, Dale, **III:**103
Carnegie Foundation for the Advancement of Teaching, **I:**81
Carnegie Steel Company, **I:**60
Carothers, W. H., **III:**80
Carousel, **IV:**98
Carpathia, **I:**78
Carpenter, M. Scott, **IV:**85
Carpenters, **V:**92
Carranza, Venustiano, **I:**53
Carrel, Dr. Alexis, **II:**82
Carrel suture, **II:**82
Carroll, Diahann, **V:**98
Carroll, Earl, **III:**99
Carson, Johnny, **V:**99
Carson, Rachel, **IV:**89; **V:**68
Carter, Elliott, **IV:**105
Carter, Howard, **II:**81
Carter, Jimmy, **II:**32; **V:**29, 39, 64; **VI:**12–15, 16, 17, 50–51, 59, 100
  economy and, **VI:**13–14, 15, 64
  foreign policy of, **VI:**14–15, 30
Carter, John Garnet, **III:**113
Carter, Rosalyn, **VI:**13
Caruso, Enrico, **I:**95
Carver, George Washington, **III:**32
Casey, William, **VI:**17
Cash, Johnny, **V:**93
Castle, Irene, **I:**117
Castle, Vernon, **I:**117
Castro, Fidel, **IV:**24, 34, 60, 61; **V:**42, 43; **VI:**22
Catcher in the Rye, The, **IV:**116
Cather, Willa, **I:**97
Cathode ray, **I:**83–84
Cat in the Hat, The, **IV:**103
Cats, **VI:**101
Catt, Carrie Chapman, **I:**18; **II:**22, 23–24
CBS, **IV:**93; **V:**98; **VI:**91
Ceausescu, Nicolae, **VI:**45
Centennial, **V:**96
Center for the Study of Responsive Law, **V:**67
Central America, **VI:**22
Central Intelligence Agency (CIA), **IV:**25, 34, 55, 61; **V:**36, 43; **VI:**11, 60
Central Pacific Railroad, **I:**25
Central Powers, **I:**31, 33, 50, 51, 52; **II:**49. *See also* World War I
Certain People of Importance, **II:**93
Ceylon, **IV:**52
Chad, **VI:**54
Chadwick, James, **III:**77, 79
Chaffee, Roger, **V:**77
Chain, Ernst, **II:**82–83
Chain letter craze, **III:**24
Challenger, **VI:**88–89
Chamberlain, Neville, **III:**43, 45
Chamberlain, Wilt, **III:**110; **IV:**110–111; **V:**106, 114
Chambers, Whittaker, **IV:**25
Chamorro, Violeta, **VI:**60
Chamoun, Camille, **IV:**55
Chandler, Raymond, **III:**104
Chaney, James, **V:**19
Chaney, Lon, **III:**98
Chaplin, Charlie, **I:**105; **II:**98; **VI:**100
Chapman, Mark David, **VI:**98
Charities, **I:**65, 67
Charleston, Oscar, **II:**110
Charlie McCarthy, **III:**96
Chávez, César, **V:**69, 70
"Checkers" speech, **IV:**19
Cheeseborough, Robert, **III:**85
Cher, **IV:**94; **V:**92
Chernenko, Konstantin, **VI:**41, 61
Chernobyl, **VI:**81
Chevrolet, Louis, **I:**70
Chicago, **I:**79, 102; **II:**18
Chicago (music group), **V:**93
Chicago Poems, **I:**97
Chico and the Man, **V:**99
Child labor, **I:**16
Children, **IV:**14, 88, 92
Children's Television Workshop, **V:**98
Chile, **V:**42, 43; **VI:**60
China, **I:**37, 57; **II:**53–54; **III:**43, 56; **IV:**18, 21, 40–41, 42–45; **V:**14, 27, 48, 50, 51–52, 52, 53; **VI:**14, 22, 56, 57–58
  civil war in, **IV:**42–44
  immigration from, **I:**25
  imperialism and, **I:**43–45
  Japanese war with, **I:**42
  Open Door policy and, **I:**14, 44
  World War I and, **I:**50
Chinese Communist party, **I:**44; **II:**54
Chinese Exclusion Act (1882), **I:**25
Chinese Revolution, **I:**45
Chinese Revolutionary party, **I:**44
Chisholm, Shirley, **II:**24
Chlorofluorocarbons (CFCs), **V:**81; **VI:**79
Chopin, Kate, **I:**96
Chorus Line, A, **V:**101; **VI:**101
Christian Democratic party (West German), **IV:**49; **V:**43, 44
Christo, **VI:**102
Chrysler, Walter P., **II:**68
Chrysler Building, **II:**19, 103
Chrysler Corporation, **II:**68; **IV:**69; **VI:**73
Church, Ellen, **III:**12
Churchill, Winston, **II:**53; **III:**30, 43, 45, 46, 47, 48, 51, 53, 55, 96; **IV:**38, 39; **V:**54, 56
Cimino, Michael, **VI:**95
Cinemax, **VI:**92
Citation (racehorse), **IV:**115–116
Citibank, **II:**64
Cities, **I:**12, 14, *20,* 45; **IV:**15–16; **VI:**22, 23–24
Citizen Kane, **III:**95
Civil defense, **IV:**80
Civil disobedience, **II:**55
Civilian Conservation Corps (CCC), **III:**21, 64, 65
Civil Rights Act (1957), **IV:**31–32
Civil Rights Act (1964), **V:**13, 14, 19–20, 30, 31, 70
Civil Works Administration, **III:**64, 70
Clancy, Tom, **VI:**103
Clapton, Eric, **VI:**97
Clark, Dr. Barney, **VI:**84
Clarke, Edward Y., **II:**33
Class divisions
  in Britain, **I:**39
  in Japan, **VI:**56
  in Mexico, **V:**41
  in U.S., **I:**59, 61, 62; **II:**20, 21–22, 60; **IV:**16, 65–66, 89; **V:***23;* **VI:***19, 20,* 20, 25, 33, 35, 66, 77
Classical music, **II:**102
Clavell, James, **V:**96
Clay, Cassius. *See* Ali, Muhammad
Clayton Antitrust Act (1914), **I:**31, 73
Clean Air Acts (1963, 1967), **V:**68
Clear and Present Danger, **VI:**103
Clemenceau, Georges, **II:**12, 36, 37, 38
Clemens, Roger, **VI:**110
Clemente, Roberto, **V:**109
Cleveland, **I:**16–17; **II:**18
Cleveland, Grover, **I:**19
Clifton, Nat "Sweetwater," **IV:**110
Cliquot Club Eskimos, **II:**102
Clockwork Orange, A, **V:**100
Close Encounters of the Third Kind, **VI:**94
CNN Headline News, **VI:**91
Coal miners, **I:**13
Cobb, Ty, **I:**111, 112; **II:**109; **III:**109
COBE, **VI:**86
Coca-Cola, **II:**28
Cody, William F. "Buffalo Bill," **I:**109
Cohan, George M., **I:**93, 94
Colbert, Claudette, **III:**94
Cold War, **IV:**19–27, 37–42, 64, 84, 113. *See also* Communist threat
  atomic bomb and, **IV:**79–81
  beginning of, **III:**55
  Kennedy's policy and, **IV:**34–35
Cole, Nat "King," **IV:**102
Collective farming, **IV:**45
Collective farms, **II:**44; **III:**40
College basketball, **IV:**110, 111
College football, **II:**110–111; **IV:**111, 113; **V:**111, 112
College Football Hall of Fame, **IV:**113
College sports, **I:**109, 112–113; **VI:**112–113
Collett, Glenna (Vare), **II:**115; **III:**113
Collins, Michael, **V:**77, 78
Collins, Phil, **VI:**98
Colombia, **V:**43; **VI:**34, 39, 59
Colonization. *See* Imperialism
Colson, Charles, **V:**27
Coltrane, John, **IV:**102
Columbia (space shuttle), **VI:**88
Columbia Broadcasting Company, **II:**81
Columbia Broadcasting System (CBS), **II:**81
Columbia Pictures, **III:**92; **VI:**72, 94
Comaneci, Nadia, **IV:**110; **VI:**107
Commerce, **II:**62–64. *See also* Business; Trade
Commercial Cable Company, **II:**79
Committee for a Sane Nuclear Policy (SANE), **IV:**80
Committee for Industrial Organizations (CIO), **III:**71, 72–73
Committee on Consumer Interest, **V:**66
Committee on Public Information (CPI), **I:**33
Committee to Re-elect the President (CREEP), **V:**28
Common Business Oriented Language (COBOL), **IV:**83
Common Market, **IV:**48, 70; **V:**27, 47; **VI:**38, 46–49, *47*
Common Sense Book of Baby and Child Care, The, **IV:**88
Commonwealth of Independent States **VI:**43–44
Communism, **II:**41, 42, 54; **IV:**38, 40–41, 49; **V:**14, 55, 56; **VI:**57
  collapse of, **VI:**40–46
  Red Scare and, **II:**30–31
  War Communism and, **II:**42–43
Communist party, **II:**43, 54; **IV:**24, 26, 37; **V:**50, 51, 55; **VI:**42, 43, 45
  Chinese, **I:**44; **IV:**42–44
  French, **IV:**48
  Italian, **IV:**49
Communists, **I:**45
Communist threat, **IV:**18, 24–27, 39–40, 57, 61, 95. *See also* Cold War
Como, Perry, **IV:**102
Compact disks (CDs), **VI:**97
Company, **V:**101
Competition
  in automobile industry, **I:**68, 70
  trusts and holding companies and, **I:**65, 66
Complete Book of Running, The, **VI:**105
Compton, Arthur, **III:**79
CompuServe, **VI:**72
Computerized axial tomography (CAT) scan, **V:**84
Computers, **III:**83; **IV:**65, 81, 83, 84; **V:**84–85; **VI:**71–72, *79,* 85–86
Computing-Tabulating-Recording Company, **II:**69
Concentration camps
  German, **III:**50–51, 52
  Soviet, **III:**40
  U.S., **III:**22, 32–33
Concorde, **V:**47, 72
Coney Island, **I:**92
Confessions of Nat Turner, The, **V:**96
Congo, **I:**36; **IV:**56; **V:**56
Congress, **VI:**13
Congress of Industrial Organizations (CIO), **III:**73; **IV:**73, 74
Congress of Racial Equality (CORE), **III:**29, 32; **IV:**28, 31; **VI:**25
Connie's Inn, **II:**89

Connor, Dennis, **VI:**116
Connors, Jimmy, **V:**113; **VI:**113–114
Conrad, Charles, Jr., **V:**76
Conservation, **I:**116; **III:**24, 81–82; **V:**14
Conservatism, **VI:**16, 27, 59, 61
Conservative party,
British, **V:**46–47
Canadian, **V:**40; **VI:**61
Colombian, **VI:**59
Consolidated Rail Corporation (Conrail), **VI:**74
Constitution, U.S.
Eighteenth Amendment to, **II:**24, 26
Equal Rights Amendment and, **V:**30, 31; **VI:**26
Fifteenth Amendment to, **II:**22
Fourteenth Amendment to, **I:**19; **II:**22; **IV:**28
Nineteenth Amendment to, **I:**18, **II:**23
Seventeenth Amendment to, **I:**22
Sixteenth Amendment to, **I:**30
Twentieth Amendment to, **III:**19
Twenty-fifth Amendment to, **V:**26
Twenty-first Amendment to, **III:**21
Twenty-fourth Amendment to, **IV:**33
Twenty-second Amendment to, **IV:**17
Twenty-sixth Amendment to, **V:**32
Consumer Advisory Council, **V:**66
Consumer Federation of America, **V:**66
Consumer goods, **II:**19–20, 63, 64–65; **III:**82–84; **IV:**63, 66, 68; **V:**61, 62, 68
Consumerism, **IV:**68; **V:**66–67; **VI:**76
Consumer Product Safety Commission, **V:**66–67, **VI:**76
Containment policy, **IV:**20
Contras, **VI:**20, 31–32, 59–60
Cook, Frederick, **I:**89
Cook, Captain James, **I:**89
Coolidge, Calvin, **II:**13, 15–16, 56, 60, 66, 71; **III:**32
Cooper, Chuck, **IV:**110
Cooper, Gary, **III:**94, 95, 109
Cooper, Jackie, **III:**94
Cooper, L. Gordon, Jr., **IV:**85; **V:**76
Cooperatives, farming, **I:**74
Copland, Aaron, **III:**102
Coppola, Francis Ford, **V:**101; **VI:**95
Coral Sea, Battle of the, **III:**57, 88
Corbett, James J. "Gentleman Jim," **I:**113; **III:**110
Corcoran, Fred, **III:**113
Corn prices, **III:***68*
Corporations, **I:**64–67; **II:**62–63; **IV:**68, 70–71, 74; **V:**70; **VI:**65, 67–70, 75, 77, 106. *See also* Business
Correll, Charles, **III:**96
Corrigan, Douglas "Wrong Way," **III:**116
Corsica, **VI:**49
Cortisone, **IV:**88
Cosby, Bill, **V:**98; **VI:**102
Cosby Show, The, **VI:**93
Cosell, Howard, **V:**112
Cosmopolitan magazine, **I:**99
Costa Rica, **II:**56; **V:**43; **VI:**59, 60
Costello, Lou, **IV:**94
Cotton Bowl, **III:**109
Cotton Club, **II:**89
Coughlin, Father Charles E., **III:**97–98
Council of Economic Advisers, **IV:**64
Council of People's Commissars, **II:**42
Counterculture, **V:**32–33
Country music, **V:**93
Court, Margaret Smith, **V:**113
Cousins, Norman, **III:**97
Cousy, Bob, **IV:**111
Cox, James M., **II:**13
Crabbe, Buster, **III:**110
Crane, Stephen, **I:**101, 105
Crawford, Joan, **II:**100; **III:**93
Credit, **II:**65–66, 72–73; **IV:**64, 67; **V:**59–60
Creel, George, **I:**33
Creole Jazz Band, **II:**88, 89
Crick, Francis, **IV:**86, 87; **V:**86
Crime, **II:**26
during Depression, **III:**16
Crisis, The, **I:**21, 99
Crosby, Bing, **III:**95, 96; **IV:**115
Crossword puzzles, **I:**117; **II:**106
Crouse, Russell, **III:**99
Crump, Diane, **V:**106, 108
C-SPAN, **VI:**91
Cuba, **II:**57; **III:**37; **IV:**34, 35, 60, 61; **V:**42, 43, 49; **VI:**22, 23
Cuban missile crisis, **IV:**61
Cuban Revolution, **IV:**60
Cubist painters, **I:**102
Cullen, Countee, **II:**90
Cultural Revolution, **V:**51–52; **VI:**57
Culture, **II:**89–91
cummings, e. e., **II:**93
Cunningham, Glenn, **III:**110
Curie, Marie, **I:**84
Curie, Pierre, **I:**84
Curry, John Steuart, **II:**102; **III:**105
Curtis, Cyrus, **I:**101
Curtiss, Glenn, **I:**87–88
Cusak, John, **V:**102
Czechoslovakia, **II:**37, 46; **III:**38, 43, 44; **IV:**39; **V:**50–51; **VI:**40, 44, 45

Daley, Richard, **VI:**13
Dallas, **VI:**92–93
Danbury Hatters case, **I:**73
Dance, **I:**94, 117; **II:**89, 96–97; **III:**101; **IV:**105; **V:**93–95, 101–102
Darwin, Charles, **I:**86; **II:**85
Daugherty, Harry, **II:**14
David, Dwight F., **I:**115
Davies, Arthur B., **I:**102
Davies, Bobby, **VI:**113
Davis, Benjamin, Jr., **IV:**33
Davis, Bette, **III:**94; **VI:**100
Davis, Miles, **IV:**102
Davis, Victor, **VI:**113
Davy Crockett, **IV:**116
Dawes, Charles G., **II:**49
Dayan, General Moshe, **V:**36–37
Daylight saving time, **I:**33
D day, **III:**53–55
DDT, **III:**82; **IV:**89; **V:**68, 80, 81
Dean, "Daffy," **III:**108
Dean, "Dizzy," **III:**108; **V:**113
Dean, James, **IV:**97, 116
Dean's December, The, **VI:**103
Dear Abby, **IV:**117
Death of a President, The, **V:**96
Death of a Salesman, **IV:**99
"Death of the Ball Turret Gunner, The," **III:**104
Debt crisis, **VI:**59–60
Decker, Mary (Slaney), **VI:**108
Declaration of Lima, **III:**37
de Coubertin, Baron Pierre, **I:**109
Deer Hunter, The, **VI:**95
Defense Department, **IV:**24, 25
De Forest, Lee, **I:**79
Degas, Edgar, **I:**105
de Gaulle, Charles, **III:**54; **IV:**48; **V:**45–46
De Klerk, F. W., **VI:**54–55
de Kooning, Willem, **III:**105; **IV:**105
Delicate Balance, A, **V:**102
De Mille, Cecil B., **II:**100
Demokratiztsiya, **VI:**41
Dempsey, Jack, **II:**112–113; **VI:**113
Deng Xiaoping, **VI:**57, 58
Denmark, **I:**49; **III:**44–45; **IV:**40; **VI:**47
Deoxyribonucleic acid (DNA), **IV:**86–87; **V:**86
Department of Agriculture, **V:**68
Department of Commerce and Labor, **I:**67
Department of Health, Education, and Welfare, **IV:**18
Department of Housing and Urban Development (HUD), **V:**13
Department of Veterans Affairs, **VI:**29
Department stores, **I:**62
Depression, defined, **II:**59. *See also* Great Depression
Deregulation, **VI:**17, 19, 67, 73, 74
Détente, **V:**26–27, 49, 50, 52, 79, 103; **VI:**14, 30
Detroit, **I:**16–17, 68; **II:**18, 33; **IV:**102
De Valera, Eamon, **II:**47
DeVries, Dr. William C., **VI:**84
Dewey, John, **I:**86
Dewey, Thomas E., **III:**33; **IV:**17, 18
Diabetes, **II:**82
Díaz Ordaz, Gustavo, **V:**41
Dickey, Bill, **III:**108
Dickson, William, **I:**103
Dick Tracy, **III:**91, 92
Didrikson, Mildred "Babe" (Zaharias), **III:**110, 114, 115; **IV:**110
Dietrich, Marlene, **III:**92
Digital Equipment Corporation, **V:**84
Dillinger, John, **III:**16
DiMaggio, Joe, **I:**109; **III:**108, 109, 114, 115; **IV:**110
Dinner for Threshers, **II:**102
Dire Straits, **VI:**97
Dirigibles, **I:**55, 57; **II:**79
Dirks, Rudolph, **I:**99
Dirksen, Everett, **IV:**17
Dirty Harry series, **VI:**95
Disk recording, **I:**94–95
Disney, Walt, **III:**94; **V:**102
Disneyland, **II:**98; **IV:**41, 117
Disney World, **II:**98
Diversification, **IV:**70
Doby, Larry, **IV:**107
Dr. Strangelove, **V:**100
Doctorow, E. L., **V:**96
Doctors, **V:**68
medical schools and, **I:**81–82
Dodge, **II:**68
Dolby, R. M., **V:**86
Dollar diplomacy, **I:**57; **II:**56
Domagk, Gerhard, **III:**84
Dominican Republic, **II:**57; **V:**43
Domino theory, **IV:**22
Donahue, Phil, **VI:**93
"Don't Be Cruel," **IV:**101
Doolittle, Lieutenant Colonel James H., **III:**57
Doonesbury, **V:**96
Doors, The, **V:**92
Dorsey, Jimmy, **III:**100
Dorsey, Tommy, **III:**100, 102
Do the Right Thing, **VI:**96
Doubleday, Abner, **III:**107, 109
Doughboys, **I:**32
Douglas, Aaron, **II:**90
Douglas, James "Buster," **VI:**115
Douglas, William O., **III:**22; **VI:**17
Dow-Jones industrial average, **II:**63–64; **VI:***68*
Dracula, **III:**92
Draft, **I:**32
Dragnet, **IV:**92
Drama, **II:**90, 96; **IV:**92–93, 99
Dreamland, **I:**92
Drexel Burnham Lambert, **VI:**69
Dreyfus, Alfred, **I:**46; **II:**50
Dreiser, Theodore, **I:**97
Drive-in movies, **III:**113; **IV:**67, 97
Drop City, U.S.A., **V:**33
Drugs, **IV:**87–89
development of, **III:**84–86
illegal, **V:**33; **VI:**21, 24, 33, 34, 39, 59, 112
sports and, **VI:**107, 112
Dual monarchy, **I:**47
Dubček, Alexander, **V:**50
Du Bois, W. E. B., **I:**21, 22, 99; **II:**90; **IV:**23
Duchamp, Marcel, **I:**102
Dukakis, Michael, **VI:**20, 25
Duke, James Buchanan, **I:**64
Dulles, John Foster, **IV:**22
Dunaway, Faye, **V:**100
Duncan, Isadora, **II:**96, 100
Dunkirk, evacuation from, **III:**45
Duran, Duran, **VI:**92
Durant, William, **I:**68, 70
Duryea, Charles, **I:**67–68
Duryea, J. Frank, **I:**67–68, 114
Dust Bowl, **III:**15, *17,* 67, *67*
Dylan, Bob, **V:**91–92
Dynasty, **VI:**92
Dzugashvili, Joseph. *See* Stalin, Joseph

E. R. Thomas Motor Company, **I:**87
Eagle (lunar module), **V:**77
Earhart, Amelia, **III:**86
Early Bird satellite, **V:**76, 79
Early Sunday Morning, **III:**105
Earth Day, **V:**80
Earthquakes, **V:**53, 87; **VI:**32, 51
in Japan, **II:**53
Eastern Europe, **III:**38
Easter Rebellion, **II:**47
East Germany, **VI:**40, 44, 45–46
Eastman, George, **I:**83, 104
Eastman Kodak Company, **I:**83
Eastwood, Clint, **VI:**95
Easy Rider, **V:**101
Echeverría Alvarez, Luis, **V:**41–42
Economic Opportunity Act (1964), **V:**13, 14
Economic Recovery Tax Act, **VI:**17
Economy, **I:**11; **II:***11,* 17–22, 59–62, 70–73; **III:**24; **IV:**16–17, 63–66, 72, 77; **V:**29, 59–64, 70; **VI:**13–17, 19–21, 24, 63–66. *See also* Business; Great Depression; New Deal
Canadian, **V:**41; **VI:**61

Chinese, **VI:**57
European, **IV:**45–49; **V:**43–44, 46–47, 50
German, **VI:**46
global, **V:**70; **VI:**38–39, 72
Hoover's policies and, **III:**11–13
information, **VI:**71–72
Iranian, **VI:**50–51
Japanese, **V:**53; **VI:**56
Latin American, **IV:**58; **V:**42
Mexican, **V:**41–42; **VI:**60
Soviet, **IV:**37–38; **V:**48; **VI:**41
World War I and, **I:**57, 74; **II:**36, 45–46, 59, 64
during World War II, **III:**73–75
Ecosystem, global, **VI:**39–40
Eddington, Sir Arthur, **I:**85–86
Eddy, Nelson, **III:**94
Ederle, Gertrude, **I:**109; **II:**117
Edison, Thomas, **I:**60, 77, 78, 94, 103–104; **III:**32; **V:**79
Edison Company, **I:**104
Ed Sullivan Show, The, **IV:**101; **V:**90
Education, **I:**86; **IV:**11–12, 65, 74; **V:**13, 14, 31; **VI:**21, 22, 35. *See also* Schools
of doctors, **I:**81–82
of immigrants, **I:**25
of managers, **II:**63; **IV:**71
in Turkey, **II:**51
of women, **I:**19, *19*
Education Act (1972), **V:**31
Edward VII, king of England, **I:**39
Edward VIII, king of England, **III:**36
Edwardian Period, **I:**39
Egypt, **I:**36; **II:**52; **III:**36, 49–50; **V:**35–38, 39, 60; **VI:**14, 49–50
Ehrlichman, John, **V:**27
Eighteenth Amendment, **II:**24, 26
Eight Week Cholesterol Cure, The, **VI:**102
Einstein, Albert, **I:**84–87; **II:**83; **III:**42, 79; **IV:**23, 83
Einstein, "Izzy," **II:**28–29
Eisenberg, David, **IV:**112
Eisenhower, Dwight D., **III:**30, 46, 51, 54; **IV:**14, 18–19, 20, 22, 27, 59, 64, 81, 94, 115; **V:**14, 24, 27
civil rights and, **IV:**29, 30, 31
foreign policy of, **IV:**22–24, 42, 53, 55, 61
Elderly, **VI:**28
Elections, **I:**22; **III:**22. *See also* Vote
Eastern European, **VI:**44, 45
Indian, **V:**54
in occupied countries, **IV:**38, 39
Pakistani, **VI:**49
presidential, **I:**29–30, *30*, 31; **II:**13–14, 16, 23, 57, 80; **III:**17–19, 23, 28, 33; **IV:**17–19, 33, 94; **V:**13, 17, 24–25, 27, 29, 63, 64; **VI:**12–13, 16, 17, 18, 19, 20–21, 23, 25, 31, 64, 100
Progressive reform of, **I:**16
Electric appliances, **II:**65, 76–77
Electricity, **I:**77–78; **II:**63; **IV:**66, 76, 81; **V:**61, 65, 66, 68, 79–80
Electric-powered machines, **II:**63
Electric streetcars, **I:**64, 117
Electron microscope, **III:**87
"Elegy for a Dead Soldier," **III:**104
Elementary and Secondary Education Act (1965), **V:**13, 14
Eliot, T. S., **I:**101; **II:**94; **V:**102
Elizabeth, princess of England, **III:**92
Elkins Act (1903), **I:**63
Ellington, Edward Kennedy "Duke," **II:**89, 102; **III:**100, 101
Ellington, Mercer, **III:**101
Ellis Island, **I:**24; **VI:**21–22
Ellison, Ralph, **IV:**28
El Penitente, **IV:**105
El Salvador, **VI:**31, 60
Emergency Banking Relief Act (1933), **III:**20, 69
Emergency Petroleum Allocation Act, **V:**66
Emergency Price Control Act (1942), **III:**75
Emergency Quota Act (1919), **II:**31
Emperor Jones, The, **II:**96
Empire State Building, **III:**82, 92
Empire Strikes Back, The, **VI:**94
Employment, **I:**12, 16, 67, 71–73; **II:**19–20, 21–22; **III:***17;* **IV:**11, 12, *15*, 17, 18, 64, 66, 71–74; **V:**69–70, 71; **VI:**19, 24, 28, 69, 70, 72, 75, 77. *See also* Labor movement; Unemployment
of blacks, **II:**17
industrialization and, **I:**12–13, 61
racial discrimination in, **III:**29, 32
wages and, **I:**12–13, **I:**20, 62, 67, 69, 71
of women, **I:**18–19; **II:**22–23, 62; **III:**25, 32, 70, 74; **IV:**14–15, 65; **V:**30, 31, 70; **VI:**24, 26, 28, 75
workforce and, **II:**60–62
working conditions and, **I:**67, 71
World War I and, **I:**74
during World War II, **III:**31, 74, 75
Employment Act (1946), **IV:**17, 64
Energy, **VI:**13, 15
Energy crunch, **V:**64–66, *65*
England. *See* Britain
English Channel, **II:**117
English Channel Tunnel, **VI:**89
ENIAC, **IV:**82; **V:**85
Eniwetok, **IV:**80
Entente Cordiale, **I:**46
Entertainment, **I:**91–92
Entrepreneurs, **VI:**70
Environmentalism, **V:**25, 68, 79–81; **VI:**76
Environmental movement, **IV:**89
Environmental Protection Agency (EPA), **V:**25, 68; **VI:**80
EPCOT center, **VI:**117
Equal Opportunity Act, **V:**70
Equal Pay Act (1963), **V:**30
Equal Rights Amendment (ERA), **V:**30, 31; **VI:**26
Erhard, Ludwig, **V:**43
Eritrea, **VI:**54
Ervin, Sam, **VI:**17
ESPN, **VI:**92, 106
Esquire magazine, **VI:**101
Estonia, **II:**37; **III:**41; **IV:**38; **VI:**43
E.T.—The Extra-Terrestrial, **VI:**94
Ethiopia, **I:**38; **III:**39; **V:**56; **VI:**39, 51, 53, 54
Ethnic groups, **I:**24. *See also* Race relations
Europe '92, **VI:**46–49
European Assembly, **VI:**47
European Community (EC), **VI:**38, 46–49, *47*. *See also* European Economic Community (EEC)
European Economic Community (EEC), **IV:**48, 70; **V:**27, 47. *See also* European Community (EC)
European Monetary System, **VI:**47
European Recovery Program, **IV:**20, 40, 46, 47, 49
European Space Agency, **VI:**88
Eustis, Dorothy Harrison, **II:**73
Evangelists, **II:**97
Evans, Hiram Wesley, **II:**33
Everly Brothers, **IV:**101
Evert, Chris, **IV:**110; **V:**113; **VI:**114
Evolutionary biology, **I:**86; **II:**84–85
Ewry, Ray, **III:**110
Executioner's Song, The, **VI:**103
Exorcist, The, **V:**96
Experiments in Art and Technology (EAT), **V:**103
Exploration, **I:**88–89
Explorers, **IV:**84–85
Expo '67, **V:**40
Exxon Valdez, **VI:**81

F. W. Woolworth Company, **I:**61
Factories, **I:**35, 59; **IV:**65, 69. *See also* Employment; Industrialization
Fads, **II:**107; **IV:**117
Fail-Safe, **IV:**103
Fairbanks, Douglas, Jr., **I:**33; **II:**100; **III:**116
Fair Deal, **IV:**17, 18
Fair Employment Practices Commission (FEPC), **III:**29, 32
Fair Employment Practices Committee, **II:**61
Fair Labor Standards Act (1938), **III:**20, 24
Faldo, Nick, **VI:**116
Falkland Islands War, **VI:**47, 48
Fall, Albert, **II:**14–15
Fallingwater (building), **I:**100; **III:**105
Fallout, **IV:**22, 80
Falwell, Jerry, **VI:**16
Family Limitation, **I:**82
Famines, in USSR, **II:**41
Fantasia, **III:**94
Fantasticks, The, **IV:**99
"Farm Aid," **VI:**99
Farm Credit Administration, **III:**65
Farmer, James, **IV:**28; **VI:**25
Farming, **I:**12, 70; **II:**21, 60, 71, *71;* **IV:**46, 64, *74*, 76–77; **V:**48, 54, 69, 70; **VI:**19, 22–23, 76, 77
collective, **II:**44; **III:**40; **IV:**45
during Depression, **III:**14–15, 69, 81–82
industrialization and, **I:**73–75
New Deal and, **III:**65, 66–68, 81–82
Russian, **II:**41
after World War I, **II:**45, 46
World War I and, **I:**74
during World War II, **III:**75, 82
Farm Security Administration, **III:**68
Farouk, king of Egypt, **IV:**55
Fascism, **II:**48; **III:**38, 39; **IV:**37
Fashion, **II:**106–107; **III:**117; **IV:**117; **V:**117
Fassbinder, Rainer Werner, **VI:**97
Fatherhood, **VI:**102
Father Knows Best, **IV:**92
Fathom (horse), **V:**106
Faulkner, William, **II:**93; **III:**103
Federal Art Project, **III:**105
Federal budget deficit, **VI:**19, 20, 21, 64, *65*, 65–66, 72
Federal Bureau of Investigation (FBI), **II:**30; **III:**16; **V:**26, 27; **VI:**11, 13
Federal Communications Commission (FCC), **II:**80; **IV:**94
Federal Deposit Insurance Corporation (FDIC), **III:**21, 69; **VI:**67
Federal Emergency Relief Agency, **III:**70
Federal Energy Office, **V:**65
Federal Farm Board, **II:**72
Federal Music Project, **III:**100–102
Federal Radio Commission, **II:**80
Federal Republic of Germany. *See* Germany, partitioning of
Federal Reserve Act, **I:**30
Federal Reserve System, **I:**73; **III:**69; **V:**63, 64
Federal Theatre Project, **III:**66, 98, 99
Federal Trade Commission, **I:**30–31; **III:**69
Federal Writers' Project, **III:**66
Feller, Bob, **III:**108–109, 115
Fellini, Federico, **IV:**98
Female Eunuch, The, **V:**97
Feminine Mystique, The, **II:**24; **IV:**14; **V:**30
Ferber, Edna, **II:**96
Ferguson, Miriam "Ma," **II:**24
Fermi, Enrico, **III:**77, 78, 79
Ferraro, Geraldine, **VI:**18
Fianna Fáil, **II:**47
Fiddler on the Roof, **V:**101, **V:**102
Field, Marshall, **I:**62
Fielder, Cecil, **VI:**110
Fields, W. C., **I:**92; **III:**94; **IV:**94
Fifteenth Amendment, **II:**22
Film trust, **I:**104
Fine arts, **I:**101–103
Fingers, Rollie, **V:**108
Finland, **II:**37, 42; **III:**41
Fire Next Time, The, **IV:**104
Fireside chats, **III:**18, 20, 69
Firpo, Luis, **II:**112
"First Fig," **II:**94
Fit for Life, **VI:**105
Fitness, **VI:**33, 105, 106
Fitzgerald, F. Scott, **II:**92, 93; **III:**98, 103
5-and-10-cent stores, **I:**61
500 Hats of Bartholomew Cubbins, The, **IV:**103
Five-Power Treaty, **II:**40
Five-Year Plans, **II:**43–44
Chinese, **IV:**45
Fixer, The, **V:**96
Flaherty, Robert, **II:**100
Flanagan, Hallie, **III:**99
Flappers, **II:**106
Flashdance, **VI:**92, 96
Flash Gordon, **III:**91
Fleming, Alexander, **II:**82
Fleming, Dr. Ernest, **I:**15
Fleming, Ian, **V:**95, 96
Fleming, Peggy, **V:**116
Flesh and the Devil, **II:**100
Flexner, Abraham, **I:**81–82
Flood, Curt, **V:**106
Florey, Howard, **II:**82–83
Floyd, Charles "Pretty Boy," **III:**16
Flutie, Doug, **VI:**111
Flynn, Errol, **III:**94
Folk music, **V:**89, 91–92
Follett, Ken, **VI:**102
Fonda, Henry, **I:**105

Fonteyn, Margot, **V:**95
Food Administration, **I:**33; **II:**59, 64
Food consumption, **IV:**68
Football, **I:**112–113; **II:**110–111; **III:**109–110, 115; **IV:***107*, 111–113; **V:**105, 106, 111–112; **VI:**109, 111–112, 113
Ford, Gerald, **V:**29, 63–64; **VI:**12, 13
Ford, Harrison, **VI:**95
Ford, Henry, **I:**68, 69, 114; **II:**64, 68–69, 75–76; **IV:**23
Ford, John, **III:**93
Ford, Whitey, **IV:**109
Ford Motor Company, **I:**68–70, 114; **II:**18, 61, 68, 77; **IV:**69, 70, 109; **VI:**72, 73, 74
Fordson tractor, **II:**71
Ford Trimotor, **II:**77
Foreign aid, **IV:**20, 46, *47*
Foreign Correspondent, **III:**95
Foreign Investment Review Agency, **V:**41
Foreman, George, **V:**107
Formosa, **I:**42; **IV:**43–44
Fort Worth, **VI:**23
For Whom the Bell Tolls, **III:**39, 103
Four-Power Treaty, **II:**40
Fourteen Points, **II:**12, 35–36
Fourteenth Amendment, **I:**19; **II:**22; **IV:**28
4'33", **IV:**105; **V:**95
Four Tops, **V:**92
Fowles, John, **V:**96
Foyt, A. J., **III:**110
France, **I:**31, 35, 45, 46; **II:**32, 40; **IV:**22, 38, 40, 48, 49; **V:**14, 45–46; **VI:**47, 48, 81
  Arab resistance and, **II:**53
  colonies of, **I:**36, 37, 38; **III:**36, 37; **IV:**48, 52–53
  economy of, **II:**36, 45
  League of Nations and, **II:**38
  World War I and, **I:**46, 47, 50; **II:**12, 36, 37, 45, 46–47, 51, 55
  World War II and, **III:**43, 44, 45, 54
Francis Ferdinand, archduke of Austria, **I:**31, 49
Francis Joseph, king of Hungary and emperor of Austria, **I:**47
Franco, Francisco, **III:**38, 39, 40; **V:**46
Franco-Prussian War, **I:**46
Frankenstein, **III:**92
Frankfurter, Felix, **III:**22
Franklin, Aretha, **V:**92
Franklin, Rosalind, **IV:**87
Fraternal organizations, **I:**115
Frazier, Brenda, **III:**116
Frazier, "Smokin' Joe," **V:**107
Freedom Riders, **IV:**31
Free-Trade Agreement, **VI:**38, 60, 61
French Canadians, **II:**33; **VI:**61
French Lieutenant's Woman, The, **V:**96
Freshman, The, **II:**99
Freud, Sigmund, **I:**83
Friday the 13th, **VI:**95
Friedan, Betty, **II:**24, 100; **IV:**14; **V:**30
Friendship, **III:**86
Friendship 7, **IV:**85; **V:**76
Frisch, Frankie, **III:**108
Frisch, Otto, **III:**78
From Here to Eternity, **IV:**103
Front for the Liberation of Quebec (FLQ), **V:**41
Frost, Robert, **II:**94
Frugal Gourmet Cooks with Wine, The, **VI:**105
Fuad I, king of Egypt, **II:**52
Fuchs, Klaus, **IV:**25–26
Fuel Administration, **II:**59
Fulbright, William, **V:**16
Fulghum, Robert, **VI:**103
Full Metal Jacket, **VI:**95
Funk, Casimir, **I:**81
Funny Face, **II:**95
Funny Girl, **V:**102

Gable, Clark, **III:**93, 94, 95, 103–104; **IV:**94
Gagarin, Yury, **IV:**85; **V:**75
Galbraith, John Kenneth, **IV:**68, 71
Gallico, Paul, **II:**105
Galloping Gaucho, **II:**98
Galveston, **I:**20
Gandhi, Indira, **V:**54; **VI:**58
Gandhi, Mohandas K. (Mahatma), **I:**41; **II:**55; **III:**35, 36; **IV:**32, 51; **V:**69
Gandhi, Rajiv, **VI:**58
Gangsters, **II:**26
Garbo, Greta, **II:**99, 100; **III:**92
Garcia, Alan, **VI:**59
García Márquez, Gabriel, **VI:**103
Garfunkel, Art, **V:**92
Garland, Judy, **III:**95
Garner, John Nance, **III:**17
Garvey, Marcus, **II:**18, 56
Gates, William, III, **VI:**70, 85
Gathers, Hank, **VI:**113
Gaullists, **IV:**48
Gaylor, Wood, **II:**103
Gaynor, Janet, **II:**99–100
Gay rights, **VI:**29
Gehrig, Lou, **II:**109; **III:**108, 109, 110, 115
Geisel, Theodor (Dr. Seuss), **IV:**103; **VI:**100
Gekko, Gordon, **VI:**69
Geldof, Bob, **VI:**99
Gemayel, Bashir, **VI:**52
Gemini missions, **V:**76
General, The, **II:**99
General Motors (GM), **I:**68, 70; **II:**68, 69; **IV:**68, 69, 70; **V:**67; **VI:**73, 74, 75
Genetic engineering, **V:**86, 87; **VI:**87
Genetics, **I:**83; **IV:**86–87
Geneva, Switzerland, **II:**37
Gentry, Bobbie, **V:**93
Georgia (country), **II:**42
German-Americans, **I:**31
German Democratic Republic. *See* Germany, partitioning of
Germany, **I:**35, 45, 54; **II:**32; **IV:**37, 38, 46, 48–49; **V:**43–44, 49, 50, 61; **VI:**40, 44, 45–46, 47, 48–49, 81. *See also* Hitler, Adolf
  aircraft of, **III:**87
  colonization by, **I:**36, 38, 46–47
  economy of, **II:**45–46
  League of Nations and, **II:**38
  partitioning of, **IV:**38, *39*, 40, 48, 49
  Spanish Civil War and, **III:**39
  Third Reich of, **III:**41–42
  unemployment in, **II:***35*
  war reparations and, **II:**12, 36, 37, 45, 48; **IV:**38
  World War I and, **I:**31–32, 46–47, 49–50, 50–51, 55, 57; **II:**37, 38, 40, 48–49, 55
  World War II and, **III:**29, 39–41, 43, 44–45, 47–49, 54, 55
Gershwin, George, **II:**89, 95; **III:**98, 99, 102
Gershwin, Ira, **III:**99, 102
Ghana, **IV:**56
Ghiorso, Albert, **III:**78
Ghostbusters, **VI:**95
Giamatti, A. Bartlett, **VI:**110
GI Bill, **IV:**11–12, 17, 64, 65
Gibson, Charles Dana, **I:**99
Gibson, Debbie, **V:**102
Gibson, Josh, **IV:**107
Gibson Girl, **I:**99
Gillespie, Dizzy, **III:**101; **IV:**102
Gillette, **IV:**109
Ginsburg, Douglas, **VI:**27
Giscard d'Estaing, Valéry, **V:**46
Glasnost, **VI:**41, 43
Glass-Steagall Banking Act (1933), **III:**20
Gleason, Jackie, **IV:**92
Glenn, John H., Jr., **II:**32; **IV:**85; **V:**76
Global politics, **VI:**39
Global village, **VI:**37–38, 72
Glyn, Elinor, **II:**99
Goddard, Robert, **II:**79
Godfather, Part II, The, **V:**101
Godfather, The, **V:**100, 101
Godzilla, **IV:**98
Goethals, Colonel George, **I:**79
Going My Way, **III:**95
Golden Boy, **III:**98
Goldmark, Dr. Peter, **IV:**100
Gold Reserve Act (1934), **III:**69
Gold Rush, The, **II:**98
Goldwater, Barry, **V:**13
Goldwyn, Samuel, Jr., **III:**95; **IV:**96
Golf, **I:**115; **II:**114–115; **III:**113–114, 115; **IV:**114–115; **V:**106, 110; **VI:**115–116
Gompers, Samuel, **I:**72, 74
Gone with the Wind (film), **III:**94, 103–104
Gone with the Wind (novel), **III:**103
Goodbye Columbus, **IV:**104
Good Earth, The, **III:**104
Gooden, Dwight, **V:**113
Good Housekeeping magazine, **IV:**66
Goodman, Andrew, **V:**19
Goodman, Benny, **III:**100, 101; **VI:**100
"Good Morning, Starshine," **V:**102
Good Neighbor policy, **II:**57; **III:**27, 37–38; **IV:**59
Gorbachev, Mikhail, **VI:**21, 32, 38, 43, 45, 48, 49, 51, 58
  collapse of communism and, **VI:**41–44
Gorbachev, Raisa, **VI:**42
Gordy, Berry, Jr., **IV:**102; **V:**92
Gore, Albert, Jr., **IV:**23
Gorgas, Dr. William, **I:**79
Göring, Hermann, **IV:**38
Gosden, Freeman, **III:**96
Gospel of Wealth, The, **I:**67
Go Tell It on the Mountain, **IV:**104
Gould, Chester, **III:**91
Government bureaucracy, **VI:**16–17
Government of Ireland Act (1920), **II:**47
Government spending, **IV:**70–71, *79;* **VI:**17, 19–20, 35, 64, 66
Grable, Betty, **III:**75
Graduate, The, **V:**100, 101
Graf, Steffi, **V:**113; **VI:**113
Graham, Martha, **II:**96–97; **III:**102; **IV:**105
Graham, Otto, **IV:**112
Grand Hotel, **II:**99
Grand Ole Opry, **II:**101
Grange, Harold "Red," **II:**105, 111
Grant, Cary, **III:**94, 95; **VI:**100
Grapes of Wrath, The, **III:**67, 104
Grasso, Ella, **V:**31
Grateful Dead, **V:**92
Gravity's Rainbow, **V:**96
Gray, Harold, **III:**92
Gray Panthers, **VI:**28
Graziano, Rocky, **VI:**113
Great Atlantic and Pacific Tea Co. (A&P), **II:**67
Great Britain. *See* Britain
Great Depression, **II:**45, 72–73; **III:**13–17, 61–73, *63*, 107; **IV:**58, 63, 72, 77
  effects of, **III:**14, 63–64
  farming during, **III:**69
  Hoover's response to, **III:**11–13
  labor movement during, **III:**70–73
  New Deal and. *See* New Deal
  unemployment and, **III:**11, 14, 17, 62
Great Gatsby, The, **II:**92
Great Lakes Quality Agreement, **V:**68
Great Leap Forward, **IV:**45
Great Northeast Blackout of 1965, **V:**79–80
Great Society, **V:**11, 13, 14, 25, 26, 68
Great Train Robbery, The, **I:**103, 104
Great White Fleet, **I:**28, 37
Greece, **II:**38, 51; **IV:**20, 39, 40; **VI:**47
  after World War I, **III:**38
  World War I and, **I:**48, 50
Green Eggs and Ham, **IV:**103
Greenhouse effect, **VI:**40, 80
Greenpeace, **VI:**40
Greer, Germaine, **V:**97
Grenada, **VI:**30
Gretzky, Wayne, **IV:**110; **VI:**115
Grey, Zane, **I:**96
Griffith, D. W., **I:**104–105
Grissom, Virgil I. "Gus," **IV:**85; **V:**76, 77
Gropius, Walter, **II:**103; **IV:**105; **V:**102
Gross national product (GNP), **IV:**63; **V:**35, 59, 70; **VI:***37*, 65
  in 1919–1929, **II:***11*
  Japanese, **V:***53*
Group Theatre, **III:**98
Groves, General Leslie, **III:**79
Guadalcanal, battle at, **III:**58
Guatemala, **IV:**25, 59–60
Guest, Edgar A., **II:**94
Guevara, Ernesto "Che," **V:**43
Guggenheim Museum, **I:**100
Guide dogs, **II:**73
Guinea, **IV:**56
Gulf of Tonkin Resolution, **V:**15
Gulf War, **VI:**26, 35, 38, 52–53, 92, 100
Gunsmoke, **IV:**92
Guomindang (Nationalist party), **I:**44; **II:**54
Guthrie, Arlo, **V:**93
Guthrie, Janet, **VI:**116
Guzman, Arbenz, **IV:**59–60

Hadden, Briton, **II**:95
Hagen, Walter, **II**:114
Hahn, Otto, **III**:78
Haight-Ashbury, **V**:32
Hair, **V**:102
Haiti, **III**:37
Halas, George, **VI**:113
Haldeman, H. R., **V**:27
Haley, Alex, **II**:100, **VI**:92
Haley, Bill, **IV**:100
Halley's comet, **I**:83
Hammer, **VI**:98
Hammerstein, Oscar, II, **II**:96; **III**:100; **IV**:98–99
Hammett, Dashiell, **III**:104
Handicapped people, **VI**:29
Handy, W. C., **I**:94; **II**:89
Hansberry, Lorraine, **IV**:99
Hapsburg Empire, **I**:47
Hardin, Lillian, **II**:89
Harding, Warren G., **II**:13–15, 16, 60, 101
Hardy, Oliver, **II**:99
Harlem Renaissance, **II**:89–91
Harlow, Jean, **III**:92, 98, 117
Harper's Bazaar, **II**:94
Harrington, Michael, **IV**:16
Harris, Joel Chandler, **I**:96–97
Harrison, George, **V**:90
Hart, Lorenz, **III**:99
Hart, Moss, **III**:99
Hart, William S., **I**:105
Harvey, Doug, **VI**:113
Hastie, William, **III**:26
Hauptmann, Bruno, **III**:12
Hawaii, **I**:14; **IV**:19
Hawaiian Eye, **IV**:92
Hawley-Smoot Tariff, **III**:12
Hay, John, **I**:19
Hayes, Janet Gray, **V**:31
Hayes, Woody, **V**:112
Hays Code, **III**:93
Haywood, William "Big Bill," **I**:73
HBO, **VI**:92
Health and Human Services, **IV**:18
Hearst, William Randolph, **I**:99
"Heartbreak Hotel," **IV**:101
Heart transplant surgery, **V**:81–82
Heath, Edward, **V**:47
Heiden, Eric, **VI**:107
Heisenberg, Werner, **II**:84
Hellman, Lillian, **III**:98
Hemingway, Ernest, **II**:93; **III**:39, 103, 104
Henderson, Fletcher, **II**:89–90
Henderson, Rickey, **V**:110; **VI**:110
Hendrix, Jimi, **V**:92, 93
Henie, Sonja, **III**:110; **V**: 113
Henson, Jim, **V**:98; **VI**:100
Henson, Matthew, **I**:89
Hepburn, Katharine, **III**:94, 95; **IV**:95
Hepburn Act (1906), **I**:63
Hertz, Heinrich, **I**:78
Hertz, John, **II**:70
Herzl, Theodor, **II**:50
Herzog, **V**:96
Hidden Persuaders, The, **IV**:68
Higher Education Act (1965), **V**:14
High society, **III**:115–116
Hijuelos, Oscar, **VI**:103
Hillary, Sir Edmund, **IV**:114
Hill Street Blues, **VI**:93
Himmler, Heinrich, **III**:52
Hinckley, John W., Jr., **VI**:16
Hindenburg, **III**:84
Hindenburg, General Paul von, **I**:51
Hindus, **I**:40; **IV**:51
Hirohito, emperor of Japan, **IV**:50; **VI**:61
Hiroshima, **III**:59, 80
Hispanics, **IV**:15–16, 74; **V**:69, 70; **VI**:18, 22, 24, 26
Hiss, Alger, **IV**:25; **V**:24
History of Standard Oil, **I**:63
Hitchcock, Alfred, **III**:95; **IV**:97–98
Hitler, Adolf, **II**:48; **III**:27–28, 38, 41, 42, 43, 47, 49, 50, 54, 55, 111; **IV**:38, 45
HIV (human immunodeficiency virus), **VI**:82, 83
Hmong people, **VI**:21
Ho Chi Minh, **III**:36; **IV**:22, 52–53; **V**:55
Ho Chi Minh City, **V**:55
Hockey, **I**:114–115; **II**:113; **IV**:116; **V**:106; **VI**:107, 115
Hoffman, Abbie, **VI**:17
Hoffman, Dustin, **VI**:95–96
Hogan, Ben, **IV**:114–115
Hog Farm, **V**:33
Holden Caulfield, **IV**:116
Holding companies, **I**:65
Holiday, Billie, **III**:101
Holiday Inn, **III**:95
Holland, Clifford M., **II**:76
Holland Tunnel, **II**:76
Holley, Robert W., **V**:86
Hollywood Canteen, **III**:95
Holmes, Larry, **VI**:114
Holocaust, **III**:52; **IV**:53
Holyfield, Evander, **VI**:115
Homecoming: Old Times, The, **V**:102
Homelessness, **VI**:35
Home Rule Bill (1920), **II**:47; **V**:47
Home to Harlem, **II**:91
Honecker, Erich, **VI**:45
Hong Kong, **VI**:56
Hoover, Herbert, **I**:33; **II**:14, 16, 24, 57, 59, 60, 63, 71, 73; **III**:11–13, 17, 19; **IV**:18; **V**:27
Hoover, J. Edgar, **II**:30; **III**:16
Hoovervilles, **III**:13, 67
Hope, Bob, **I**:92; **III**:95; **IV**:115
Hopkins, Sir Frederick Gowland, **I**:81
Hopper, Edward, **III**:105
Hopper, Grace Murray, **IV**:83
Hornet, **III**:88
Horowitz, Vladimir, **V**:94
Horse racing, **II**:109; **IV**:115–116; **V**:106
Horthy, Admiral Miklós, **II**:46
Horton, Willie, **VI**:20
Hostages, **VI**:15, 39, 50–51
Hot Five, **II**:88
Hotline, **IV**:34, 61
Hot Seven, **II**:88
Houdini, Harry (Ehrich Weiss), **I**:109; **II**:100
"Hound Dog," **IV**:101
Household appliances, **II**:65, 76–77
House Judiciary Committee, **V**:28–29
House Un-American Activities Committee (HUAC), **IV**:25, 27, 95
Housing Act (1949), **IV**:18
Housing industry, **IV**:12–13, 18, 63–64, 75
Houston Astrodome, **V**:108, 114
Howdy Doody Show, The, **IV**:92, 116
Howells, William Dean, **I**:97
How the Other Half Lives, **I**:14
How to Win Friends and Influence People, **III**:103
Hubbard, William DeHart, **II**:112
Hubbell, Carl, **VI**:113
Hubble, Edwin, **II**:84
Hubble Space Telescope, **II**:84; **VI**:88
Hudson, Henry, **I**:89
Hudson, Rock, **VI**:100
Hughes, Charles Evans, **II**:14, 39
Hughes, Langston, **II**:91; **V**:102
Hull, Bobby, **V**:106
Hull, Cordell, **III**:29
Hull House, **I**:15, 86
"Human Rights Now!" **VI**:99
Human Sexual Response, **V**:97
Humber River Bridge, **V**:77
Humphrey, Hubert H., **V**:25; **VI**:17
Hungary, **II**:37; **III**:38; **IV**:23, 39, 42; **V**:50; **VI**:44, 45
Huns, **I**:55
Hunt, Howard, **V**:28
Hunter, Jim "Catfish," **V**:108; **VI**:108
Hunt for Red October, The, **VI**:103
Hurricanes, **I**:20
Hurston, Zora Neale, **II**:90
Hussein, Faisal, **II**:51
Hussein, Saddam, **VI**:50–51, 52–53
Hussein, Sharif, **II**:50
Hutson, Don, **III**:110
Huxley, Aldous, **III**:103–104
Hyatt Roller Bearing Company, **II**:69
Hydrogen bomb, **IV**:22, 80, 81

Iacocca: An Autobiography, **VI**:103
Iacocca, Lee, **VI**:73
Ibn Saud, king of Saudi Arabia, **II**:52
Ibo people, **V**:56
Icahn, Carl, **VI**:67, 68
Ice Glare, **III**:105
Ice hockey, **I**:114–115; **II**:113; **IV**:116; **V**:106; **VI**:107, 115
Iceland, **IV**:40
"I Could Have Danced All Night," **V**:100
I'd Rather Be Right, **III**:99
"If We Must Die," **II**:91
"I Have a Dream" speech, **IV**:32
I Know Why the Caged Bird Sings, **V**:97
Il Duce. *See* Mussolini, Benito
I Led Three Lives, **IV**:103
I Love Lucy, **IV**:92
Imagism, **I**:101
Immigration, **I**:*11*, 11–12, 22–25; **VI**:21, 22–23
  to cities, **I**:*20*
Immigration Act (1965), **V**:14; **VI**:22
Immigration Control and Reform Act (1985), **VI**:23
Imperial Hotel (Tokyo), **I**:100
Imperialism
  Japanese, **I**:42–43
  justification of, **I**:37
  Western, **I**:13–14, 36–38
"Impossible Dream, The," **V**:102
Income taxes, **I**:30; **II**:16; **III**:23, 31, 75; **V**:14, 59; **VI**:64–65
India, **I**:36, 40, 41; **II**:54–55; **III**:35; **IV**:51–52; **V**:54–55; **VI**:22, 56, 58
Indiana Jones, **VI**:94–95
Indiana Jones films, **VI**:95
Indianapolis, **II**:33
Indianapolis 500, **VI**:116
Indianapolis *Times,* **V**:97
Indian Mutiny of 1857, **I**:36
Indian Reorganization Act (1934), **III**:26
Indochina, **I**:36; **III**:28, 36; **V**:45; **VI**:22
Indonesia, **III**:36; **IV**:51; **V**:55; **VI**:56
Industrialization, **I**:12–13, 45, 47, 59–60, 61; **II**:29, 68–69
  automobile industry and, **I**:67–70
  factory workers and, **I**:12–13
  farming and, **I**:73–75
  international trade and, **I**:35–36
  of Japan, **I**:42
  Progressivism and, **I**:14
  Russian, **II**:43–44
Industrial Light and Magic, **VI**:95
Industrial Revolution, **I**:35, 59. *See also* Industrialization
Industrial Workers of the World (IWW), **I**:73
Industry, **IV**:46, 47, 58, 65, 69; **V**:41, 42, 47, 53, 54; **VI**:70–72
  during World War II, **III**:73–74
Infantile paralysis, **III**:19, 85; **IV**:87
Infectious diseases, **I**:81; **II**:82–83; **IV**:88
Inflation, **II**:36, 45–46; **IV**:16–17, 72; **V**:41, 53, 59, 60, 61, *62*, 62–63, 64, 70; **VI**:13, 19, 20, 63, 64, 65
Influenza epidemic of 1918-1919, **I**:81
Information economy, **VI**:71–72
Inkatha movement, **VI**:55, 56
Installment purchasing, **II**:65–66; **IV**:67
Institutional Revolutionary Party (PRI) (Mexican), **VI**:60
Instrumentalism, **I**:86
Insulin, **II**:82
Integrated circuit, **V**:84
Intel Corporation, **V**:85
Intelsat satellites, **V**:76, 79
Inter-American Treaty for Reciprocal Assistance, **IV**:59
Intercollegiate Athletic Association, **I**:112
Interest rates, **V**:63, 64; **VI**:15, 65, 67
Internal Revenue Service (IRS), **V**:26
International Brigade, **III**:39
International Business Machines (IBM), **II**:69; **V**:84–85; **VI**:85
International Church of Foursquare Gospel, **II**:97
International Conference on Amateurism, **I**:109
International Court of Justice, **II**:38
International Ladies Garment Workers Union, **I**:12; **III**:98
International Military Tribunal, **IV**:38
International Style, **IV**:105
International trade, **I**:35–36, 54; **II**:46, 56; **IV**:46, 58; **V**:41, 43–44, 50, 53, 62, 63, 70–71; **VI**:15, 38–39, 56, 59, 66, 72, 73, 74, 77
Interstate Commerce Act (1887), **I**:63
Interstate Commerce Commission, **I**:63–64
Interstate Highway Act (1956), **IV**:74–77
In the Heat of the Night, **V**:101
Intifada, **VI**:51
Invasion from Mars, **III**:97

Inventions, **I:**77–79, 87–88; **II:**77, 82; **IV:**82
Invisible Man, **IV:**28
Ionesco, Eugène, **IV:**99
Iran, **II:**52; **IV:**25, 55; **VI:**15, 49, 50
Iran-Contra scandal, **VI:**20, 31–32, 60
Iran-Iraq War, **VI:**53
Iraq, **II:**53; **III:**36; **V:**36, 38; **VI:**21, 32, 49, 50–51, 52–53, 53. *See also* Gulf War
Ireland, **I:**39–40; **II:**32, 47; **VI:**47, 49
Irish Free State, **II:**47
Irish Republican Army (IRA), **II:**47; **V:**47, 49
Irish Republican Brotherhood, **II:**47
Iron Curtain, **IV:**39–41, 42
Iron Guard, **III:**38
Ironweed, **VI:**103
Irrigation projects, **I:**75
Irving, John, **III:**98
Isolationism, in 1930s, **III:**27, 35
Israel, **IV:**53–55; **V:**35, 38–39, 49; **VI:**21, 49–50, 51–52
  Six-Day War and, **V:**35–37
  Yom Kippur War and, **V:**38, 60
It, **II:**99
Italian East Africa, **III:**39
Italy, **I:**23; **II:**32, 40; **IV:**37, 40, 46, 48–49; **VI:**47, 81
  economy of, **II:**45
  under Mussolini, **III:**39–40
  Spanish Civil War and, **III:**39
  World War I and, **I:**50, 51, 52; **II:**12, 36, 37, 45, 47–48, 51
  World War II and, **III:**29, 39–40, 44, 51, 53
Itasca, **III:**86
It Can't Happen Here, **III:**99
It Happened One Night, **III:**94
"I've Grown Accustomed to Her Face," **V:**100
Ives, Charles, **I:**102–103
I Was a Teen-age Werewolf, **IV:**97
Iwo Jima, Battle of, **III:**59

J. C. Penney, **I:**61; **II:**67
Jackson, Jesse, **III:**32; **VI:**18, 25
Jackson, Leroy, **VI:**113
Jackson, Michael, **VI:**98
Jackson, Reggie, **IV:**110; **V:**108; **VI:**108
Jackson, Robert H., **III:**22
Jackson State University, **V:**18
Jacobs, Helen Hull, **III:**113
Jagger, Mick, **V:**91
James, Harry, **III:**100, 102
James, Henry, **I:**101; **V:**97
James Bond, **V:**95–96
Jameson, Betty, **III:**113
Jane Fonda's Workout Book, **VI:**105
Jannings, Emil, **II:**99
Japan, **I:**25, 35; **II:**40, 53; **III:**38; **IV:**17, 37, 43, 50, 79; **V:**27, 52, 53, 61, *62;* **VI:**22, 56, 71, 72, 74
  China and, **II:**54
  empire of, in 1942, **III:***56*
  modernization of, **II:**53
  Pearl Harbor attacked by, **III:**27, 29, 30, 56
  war with China, **I:**42
  war with Russia, **I:**28, 43, 45
  westernization of, **I:**41–43
  World War I and, **I:**50; **II:**36, 37
  World War II and, **III:**28, 29, 40, 41, 43, 56, 59
Japanese-Americans, **II:**33
  imprisonment of, **III:**22, 32–33
Jarrell, Randall, **III:**104
Jarvis, Gregory, **VI:**89
Jaws, **V:**96
Jazz, **I:**94; **II:**87–89, 102; **III:**100–101; **IV:**102
Jazz Singer, The, **II:**100
Jefferson Airplane, **V:**92, 93
Jefferson Memorial, **III:**105
Jeffries, Jim, **I:**113, 114
Jenner, Bruce, **VI:**107
Jenney, William LeBaron, **I:**79
Jerusalem, **V:**36, 37; **VI:**49, 51
Jet aircraft, **III:**87
Jewett, Sarah Orne, **I:**96
Jews, **III:**38; **VI:**49. *See also* Israel
  anti-Semitism and, **I:**46; **II:**33, 50; **V:**70
  emigration from Russia, **I:**45
  Hitler's persecution of, **III:**41, 42, 48, 50–51, 52
  immigration of, **I:**23
  immigration to Palestine, **III:**36–37; **IV:**54
  Israel and, **IV:**53–55
  Palestine Problem and, **II:**49–53
Jiang Jie-shi (Chiang Kai-shek), **II:**54; **IV:**43, 44, **V:**54
Jim Crow laws, **I:**20; **IV:**30
Jinnah, Mohammed Ali, **IV:**51
Jitterbug, **III:**101
Jive talk, **III:**101
Job, The, **II:**62
Jobs, Steven, **VI:**70, 85
Joe's Bed-Stuy Barbershop: We Cut Heads, **VI:**96
John, Elton, **V:**92
John F. Kennedy Center for the Performing Arts, **V:**94
John P. Grier (racehorse), **II:**109
John Paul II, pope, **VI:**46
Johns Hopkins Medical School, **I:**82
Johnson, Andrew, **VI:**13
Johnson, Ben, **VI:**107, 112
Johnson, Byron Bancroft "Ban," **I:**111
Johnson, Earvin "Magic," **VI:**83, 111, 113
Johnson, Jack, **I:**113–114
Johnson, Lady Bird, **V:**12
Johnson, Lyndon, **IV:**33, 34, 35; **V:**11–15, 21, 25, 27, 43, 59, 60, 66, 97, 98; **VI:**11, 18, 63
  civil rights and, **V:**19, 21, 23
  Great Society of, **V:**11, 13, 14, 25, 26, 68
  Vietnam War and, **V:**13, 14–15, 17
Johnson, Robert, **VI:**97
Johnson, Sam, **V:**12
Johnson, Virginia, **V:**97
Johnson, Walter "Big Train," **I:**111–112; **III:**109
Johnson's Wax corporate headquarters, **I:**100
Joliot-Curie, Frédéric, **III:**86
Joliot-Curie, Irène, **I:**84; **III:**86
Jolson, Al, **II:**100
Jonathan Livingston Seagull, **V:**95
Jones, James, **IV:**103
Jones, Mary Harris, **III:**70
Jones, Robert Tyre "Bobby," **II:**114, 116
Joplin, Janis, **V:**92, 93
Joplin, Scott, **I:**94
Jordan, **III:**36; **IV:**54, 55; **V:**36, 38; **VI:**51
Jordan, Michael, **VI:**111, 113
Jordan Motor Cars, **II:**66
Joshua Tree, The, **VI:**98
Jou En-lai (Chou En-lai), **V:**51
Joyce, James, **II:**94
Joy of Music, The, **V:**94
Judd, Donald, **V:**103
Julius's Annex, **II:**103
Jungle, The, **I:**14, 27, 97
Jupiter, **V:**79

Kaltenborn, H. V., **III:**97
Karami, Omar, **VI:**52
Karloff, Boris, **III:**92
Kaufman, George S., **III:**99
KDKA, **II:**80
Keaton, Buster, **II:**99
Kefauver, Estes, **IV:**94
Keller, Charlie, **VI:**113
Kelley, Florence, **I:**15–16, 17
Kellogg, William Keith, **I:**63
Kellogg-Briand Pact (1928), **II:**40
Kellogg Company, **I:**63
Kelly, Gene, **IV:**95
Kelly, George "Machine Gun," **III:**16
Kelly, Grace, **IV:**99
Kelly, Judge Patrick, **VI:**26
Kelly, "Shipwreck," **II:**107
Kennan, George, **IV:**20
Kennedy, Anthony M., **VI:**27
Kennedy, Edward, **III:**32
Kennedy, John F., **I:**19; **III:**30; **IV:**22, 32, 33, 34, 48, 61, 88, 94, 99; **V:**13, 14, 19, 21, 24–25, 59, 60, 75, 79, 87
  assassination of, **IV:**35; **V:**11, 96, 97; **VI:**92
  foreign policy of, **IV:**34–35
  New Frontier of, **IV:**33–34
  space program and, **IV:**85–86
Kennedy, Robert F., **V:**17, 25, 27, 98
Kennedy, William P., **VI:**103
Kent State University, **V:**18
Kentucky Derby, **V:**106
Kenya, **III:**36
Kenyatta, Jomo, **IV:**57
Kerensky, Alexander, **I:**52
Kern, Jerome, **II:**96
Kerner Report, **V:**23
Kerouac, Jack, **IV:**104
Kerr, Jean, **IV:**103
Kettering, Charles, **I:**70
Keynes, John Maynard, **VI:**64
Keystone Cops, **I:**105
Key to Rebecca, The, **VI:**102
Khmer Rouge, **V:**55; **VI:**57
Khomeini, Ayatollah Ruhollah, **II:**52; **IV:**55; **VI:**15, 50–51, 51, 53, 61, 103
Khorana, Har Gobind, **V:**86
Khrushchev, Nikita, **IV:**23, 34–35, 41–42, 61; **V:**24, 37, 48; **VI:**42
Kid Brother, The, **II:**99
Kidney transplant, **IV:**87
Kids Say the Darndest Things, **IV:**103
Kiernan, John, **II:**105, 106
Kiev, **III:**48
Killy, Jean Claude, **V:**116
Kim Il Sung, **IV:**21
King, Billie Jean, **III:**110; **V:**112–113
King, Carole, **V:**92
King, Martin Luther, Jr., **II:**32; **IV:**31, 32–33; **V:**16, 17, 19, 20, 21, 23–24, 27, 69, 98; **VI:**18, 103
King, Rodney, **VI:**24
King, Stephen, **VI:**103
King and I, The, **IV:**98
King Kong, **III:**92
King Tut's tomb, **II:**81; **V:**50
Kinshasa, **V:**56
Kipling, Rudyard, **I:**37
Kirov Ballet, **V:**95
Kissinger, Henry, **V:**18, 26–27, 39, 52, 71
Kitchener, Lord Horatio Herbert, **I:**38, 40
Kitt Peak National Observatory, **V:**86
Knight, Gladys, **V:**92
Knight-Ridder, **VI:**100
Knights of Labor, **I:**71
Knoll, Max, **III:**87
Knopf, Alfred, **II:**91
Koch, Howard, **III:**97
Kohl, Helmut, **VI:**46, 48–49
Koppel, Ted, **VI:**100
Korea, **I:**42, 43; **IV:**18, 20–22, **VI:**22
Korean War, **IV:**21, 22, 23, 41, 43–44, 50
Kosygin, Aleksey, **V:**48
Koufax, Sandy, **V:**109
Kowalski, Robert E., **VI:**102
Kraft Television Theatre, **IV:**92, 93
Kramer vs. Kramer, **VI:**95
Krantz, Judith, **VI:**102
Kreisler, Fritz, **II:**88
Krenz, Egon, **VI:**45
Kreps, Juanita Morris, **V:**64
Kreuger, Ivar, **III:**38
Kristallnacht, **III:**41
Kristensen, Leonard, **I:**89
Kroc, Ray, **IV:**68
Krock, Arthur, **III:**20
Kubrick, Stanley, **V:**100; **VI:**95
Ku Klux Klan (KKK), **II:**32–33; **IV:**31; **V:**19
Kundera, Milan, **VI:**103
Kuwait, **VI:**21, 32, 52–53, 81. *See also* Gulf War

L.A. Law, **VI:**93
Labor-Management Act (1947). *See* Taft-Hartley Act
Labor movement, **I:**31, 45, 69, 71–73; **II:**19–20; **III:***73;* **IV:**17, 72–74; **V:**69–70; **VI:**77. *See also* Unions
  during Depression, **III:**14, 17, 70–73
  Red Scare and, **II:**30–31, 61
  union membership and, **I:***71*
  women and, **I:**18–19
  during World War I, **I:**33, 74
  during World War II, **III:**73
Labor Relations Act (1935), **IV:**72
Labor Stage, **III:**98
Labour party (British), **I:**39; **IV:**48; **V:**46, 47
Ladies' Home Journal, **I:**100, 101
Lady Be Good!, **II:**95
Lafayette Escadrille, **I:**88
La Follette, Robert, **I:**16
LA Gear, **VI:**66
Lake Erie, **V:**80
Laker Airways, **VI:**74
Land, Edwin, **IV:**84
Landers, Ann, **IV:**117
Landis, Judge Kenesaw Mountain, **II:**107; **III:**107, 110
Landon, Alfred M., **III:**23
Lane, Mark, **V:**96
Langley, Samuel, **I:**87, 88
Laos, **IV:**25, 48, 52–53; **V:**55; **VI:**21, 22
Lardner, Ring, **II:**105
Larkin Administrative Building, **I:**100

Larsen, Don, **IV:**110
Lasers, **IV:**83–84; **V:**86–87
Late Night with David Letterman, **VI:**94
Latin America, **I:**29, 31; **II:**56–57; **III:**37–38; **IV:**58–61; 72 **V:**42–43; **VI:**14, 22, 59–60, 72
Latvia, **II:**37; **III:**41; **IV:**38; **VI:**43
Laugh-In, **V:**100
Lauper, Cyndi, **VI:**92
Laurel, Stan, **II:**99
Laurel and Hardy, **III:**94
Laurents, Arthur, **IV:**99
Laver, Rod, **IV:**115
Law and Order League, **I:**102
Lawler, Dr. Richard, **IV:**87
Lawn tennis, **I:**108–109, 115
Lawrence, Florence, **I:**104
Lawrence Welk Show, The, **V:**98
Lazarus, Emma, **II:**32
League of Nations, **II:**11, 12–13, 37, 38–39, 55; **III:**39, 42, 43; **IV:**54
League of Women Voters, **II:**24; **V:**31
Leary, Timothy, **V:**33
Leave It to Beaver, **IV:**92
Leavitt, David, **VI:**103
Lebanese Front, **VI:**51
Lebanon, **III:**37; **IV:**55; **VI:**31, 39, 49, 51–52
Lebensraum, **III:**42
Le Carré, John, **V:**96; **VI:**103
Le Corbusier, **IV:**105
Lee, Spike, **VI:**96, 97
Legion of Decency, **III:**93
Leigh, Vivien, **III:**103
Leipzig, **VI:**44
Leisure, **I:**91–92, 115–117; **II:**69–70, 106–107; **III:**115–117; **IV:**116–117; **V:**117; **VI:**116–117
Lemieux, Mario, **V:**113
LeMond, Greg, **VI:**116
Lend-Lease, **III:**28
Lenin, Vladimir Ilyich, **I:**52; **II:**40, 41–43
Leningrad, **III:**48
Lennon, John, **V:**90; **VI:**98
Leno, Jay, **V:**99
Leopold II, king of Belgium, **I:**36, 38
Léopoldville, **V:**56
Lerner, Alan Jay, **IV:**99
Lesage, John, **V:**40
Les Miserables, **VI:**101
Letterman, David, **V:**99
Levitt, William, **IV:**64
Levitt and Sons, Inc., **IV:**64
Levittown, New York, **IV:**13, 64, 94
Lewis, John L., **III:**71, 73
Lewis, Sinclair, **II:**62, 92; **III:**99
Lexington, **III:**87
Libby, Willard, **IV:**86
Liberal-Democratic party (Japanese), **V:**53; **VI:**56
Liberal party
British, **I:**39
Canadian, **V:**40
Colombian, **VI:**59
Liberia, **I:**38
Liberty, **VI:**116
Liberty Bonds, **I:**33; **II:**64
Libraries, **I:**95
Libya, **V:**49; **VI:**30
Life expectancy, **I:**81
Life magazine, **II:**94; **IV:**94, 97, 99
Lifestyles of the Rich and Famous, **VI:**93
Light in August, **III:**103
"Light My Fire," **V:**92
"Like a Rolling Stone," **V:**91–92
"Like a Virgin," **VI:**98
Li'l Abner, **III:**91
Lin, Maya Yang, **VI:**99
Lincoln, **VI:**103
Lindbergh, Anne Morrow, **III:**12
Lindbergh, Colonel Charles A., Jr., **II:**78, 82, 101; **III:**12; **V:**27
Lindsay, Vachel, **II:**91
Lindsey, Harold, **III:**99
Linkletter, Art, **IV:**103
Liston, Sonny, **V:**106
Lithuania, **II:**37; **III:**41; **IV:**38; **VI:**43
Little Caesar, **III:**92
Little Entente, **III:**38
Little Foxes, The, **III:**98
Little Night Music, A, **V:**101
Little Orphan Annie, **III:**91–92
Little Rock, Arkansas, **IV:**30
"Live Aid," **VI:**99
Living Newspaper, The, **III:**99
Living standard, **I:**61; **II:**20, 65–66, *66;* **IV:**16, 65, 66, 77; **VI:**75
Soviet, **V:**48
Livingstone, David, **V:**97
Lloyd, Harold, **II:**98–99
Lloyd George, David, **II:**12, 36
Locke, Alain, **II:**90
Lodge, Henry Cabot, **II:**12–13, 32; **IV:**33
Loewe, Frederick, **IV:**99
Lombardi, Vince, **IV:**113; **V:**111, 113
London, **I:**79
London, Jack, **I:**97, 109
Lonely Crowd, The, **IV:**104
Lone Ranger, The, **IV:**92
Long, Huey, **III:**97
Long, Lutz, **III:**111
Long March, **IV:**43, 44
Look magazine, **IV:**94
Lopez, Vincent, **II:**102
Lorenzo, Frank, **VI:**68
Loring, Eugene, **III:**102
Los Angeles, **IV:**76
Lost generation, **II:**93
Lost Language of Cranes, The, **VI:**103
Louganis, Greg, **VI:**108
Lou Gehrig's disease, **III:**109
Louis, Joe, **III:**112, 115; **VI:**113
Love Canal, New York, **VI:**15, 80
Love Me Tender, **IV:**101
"Love Song of J. Alfred Prufrock, The," **I:**101
Love Story, **V:**96
Lowell, Percival, **III:**84
Lowndes County Freedom Organization, **V:**22
LSD, **V:**33; **VI:**34
Lucas, George, **VI:**94, 95
Luce, Henry R., **II:**95; **IV:**111
Lucky Strike cigarettes, **II:**66
Ludendorff, General Erich Friedrich Wilhelm, **I:**51
Luftwaffe, **III:**44, 47
Lugosi, Bela, **III:**92
Lumière brothers, **I:**103
Luna Park, **I:**92
Lupica, Mike, **VI:**112
Lusitania, **I:**31
Luxembourg, **IV:**40, 48; **VI:**47
Lvov, Georgy, prince of Russia, **I:**52
Lyme disease, **VI:**82
Lynch, David, **VI:**93
Lynchings, **I:**20; **II:**31–33
Lynn, Loretta, **V:**93
MacArthur, General Douglas, **III:**54, 58; **IV:**21, 22, 50
McAuliffe, Christa, **VI:**88, 89
McCarran Act (1950), **IV:**24
McCarthy, Eugene, **V:**17
McCarthy, Joseph, **IV:**23, 24–25, 26, 27, 94
McCarthyism, **IV:**27
McCartney, Paul, **V:**90
McClure, S. S., **I:**99
McClure's magazine, **I:**99, 101
McCollum, Elmer V., **I:**81
McCormack, John, **V:**11
McDaniel, Hattie, **III:**103–104
MacDonald, Jeanette, **III:**94
McDonald, Maurice, **IV:**68
McDonald, Richard, **IV:**68
McDonald's, **IV:**68
McDowall, Roddy, **III:**94
McEnroe, John, **VI:**114
McGovern, George, **V:**27
McGraw, John, **I:**111
Ma Chiang (Chinese game), **II:**107
Machine gun, **I:**53–54
McInerney, Jay, **VI:**103
Mack, Connie, **I:**111
McKay, Claude, **II:**91
McKinley, William, **I:**19, 27
"Mack the Knife," **IV:**99
McLuhan, Marshall, **V:**85
McMahon, Ed, **V:**99
McNair, Ronald, **VI:**89
McNamee, Graham, **II:**101
McNary-Haugen Bill, **II:**71
MacNeil-Lehrer News Hour, The, **VI:**100
McPherson, Aimee Semple, **II:**96, 97
Macy, Rowland H., **I:**62
Macy's department store, **I:**62
Madison Square Garden network, **VI:**106
Madonna, **VI:**92, 98
Madrid, **III:**38
Magazines, **I:**61, 97–98, 99, 101; **II:**93, 94, 95; **III:**115, 117; **IV:**66, 89, 94, 97, 111; **VI:**33, 100–101
Maginot Line, **III:**45
Mah-jongg, **II:**107
Mailer, Norman, **IV:**103; **V:**16, 96; **VI:**103
Mail-order businesses, **I:**61
Mail service, **II:**77
Maiman, Theodore H., **IV:**83; **V:**86
Main Street, **II:**92
Major, John, **VI:**48
Malamud, Bernard, **IV:**104; **V:**96
Malaria, **I:**79
Malawi, **V:**57
Malaya, **III:**36, 57; **IV:**52
Malaysia, **IV:**52; **VI:**56
Malcolm X, **IV:**33; **V:**21–22, 96–97
Malpractice insurance, **V:**68
Maltese Falcon, The, **III:**104
Management, **II:**63; **IV:**71, 74
Manchester, William, **V:**96
Manchuria, **I:**43; **III:**28, 43
Mandela, Nelson, **IV:**58; **VI:**55, 99
Man for All Seasons, A, **V:**101
Manhattan Project, **III:**79; **IV:**79
Mann Act, **I:**114
Man Nobody Knows, The, **II:**66
Man of La Mancha, **V:**102
Man o' War, **II:**109
Mantle, Mickey, **IV:**109, 110
Mao Ze-dong (Mao Tse-tung), **II:**54; **IV:**43, 44, 45; **V:**48, 50, 51–52; **VI:**57, 61
Mapplethorpe, Robert, **VI:**102
Marble Faun, The, **II:**93
Marchand, Captain J. B., **I:**38
"March of Time," **III:**96–97
March on Washington for Jobs and Freedom, **II:**61
Marciano, Rocky, **IV:**116; **V:**113; **VI:**114
Marconi, Guglielmo, **I:**78; **II:**79
Marconi Wireless Telegraph Company, **II:**79
Marcos, Ferdinand, **VI:**57, 61
Marcus Welby, M.D., **V:**100
Margaret, princess of England, **III:**92
Mariam, Mengistu Haile, **V:**56; **VI:**53
Mariner probes, **V:**79
Maris, Roger, **IV:**109; **VI:**113
Married with Children, **VI:**93
Mars, **V:**79
Marsh, Daniel, **IV:**94
Marsh, Reginald, **II:**103; **III:**105
Marshall, George C., **IV:**40, 43–44
Marshall, Thurgood, **IV:**29; **V:**21; **VI:**27
Marshall Plan, **IV:**20, 40, 46, 47, 49
Martin, Billy, **VI:**113
Martin, Dick, **V:**100
Martin, "Pepper," **III:**108
Marx, Karl, **I:**45; **II:**43, 44; **IV:**117
Marx Brothers, **I:**92; **III:**94
Maser, **IV:**83
*M*A*S*H* (movie), **V:**100
*M*A*S*H* (television show), **V:**98–99
Mass, **V:**94
Mass media, **IV:**66–67. *See also* Books; Magazines; Newspapers; Radio; Television
Mass production, **I:**69, 71
Masters, Edgar Lee, **I:**97
Masters, William, **V:**97
"Material Girl," **VI:**98
Mathewson, Christy, **III:**109
Matsushita Electric Industrial Company Limited, **VI:**94
Mattel, **IV:**117
Matthews, Victoria Earle, **I:**15
Mau Mau Society, **IV:**57
Maxwell, Elsa, **III:**116
Maxwell Company, **II:**68
Mayer, Louis B., **III:**93
May Fourth Movement, **II:**53–54
Mays, Willie, **IV:**15–16, 107; **V:**109
MCA, **VI:**94
Meany, George, **IV:**73
Meat-packing industry, **I:**14, 27, 66
Medical Care Act (1965), **V:**13, 14
Medical insurance, **II:**62; **IV:**66; **V:**13, 14, 40, 60; **VI:**28, 77, 84
Medical schools, **I:**81–82
Medicine, **I:**79, 81–83; **II:**81–83; **III:**84–86; **IV:**87–89; **V:**81–84; **VI:***82,* 82–84
Medium, The, **IV:**93
Medwick, "Ducky," **III:**108
Meech Lake Accord, **VI:**61
Meet Me in St. Louis, **III:**95
Meiji Restoration, **I:**42
Mein Kampf, **II:**49, **III:**42
Meir, Golda, **V:**38, **VI:**61
Melamine formaldehyde, **III:**80
Mellon, Andrew, **II:**14, 16, 73
Melting pot, **I:**23–24
Melting Pot, The, **I:**23
Mencken, H. L., **III:**92–93, 94, 105
Mendel, Johan Gregor, **I:**83, **IV:**86

Menotti, Gian Carlo, **IV**:93
Mercury (planet), **V**:79
Mercury spacecraft, **V**:75–76
Meredith, James, **IV**:30; **V**:21
Mergers, **I**:64–65, 75; **IV**:71; **VI**:65
Merman, Ethel, **III**:99, 101
Messenger magazine, **II**:61
Messerschmitt 262, **III**:87
Metalious, Grace, **IV**:103
Metro-Goldwyn-Mayer (MGM), **III**:92, 93
Metropolitan Opera House, **V**:94
Mexican-Americans, **II**:33
Mexico, **I**:53; **II**:32, 56, 57; **IV**:60–61; **V**:41–42, 43; **VI**:22, 40, 59, 60
Miami Vice, **VI**:92
Michael, George, **VI**:98
Michaels, Al, **VI**:107
Michener, James, **V**:96
Mickey Mouse, **II**:98
Mickey Mouse Club, The, **IV**:92, 116
Microprocessors, **VI**:85–86
Microsoft Corporation, **VI**:70, 85
Middle class, **IV**:58, 65, 66, 72, 74, 89, 104, 117; **VI**:23
Middle East, **II**:49–53, *50*; **V**:35–39; **VI**:49–53. *See also* Arab oil embargo
Midnight's Children, **VI**:103
Midway, Battle of, **III**:57–58, 88
Miës van der Rohe, Ludwig, **II**:103; **IV**:105
Migration, **II**:17–19; **IV**:65, 74, 21–22; **VI**:77
  to cities, **II**:29; **IV**:15–16
Mikan, George, **IV**:110
Military, **I**:28; **III**:28, 32, *43*; **V**:*11*, 54; **VI**:26, 46
  World War I and, **I**:32, 49, 50–51
Milken, Michael, **VI**:69
Millay, Edna St. Vincent, **II**:94
Miller, Arthur, **I**:105; **IV**:99
Miller, Glenn, **III**:100
Miller, Marvin, **VI**:109
Millett, Kate, **V**:97
Mills, Billy, **V**:115
Minimalism, **V**:103
Minimum Wage Law (1966), **V**:14
Minor-league baseball, **II**:110
Minow, Newton, **IV**:94
Miracles (music group), **V**:92
Miss America contest, **II**:106
Mission: Impossible, **V**:99
Miss Saigon, **VI**:101
Mitchell, John, **V**:26, 28
Mitchell, Margaret, **III**:103
Mitchell, William L. "Billy," **I**:88; **II**:77
Mitterrand, François, **VI**:48
Mix, Tom, **I**:105; **III**:91
M-19 movement, **VI**:59
Moawad, Rene, **VI**:52
Mobutu, Colonel Joseph, **V**:56
Mock, Jerrie, **V**:109
Model A Ford, **II**:69
Model Cities Act (1966), **V**:14
Model T Ford, **I**:68, 69, 70; **II**:65, 69, 75–76
Modernism, **II**:103
Molyneux, George Edward Stanhope (Lord Carnarvon), **II**:81
Mona Lisa, **I**:101
Monarchies, **I**:45, 47; **II**:52
Monday Night Football, **V**:112
Monk, Thelonious, **IV**:102; **VI**:100
Monroe, James, **I**:29
Monroe Doctrine, **I**:29; **IV**:58–60
Montague, Edwin, **II**:54
Montague-Chelmsford Reforms, **II**:54
Montana, Joe, **VI**:111–112
Montgomery, Alabama, **IV**:30–31
Montgomery, Lieutenant General Bernard, **III**:50, 51
Montgomery, Lucy, **I**:96
Montgomery Ward Company, **I**:61
Montini, Cardinal Giovanni Batista (Pope Paul VI), **V**:41
Montreal, **V**:40
Moody, Helen Wills, **III**:113, 115
Moon landing, **IV**:85–86; **V**:75, 78; **VI**:92
Moon probes, **V**:76
Mop and Pail Brigade, **I**:103
Moral Majority, **VI**:16
Moran, Bugs, **II**:27
More, Sir Thomas, **V**:101
Morenz, Howie, **III**:110
Morgan, J. P., **I**:65
Morgan, Thomas Hunt, **I**:83
Morita, Akio, **VI**:98
Morning Edition, **VI**:100
Morocco, **I**:38, 46, 47; **II**:56
Morrison, Jim, **V**:92
Morrison, Toni, **VI**:103
Morrow, Dwight, **II**:57
Morton, Jelly Roll, **II**:88
Moscow, **III**:48
Mothers Against Drunk Driving (MADD), **VI**:34
Motion Picture Patents Company, **I**:104
Motion Picture Rating System, **V**:100
Motorcycle, first, **I**:87
Motown Records, **IV**:102; **V**:92
Mount Everest, **IV**:114
Mount Saint Helens, **VI**:87
Movie Channel, **VI**:92
Movies, **I**:*91*, 103–105; **II**:98–100, 117; **III**:*91*, 92–95, 113; **IV**:67, *91*, 95, 96–98, 101; **V**:100–101; **VI**:94–96
Mozambique, **IV**:56; **VI**:54
Mrs. Miniver, **III**:95
Ms. magazine, **V**:31
Muckrakers, **I**:14–15, 97, 99
Muhammad, Elijah, **V**:21
Muir, John, **I**:109, 116
Mulroney, Brian, **VI**:61
Multinational corporations, **IV**:70; **V**:70
Muni, Paul, **III**:92
Munich, **V**:49
Munich Conference, **III**:97
Munsey's magazine, **I**:99, 101
Murderers' Row, **II**:109
Murphy, Eddie, **IV**:94
Murphy, Frank, **III**:22
Murrow, Edward R., **III**:27, 97; **IV**:27
Music, **I**:93–95, 101–103; **II**:87–89, 90, 95, 102; **III**:94, 95, 99, 100–102; **IV**:97, 98–102, 105; **V**:89–95; **VI**:92, 97–99
Musical hits, 1919–1929, **II**:89
Music Television (MTV), **VI**:92
Muslim League, **I**:40
Muslims, **IV**:51, 55; **V**:45; **VI**:103
  Black, **IV**:33; **V**:21, 107; **VI**:33
Mussolini, Benito, **II**:48; **III**:38, 39, 44, 51
Mutsuhito, emperor of Japan, **I**:42
Myanmar, **IV**:52
My Fair Lady, **IV**:99; **V**:100
"My Generation," **V**:91
My Three Sons, **V**:98

Nader, Ralph, **V**:66, 67
Nader's Raiders, **V**:67
Nagasaki, **III**:59, 80
Nagy, Imre, **IV**:42
Naked and the Dead, The, **IV**:103
Namath, "Broadway Joe," **V**:105, 111, 112
Nanook of the North, **II**:100
Nansen, Fridtjof, **I**:89
Nashville Network, **VI**:92
Nasser, Colonel Gamal Abdel, **IV**:55; **V**:35, 36, 37
National Academy of Sciences, **V**:79, **V**:87
National Aeronautics and Space Administration (NASA), **II**:84; **IV**:19, 85; **V**:78; **VI**:88–89
National AIDS Memorial Quilt, **VI**:83
National American Woman Suffrage Association (NAWSA), **I**:18; **II**:22, 23
National Association for the Advancement of Colored People (NAACP), **I**:21, 99; **III**:29, 32; **IV**:28, 29; **V**:21
National Baseball Hall of Fame, **III**:107, 109; **IV**:108
National Basketball Association (NBA), **IV**:110; **VI**:107, 110–111
National Basketball League (NBL), **IV**:110
National Broadcasting Company (NBC), **II**:81
National City Bank, **II**:64
National Collegiate Athletic Association (NCAA), **I**:112; **IV**:113, 114; **V**:112; **VI**:113
National Consumers' League, **I**:15–16
National Education Association, **V**:70
National Endowments for the Arts and the Humanities (1965), **V**:14, 102–103
National Environmental Policy Act (1969), **V**:68
National Football League (NFL), **II**:111; **IV**:112; **VI**:111
National Geographic magazine, **II**:94
National Guard, **II**:31; **IV**:30
National Health Insurance, **IV**:48
National Health Service, **V**:46
National Hockey League, **II**:113
National Industrial Recovery Act (1933), **III**:20, 64–65
Nationalism, **I**:42, 47, 48; **III**:35–38; **IV**:51, 55; **VI**:57
Nationalist Army, **IV**:43
Nationalist China, **I**:44
Nationalist Movement, **VI**:51
Nationalist party (Guomindang), **I**:44, 54
Nationalization, **IV**:47
National Labor Relations Act (1935), **III**:20, 22–23, 71
National Labor Relations Board, **I**:69; **III**:23, 71
National League, **IV**:109
National Organization for Women (NOW), **II**:24; **V**:30–31
National Origins Acts (1921, 1924), **II**:32
National parks, **I**:27, 116; **III**:24–25
National party, **VI**:55
National Prohibition Act (1920), **II**:26
National Public Radio, **VI**:100
National Recovery Administration (NRA), **III**:21, 64, 65
National Rifle Association (NRA), **VI**:16
National Security Act (1947), **IV**:25
National Security Council (NSC), **IV**:25, **VI**:31
National Socialist (Nazi) party, **II**:48; **III**:41; **IV**:38
National System of Interstate and Defense Highways, **IV**:75, *75*
National Traffic and Motor Vehicle Safety Act (1966), **V**:67
National War Labor Board, **I**:33, 74
National Woman's Party (NWP), **I**:18; **II**:22, 23; **V**:31
National Women's Political Caucus, **V**:31
Nation at Risk, A, **VI**:35
Nation of Islam, **V**:21
Native Americans, **IV**:15–16; **V**:18
  vote and, **II**:23
Native Son, **III**:104
Nativism, **I**:23
Natural Gas Pipeline Safety Act (1968), **V**:67
Nautilus, **IV**:81
Navratilova, Martina, **VI**:113, 114
Nazis. *See* National Socialist party
NBC, **IV**:93; **V**:98; **VI**:91
Negri, Pola, **II**:100
Negro baseball leagues, **II**:110; **III**:107, 108; **IV**:107
Negro World, **II**:18
Nehru, Jawaharlal, **IV**:51–52; **V**:54
Nelson, Byron, **III**:113
Nelson, Gaylord, **V**:81
Neoprene, **III**:81
Neptune, **VI**:89
Netherlands, **I**:37; **IV**:40, 48; **VI**:47, 81
Netherlands East Indies, **III**:36
Neutrality Acts (1935, 1936, 1937), **III**:27
Newcombe, John, **V**:113
New Deal, **III**:19–27, 64–70, 97; **IV**:16
  agencies of, **III**:20–22, 64–66, 70
  banking and, **III**:68–69
  economic innovations of, **III**:65–66
  farming and, **III**:66–68
  first, **III**:20–22, 64–65
  impact of, **III**:24–26, 64
  labor movement and, **III**:70–73
  second, **III**:22–23, 64
New Economic Mechanism, **V**:50
New Economic Policy (NEP), **II**:42–43
New Federalism, **V**:26
New Freedom program, **I**:30–31
New Frontier, **IV**:33, 34
New Kids on the Block, **VI**:97
Newlands Reclamation Act (1902), **I**:75
Newman, Paul, **IV**:93
New Mexico, **I**:25
New Negro, The, **II**:90
New Orleans, **II**:87
New Orleans Rhythm Kings, **II**:89
News broadcasting, **II**:101; **IV**:39, 94; **VI**:38, 91, 92, 99–101
Newspapers, **I**:61, 97–99, 117; **II**:92–93, 94; **IV**:94; **VI**:100
  black, **II**:18
Newton, Sir Isaac, **I**:83; **II**:83, 84
Newton-John, Olivia, **V**:92
New Wave music, **IV**:102

New York City, **I:**79–80, 93, 105; **II:**18; **IV:**105; **V:**32, 70; **VI:**12, 22, 24, 25, 29
New York City Ballet, **V:**95
New York *Daily News*, **II:**94
New Yorker magazine, **II:**94, **II:**95; **IV:**89
New York *Morning Journal*, **I:**99
New York Philharmonic Orchestra, **V:**94
New York Shakespeare Festival, **VI:**101
New York Stock Exchange, **V:**64
New York Sunday World, **I:**117
New York *World*, **I:**99
New York *World Journal Tribune*, **V:**97
New York Yacht Club, **VI:**116
New York Yankees, **IV:**109–110; **VI:**106, 108–109
New Zealand, **I:**39
Nicaragua, **I:**28, 57; **II:**55, 56–57; **III:**37; **VI:**31; **VI:**59–60
Nicholas II, czar of Russia, **I:**52; **II:**40
Nickelodeons, **I:**104
Nicklaus, Jack, **III:**110; **IV:**115; **V:**110; **VI:**115, 116
Nigeria, **VI:**81
Nightline, **VI:**100
Night of the Barricades, **V:**45–46
Nike, **VI:**66
Nimitz, Admiral Chester William, **III:**58
Nineteenth Amendment, **I:**18; **II:**23
Ninotchka, **II:**99
Nirenberg, Marshall W., **V:**86
Nixon, Richard M., **I:**19; **IV:**19, 25, 33, 41, 94; **V:**17–19, 24–29, 41, 50, 60, 62–63, 64–65, 68, 77, 96, 98; **VI:**11, 13, 18, 57, 61
  foreign policy of, **V:**26–27, 52
  Watergate scandal and, **V:**27–29
Nobel Prize winners, **I:**28, 36, 83, 84, 85; **II:**13, 82, 83, 92; **III:**37, 46, 78, 83; **IV:**33, 59–60, 81, 86, 87, 89; **V:**40, 44, 48, 81, 82, 86; **VI:**15, 44
No Man's Land, **V:**102
No Name in the Street, **V:**97
Noonan, Frederick J., **III:**86
Norge, **II:**79
Noriega, Manuel, **VI:**21, 60
Normandy invasion, **III:***53*, 53–55
Norris, Frank, **I:**97
Norris, Kathleen, **II:**93
North
  migration to, **I:**20, 22; **II:**17–19
North, Lieutenant Colonel Oliver, **VI:**31
North Africa, World War II in, **III:**49–50
North Atlantic Treaty Organization (NATO), **IV:**20, 40; **V:**45
Northeast Rail Service Act, **VI:**74
Northern Expedition, **II:**54
Northern Ireland, **V:**47; **VI:**49
Northern Securities Company, **I:**27
North Pole, **I:**89; **II:**78
Norton, Ken, **VI:**114
Norway, **III:**44–45; **IV:**40
Notes of a Native Son, **IV:**104
Nothing Down: How to Buy Real Estate with Little or No Money Down, **VI:**102
Notre Dame, **II:**110–111
Novello, Dr. Antonia, **VI:**26
Nuclear accidents, **VI:**15, 81
Nuclear arms control, **VI:**21, 29, 32, 39
Nuclear fission,**III:**77–80
Nuclear power, **V:**65, 66, 80; **VI:**13, 15
Nuclear weapons, **V:**54, 87
Nude Descending a Staircase, **I:**102
Nuremberg Laws, **III:**41
Nuremberg trials, **IV:**38
Nureyev, Rudolf, **V:**95
Nylon, **III:**80–81

O. Henry (William Sydney Porter), **I:**97
Oakland Athletics, **V:**108
Oakley, Annie, **II:**32, 100
Obote, Milton, **V:**57
O'Brien, Margaret, **III:**94
Occupational Safety and Health Administration (OSHA), **V:**25, 67
O'Connell, Helen, **III:**101
O'Connor, Sandra Day, **III:**32; **VI:**27
Octopus, The, **I:**97
Odd Couple, The, **V:**102
Odets, Clifford, **III:**98
Off-Broadway, **IV:**99
Office machines, **III:**83–84
Office of Civil Defense, **III:**31
Office of Price Administration (OPA), **III:**75
Official Languages Act (1969), **V:**41
Of Thee I Sing, **III:**99
Oil, **I:**64
Oil spills, **V:**80; **VI:**81
O'Keeffe, Georgia, **II:**103; **VI:**100
Okinawa, Battle of, **III:**59
Okker, Tom, **V:**113
Oklahoma, **I:**22
Oklahoma! **IV:**97, 98
Oldenburg, Claes, **V:**103
Oldfield, Barney, **I:**114
Olds, Ransom E., **I:**68
Oldsmobile, **I:**68
Oliver, Joe "King," **II:**87, 88–89
Olivier, Laurence, **III:**95
Olympics, **I:**109–110; **II:**112, 117; **III:**110–111, 114; **IV:**113; **V:**17, 49, 115–116; **VI:**14, 30, 106–108
Olympus, **I:**109
O'Meara, Baz, **IV:**108
Omnibus Housing Act (1965), **V:**14
Onassis, Jacqueline Kennedy, **II:**32
One Flew over the Cuckoo's Nest, **V:**100
O'Neill, Eugene, **I:**93; **II:**96; **III:**98
O'Neill, Thomas P. "Tip," Jr., **VI:**42
Onizuka, Ellison, **VI:**89
On the Origin of Species, **II:**85
On the Road, **IV:**104
On the Town, **V:**94
Op art, **V:**103
Open Door policy, **I:**14, 44
Operation Barbarossa, **III:**47–49
Operation Desert Storm, **VI:**53
Operation Overlord, **III:**53–55
Oppenheimer, J. Robert, **III:**78, 79; **IV:**80–81
Orange Bowl, **III:**109
Orange Free State, **I:**40, 41
Order of Literary Patriotic Harmonious Fists (Boxers), **I:**43
Ordinary People, **VI:**95
Oregon, **V:**66
Organization for Afro-American Unity, **IV:**33
Organization Man, The, **IV:**71, 104
Organization of American States (OAS), **IV:**59
Organization of Petroleum Exporting Countries (OPEC), **V:***39*, 61, 64, 65, 70; **VI:**63
Organized crime, **II:**26; **III:**16
Original Dixieland Jazz Band, **II:**89
Orlando, Vittorio, **II:**12
Ortega, Daniel, **VI:**31
Ory, Kid, **II:**88
Oscars, **II:**99–100
Oscar winners, **III:**94, 103–104; **IV:**98
Oshimi, General Kenichi, **II:**39
Oswald, Lee Harvey, **IV:**35
Other America, The, **IV:**16
Ottoman Empire, **I:**31, 45; **II:**39, 42, 52
  World War I and, **I:**47–48, 50, 51, 57; **II:**49–50, 51
Our Bodies, Ourselves, **V:**97
Our Palestine, **V:**36
Our Town, **III:**98
Outcault, Richard Felton, **I:**99
Overland Company, **II:**68
"Over There," **I:**94
Owens, Jesse, **I:**109; **III:**110, 111, **VI:**113
Ozone layer, **VI:**79

Pacific Rim nations, **VI:**72
Packard, Vance, **IV:**68, 104
Pact of Steel, **III:**44
Paige, Leroy "Satchel," **II:**110; **III:**108; **IV:**107; **VI:**113
Pakistan, **V:**53, 54–55, 55; **VI:**49
Palestine, **III:**36–37; **IV:**53, 54; **V:**35, 36; **VI:**49
  Jewish immigration to, **II:**51, 53
Palestine Liberation Organization (PLO), **V:**36, 49; **VI:**49, 51, 52
Palestine Problem, **II:**49–53
Paley, William, **II:**81
Palmer, A. Mitchell, **II:**31
Palmer, Arnold, **IV:**115; **V:**106, 110; **VI:**115
Palmer, Jim, **V:**108
Pan-African Conferences, **II:**56
Panama, **II:**56; **VI:**21
Panama Canal, **I:**28, 29, 36, 79; **VI:**14, 59
Pan American Airways, **III:**84
Pan-American Games, **IV:**112
Pan Am flight 103, **VI:**39
Panzer divisions, **III:**45
"Papa's Got a Brand New Bag," **V:**92
Papp, Joseph, **VI:**101
Paramount, **III:**92
Paris, **II:**52, 78, 93
Paris Peace Conference, **II:**11–12, 35, 36–37, 51–52; **IV:**53
Parker, Bonnie, **III:**16
Parker, Charlie "Bird," **IV:**102
Parker, Dorothy, **II:**16
Parker, Colonel Tom, **IV:**101
Parks, Rosa, **I:**19; **IV:**30–31
Parry, William Edward, **I:**89
Partial Test Ban Treaty (1963), **IV:**22
Particle accelerators, **VI:**86
Parting the Waters, **VI:**103
Parti Quebecois, **VI:**61
Patents, **III:**89
Patten, Gilbert, **I:**96
Patton, George S., **III:**51
Paul, Alice, **I:**18; **II:**22
Paul VI, pope, **V:**41
Paz, Octavio, **V:**40
Peace Corps, **IV:**34
Peace of Vereeniging, **I:**41
Peale, Norman Vincent, **IV:**103
Peanuts, **IV:**103
Pearl Harbor, Japanese attack on, **III:**27, 29, 30, 56
Pearson, Lester, **V:**40
Peary, Robert, **I:**89; **II:**78
Pegler, Westbrook, **II:**105
Peierls, Rudolf, **III:**78
Pelé, **IV:**114; **V:**115
Penicillin, **II:**82–83; **III:**85; **IV:**88
Penn Central railroad, **V:**62
Pentagon Papers, **V:**18
People, Yes, The, **III:**104
People Express, **VI:**74
People's Republic of China, **IV:**44, 45
Perestroika, **VI:**41
Perez, Moreno, **VI:**23
Pérez de Cuéllar, Javier, **VI:**39
Perkins, Frances, **III:**25
Perry, Commodore Matthew, **I:**41–42
Pershing, General John J., **I:**32, 53
Persia, **II:**52
Persian Gulf, **VI:**30, 49. *See also* Gulf War
Peru, **V:**53; **VI:**59
Pesticides, **IV:**89
Petit, Philippe, **V:**106
Petrograd soviet, **II:**40
Petroleum Building, **II:**19
Petroleum industry, **II:**63; **V:***35*, 42, 61, 64–65, 66; **VI:**13–14. *See also* Arab oil embargo
Peyton Place, **IV:**103
Phantom of the Opera, **VI:**101
Philadelphia Story, The, **III:**95
Philanthropy, **I:**65, 67, 95
Philbrick, Herbert, **IV:**103
Philco TV Playhouse, **IV:**92
Philippines, **I:**13; **III:**36, 54, 57, 58–59; **IV:**51; **V:**52; **VI:**56–57
Philippine Sea, Battle of the, **III:**58
Phnom Penh, **V:**55; **VI:**57
Phonofilm, **II:**100
Phonograph, **I:**94–95
Photoelectric effect, **I:**85
Photo-Secession, **I:**103
Physics, **I:**83–87; **II:**83–84
Piano industry, **II:**81
Picasso, Pablo, **V:**102
Pickford, Mary, **I:**33, 105; **II:**99–100
Pie in the sky (phrase), **I:**94
Piggly Wiggly, **II:**67
Pilgrim's Progress, **I:**14
Pilsudski, Joseph, **II:**46
Pinochet, General Augusto, **V:**43; **VI:**60
Pins and Needles, **III:**98
Pinter, Harold, **V:**102
Pioneer missions, **V:**79; **VI:**89
Pips (music group), **V:**92
Pittsburgh, **II:**33
Planck, Max, **I:**84; **II:**83
Plane Crazy, **II:**98
Planned Parenthood Federation of America, **I:**82
Plastics, **III:**80–81
Plastic surgery, **II:**82
Plate tectonics, **V:**87
Platoon, **VI:**95
Platt Amendment, **I:**39; **III:**37
Player piano, **I:**93–94
Playhouse 90, **IV:**92
Plaza Suite, **V:**102

Please Don't Eat the Daisies, **IV:**103
Pledge of Allegiance, **IV:**14
Plessy, Homer, **I:**19
Pluto, discovery of, **III:**84
Poetry, **II:**90, 91, 93–94; **III:**104
Poison gas, **I:**54–55
Poitier, Sidney, **IV:**15–16, 98; **V:**101
Poker Cabinet, **II:**14
Poland, **II:**32, 37, 42, 46; **III:**44–45, 55; **IV:**38, 39; **V:**44, 50; **VI:**30, 40, 44, 45
Polaroid Land Camera, **IV:**84
Polio, **II:**13; **IV:**87
Poliomyelitis, **III:**19, 85
Pollock, Jackson, **III:**105; **IV:**105
Pollution, **VI:**39, 40
Pollution Act (1924), **II:**16
Pollyanna, **I:**96
Pol Pot, **V:**55; **VI:**57
Poltergeist, **VI:**95
Polyethylene, **III:**80
Polyvinyl chloride, **III:**80
Pompidou, Georges, **V:**46
Pop art, **V:**103
Pop music, **V:**92–93; **VI:**97–98
Popular culture, **III:**91–92
Popular fiction, 1930–1945, **III:***104*
Popular literature, **I:**95–96
Population growth, **VI:***11*
Porgy and Bess, **III:**99
Porsche, Ferdinand, **III:**40
Porter, Cole, **III:**99, 101, 102; **V:**102
Porter, Edwin S., **I:**103, 104
Porter, Eleanor Hodgman, **I:**96
Porter, William Sydney (O. Henry), **I:**97
Portnoy's Complaint, **V:**96
Portugal, **IV:**40; **V:**46; **VI:**47
Post, Charles William, **I:**63
Potsdam Conference, **III:**48, 55; **IV:**20, 39
Pound, Ezra, **I:**101; **II:**93–94
Poverty, **I:**11
Powell, Adam Clayton, **IV:**28
Powell, Lewis F., Jr., **VI:**27
Powell, Michael, **V:**116
Power of Positive Thinking, The, **IV:**103
Powers, Francis Gary, **IV:**23–24
Pragmatism, **I:**86
Prague Spring, **V:**50
Prairie Style, **I:**100
Pravda, **II:**44
President, U.S., **III:**26–27
  power of, **VI:**11
  term of, **III:**19; **IV:**17
Presidential elections, **I:**29–30, *30,* 31; **II:**13–14, 16, 23, 57, 80; **III:**17–19, 23, 28, 33; **IV:**17–19, 33, 94; **V:**13, 17, 24–25, 27, 29, 63, 64; **VI:**12–13, 16, 17, 18, 19, 20–21, 23, 25, 31, 64, 100
Presidential succession, **III:**19
President's Commission on Education, **VI:**35
President's Commission on the Status of Women, **V:**30
Presley, Elvis, **III:**98, **IV:**100–101; **VI:**100
Prices, **I:***59,* 67; **II:**45–46, *59,* 60, 64, 65, 71; **III:***61;* **IV:**16–17, *63,* 67, 72, 77; **V:***59,* 59–60, 61, 62–63; **VI:***63,* 75
Pride of the Yankees, **III:**109
Prince, **VI:**98
Princip, Gavrilo, **I:**49
Prodigy, **VI:**72
Professional Football Hall of Fame, **IV:**113
Progressive party, **I:**30
Progressivism, **I:**14–17, 32, 67, 86; **II:**22, 25
  of Theodore Roosevelt, **I:**26, 29, 63
  of Wilson, **I:**29
Prohibition, **I:**17; **II:**24–29
  repeal of, **III:**21
Project Independence, **V:**65
Project Mercury, **IV:**85
Project Vanguard, **IV:**84
Promises, Promises, **V:**102
Prontosil, **III:**84–85
Propaganda, **I:**55
Proposition 13, **VI:**16
Provincetown (Massachusetts) Players, **I:**93
Psychoanalysis, **I:**83
Public assistance, during Depression, **III:***63*
Public Citizen, Inc., **V:**67
Public Enemy (film), **III:**92
Public Enemy (music group), **VI:**98
Public Works Administration (PWA), **III:**21, 64, 65–66
Puerto Ricans, **IV:**15–16, 74
Puerto Rico, **II:**32
Pulitzer, Joseph, **I:**99, 105
Pulitzer Prize winners, **II:**93, 96; **III:**97, 99, 103, 104; **V:**96, 97, 102; **VI:**103
Pullman Company, **II:**61
Pulsars, **V:**87
Pure Food and Drug Act (1906), **I:**27
Purges, **II:**44
Purple Rain, **VI:**92, 98
Putnam, George P., **III:**86
Pyle, Ernie, **III:**97
Pyle, Howard, **I:**99
Pynchon, Thomas, **V:**96

Quadricycle, **I:**69
Quantum mechanics, **II:**83–84
Quantum theory, **I:**84–85
Quayle, Dan, **IV:**23
Quebec, **V:**40–41; **VI:**61
Queen Christina, **II:**99
Queen for a Day, **IV:**92
Quinine, **III:**85–86
Quinlan, Karen Ann, **VI:**84

Rabbit, Run, **IV:**104
Rabbit Angstrom, **V:**96; **VI:**103
Rabbit at Rest, **VI:**103
Rabbit Is Rich, **VI:**103
Rabbit Redux, **V:**96
Race relations, **I:**19–22; **II:**17, *17;* **III:**22, 26, 38; **IV:**15–16, 28–33; **V:**14, 17; **VI:**22, 96. *See also* African-Americans
  apartheid and, **IV:**56–58
  civil rights movement and, **V:**17, 19–24, 26
  Japanese-Americans and, **III:**22, 32–33
  Ku Klux Klan and, **II:**31–33
  legislation and, **IV:**31–32
  in music, **III:**100–101, 102
  in Rhodesia, **V:**57
  riots and, **VI:**24
  in South Africa, **VI:**54–56, 76, 107
  in sports, **III:**107–108, 111
  sports and, **I:**113–114
  Supreme Court decisions and, **IV:**28–30, 31
  in Union of South Africa, **I:**41
  unions and, **III:**29
  World War I and, **I:**32, 74
  World War II and, **III:**32
Radar, **III:**45, 88, 89
Radiation Control for Health and Safety Act (1968), **V:**67
Radio, **I:**79; **II:**16, 79–81, *87,* 95, 97, 101–102; **III:**83, 92, 96–98, 100–102, 115; **IV:**39, 81, 94, 100; **VI:**38, 100
Radioactivity, **I:**83–84
Radio City Music Hall, **II:**103
Radio Corporation of America (RCA), **II:**79, 81; **III:**87; **IV:**92; **V:**86
Radio Free Europe, **IV:**39
Radioisotopes, **III:**86
Radio Liberty, **IV:**39
Radio Moscow, **IV:**39
Radium, **I:**84
Radium Institute, **I:**84
Ragtime, **I:**94, 117
Ragtime (novel), **V:**96
Raiders of the Lost Ark, **VI:**95
Railroads, **I:**59, 60–61, 62–64, 75, 77; **V:**62, 70, 72
  by 1900, **I:***63*
Rainey, Gertrude "Ma," **II:**89
Rainier III, prince of Monaco, **IV:**99
Rain Man, **VI:**96
Raisin in the Sun, A, **IV:**99
Rákosi, Mátyás, **IV:**42
RAND Corporation, **IV:**82
Randolph, Asa Philip, **II:**61; **III:**29
Ranger probes, **V:**76
Rankin, Jeannette, **I:**16
Rap music, **VI:**98
Rationing, **III:**31, 75, 81
Rattle and Hum, **VI:**98
Rauschenberg, Robert, **V:**103
Rayon, **I:**78
Reader's Digest, **II:**94, 95
Reagan, Ronald, **I:**19; **IV:**95; **VI:**15, 16, 26, 27, 29, 34, 48, 50–51, 60, 61, 67, 76, 77, 89
  economy and, **VI:**16–17, 19–20, 64–65, 74
  foreign policy of, **VI:**30–32
  Iran-Contra scandal and, **VI:**31–32
Real Folks, **II:**101
Realism, **I:**96–97, 101; **IV:**99
Rebates, railroads and, **I:**63
Rebecca of Sunnybrook Farm, **I:**96
Recession, **II:**59; **IV:**64; **V:**29, 60, 61–62, 70; **VI:**19, 21, 23, 25, 39, 63, 65, 66, 70, 71
  of 1937–1938, **III:**24, 64
Reconstruction Finance Corporation, **III:**12, 13
Recreation, **II:***105*
Recycling, **V:**66; **VI:**76
Red Army, **IV:**43, 44
Red Badge of Courage, The, **I:**101
Redbook magazine, **IV:**94
Red Brigades, **V:**49
Red Guards, **V:**51, 52
Red Russians, **II:**42
Red Scare, **II:**30–31, 61
Red Sea, **V:**35
Reebok International Ltd., **VI:**66
Reed, Stanley F., **III:**22
Reed, Dr. Walter, **I:**79
Rehnquist, William H., **VI:**27
Reiner, Carl, **IV:**92
Reinhardt, Ad, **III:**105
Relativity, theory of, **I:**85–86
Religion, **II:**85, 97; **IV:**55, 104; **V:**35, 41, 47; **VI:**16, 33, 49
Remington, Frederic, **I:**99
Republic, **III:**92
Republic of China, **IV:**43–44
Republic of Korea, **IV:**21
Resettlement Administration, **III:**68
Resnik, Judith, **VI:**89
"Respect," **V:**92
Return of the Jedi, **VI:**94
Reuther, Walter, **IV:**73
Revenue bill (1942), **III:**75
"Revolution," **V:**89
Reynolds, Malvina, **IV:**13
Reza Shah Pahlavi, **II:**52; **IV:**55; **VI:**50–51
Rhapsody in Blue, **II:**89
Rhee, Syngman, **IV:**21
Rhodesia, **V:**57
Rhythm and blues (R&B), **IV:**100–101
Rice, Grantland, **II:**105, 110, 111, 114
Rich, Matty, **VI:**97
Richards, Keith, **V:**91
Rickenbacker, Captain Eddie, **I:**88
Rickey, Branch, **IV:**108
Ride, Sally K., **IV:**23; **VI:**88
Riefenstahl, Leni, **III:**111
Riesman, David, **IV:**104
Riis, Jacob, **I:**14
Ringling Bros. and Barnum & Bailey Circus, **V:**106
Rio pact, **IV:**59
Risky Business, **VI:**96
Rite of Spring, The, **I:**101
Rivera, Geraldo, **VI:**93
Rivers, Joan, **V:**99
Rizzuto, Phil, **IV:**109
RKO, **III:**92
Roads, **I:**70; **II:**70, *70;* **IV:**74–77, *75,* 117; **VI:**75
Roaring Twenties, **II:**60
Robber Barons, **I:**12, 65, 67
Robbins, Harold, **V:**96
Robbins, Jerome, **IV:**99; **V:**101–102
Robert-Houdin, Jean Eugene, **I:**109
Robeson, Paul, **II:**90; **VI:**100
Robinson, Brooks, **V:**108
Robinson, Edward G., **III:**92
Robinson, Frank, **V:**108
Robinson, Jackie, **II:**110; **III:**108; **IV:**107, 108; **V:**113
Robinson, Smokey, **V:**92
Robinson, Sugar Ray, **VI:**113
"Rock Around the Clock," **IV:**97, 100
Rockefeller, John D., **I:**12, 63, 65
Rockefeller Center, **VI:**72
Rockets, **II:**79
Rock music, **IV:**99–102; **V:**89–92
Rockne, Knute, **II:**110–111; **III:**110
Rocky films, **VI:**95
Rodgers, Richard, **III:**99, 100; **IV:**98–99
Roebuck, Alvah C., **I:**61
Roentgen, Wilhelm, **I:**83
Roethke, Theodore, **III:**104
Roe v. Wade, **VI:**27
Rogers, Ginger, **III:**92, 94
Rogers, Roy, **VI:**16
Rogers, Will, **II:**16, 67, 95; **III:**13
Rolling Stones, **V:**89, 91, 92; **VI:**97
Romania, **III:**38, 55; **IV:**39; **V:**50; **VI:**40, 45
  World War I and, **I:**48, 50

Romantic novels, **I:**96
Romeo and Juliet, **V:**95
Rommel, Field Marshal Erwin "Desert Fox," **III:**49–50
Rooney, Mickey, **III:**94
Roosevelt, Eleanor, **II:**13; **III:**18–19, 25–26, 85, 102; **IV:**23
Roosevelt, Franklin Delano, **II:**13, 57, 61; **III:**17–31, 33, 37, 48, 51, 53, 55, 56, 64, 65, 66, 68–69, 73, 79, 85, 97, 115; **IV:**17, 18, 38, 39, 59, 79; **V:**13; **VI:**18
  affliction with polio, **II:**13
  elections and, **III:**19, 23, 28, 33
  fireside chats of, **III:**18, 20, 69
  foreign policy of, **III:**27–29
  leadership style of, **III:**18
  marriage of, **III:**18–19
  New Deal of. *See* New Deal
  opposition to, **III:**23–24
  presidency changed by, **III:**26–27
  Supreme Court and, **III:**22, 23
  World War II and, **III:**29–31
Roosevelt, Theodore, **I:**14, 18, 22, 25, 26–29, 30, 37, 63, 67, 75, 107, 111, 112, 113, 116, 117; **II:**32
  foreign policy of, **I:**27–29
  labor-management relations and, **I:**73
  Panama Canal and, **I:**28, 29
  reforms of, **I:**27
Roots, **VI:**92
Rose, Pete, **VI:**109–110
Rose Bowl, **II:**81; **III:**109
Rosenberg, Ethel, **IV:**26
Rosenberg, Julius, **IV:**26
Rosencrantz and Guildenstern Are Dead, **V:**102
Ross, Diana, **IV:**102; **V:**92
Ross, Harold, **II:**95
Ross, Nellie Tayloe, **II:**24
Rossellini, Roberto, **IV:**98
Ross Ice Shelf, **VI:**80
Roth, Philip, **IV:**104; **V:**96; **VI:**103
Rothko, Mark, **III:**105; **IV:**105
Rowan, Dan, **V:**100
Rowlatt Acts, **II:**54
Royal Air Force (RAF), **III:**45, 47
Royal Ballet (London), **V:**95
Rozelle, Alvin Ray "Pete," **IV:**113; **V:**105
Rubella vaccine, **V:**84
Rubin, Jerry, **V:**32
Ruby, Jack, **IV:**35
Runyon, Damon, **II:**105
Rushdie, Salman, **VI:**103
Rush to Judgment, **V:**96
Ruska, Ernst, **III:**87
Russell, Bill, **IV:**111; **V:**114
Russia, **I:**31, 35, 45. *See also* Soviet Union
  civil war in, **II:**41, 42
  economy of, **II:**45
  Jewish emigration from, **I:**45
  revolutions in, **I:**51, 52; **II:**40–42
  Russo-Japanese War and, **I:**28, 43, 45
  World War I and, **I:**48, 49, 50, 57; **II:**36, 40
Russian Republic, **VI:**43
Ruth, George Herman "Babe," **II:**105, 108–109, 110, 116; **III:**109, 115; **IV:**110; **V:**109–110
Rutherford, Ernest, **I:**84
Rutledge, Wiley B., Jr., **III:**22
Ryan, Nolan, **VI:**110

Sabin, Albert, **IV:**87
Sacco, Nicola, **II:**31
Sadat, Anwar, **V:**37–38; **VI:**14–15, 49–50
Safety Last, **II:**98
Saigon, **V:**19, 55; **VI:**57
Saint-Mihiel, Battle of, **I:**88
St. Elsewhere, **VI:**93
Sakharov, Andrey, **VI:**61
Salazar, Antonio, **V:**46
Salinger, J. D., **IV:**116
Salk, Jonas, **IV:**87
Sandburg, Carl, **I:**97; **III:**103, 104
Sandinistas, **VI:**31, 59–60
Sandino, General César Augusto, **II:**56–57
San Francisco, **V:**32, 72
San Francisco earthquake, **I:**15; **VI:**32
Sanger, Margaret Higgins, **I:**82
Sarajevo, **I:**49
Saratoga, **III:**87, 92
Sarazen, Gene, **II:**114; **III:**113
Sarnoff, David, **II:**79, 81
Saroyan, William, **III:**99
Sartre, Jean-Paul, **IV:**104
Satanic Verses, The, **VI:**103
Satellite dish, **VI:**99–100
Satellites, **V:**76, 79
Saturday Evening Post, **I:**101; **II:**94, 106; **V:**97
Saturday Night Fever, **VI:**96
Saturday Night Live, **VI:**94
Saudi Arabia, **II:**52; **III:**36; **V:**60–61; **VI:**52
Scalia, Antonin, **VI:**27
Scarface, **III:**92
Schirra, Walter M., Jr., **IV:**85
Schlafly, Phyllis, **V:**31
Schlesinger, Arthur, **V:**96
Schmeling, Max, **III:**112
Schmidt, Helmut, **V:**44
Schmidt, Mike, **VI:**110
Schneiderman, Rose, **I:**19
Schoenberg, Arnold, **I:**101–102
School and Society, The, **I:**86
School Daze, **VI:**96
Schools, **I:**86, 95. *See also* Education
  during Depression, **III:**14
  integration of, **III:**22; **IV:**29–30
Schulz, Charles M., **II:**100; **IV:**103
Schuster, Joe, **III:**92
Schwarzenegger, Arnold, **VI:**95
Schwerner, Michael, **V:**19
Science, **I:**83–87
Scientific American magazine, **VI:**101
Scobee, Dick, **VI:**89
Scopes, John, **II:**85
Scopes trial, **II:**84–85
Scott, Robert F., **I:**89
Scottsboro case, **III:**26
Screen Actors Guild, **IV:**95
Sealab II, **V:**87
Sears, Richard W., **I:**61
Sears, Roebuck and Company, **I:**61; **II:**67
Seascape, **V:**102
Securities and Exchange Commission (SEC), **III:**22, 69
Security Council, **IV:**21
Seeing Eye, Inc., The, **II:**73
Segal, Erich, **V:**96
Seize the Day, **IV:**104
Selassie, Haile, **V:**54, 56; **VI:**53
Selective Service Act (1917), **I:**32
Selective Service and Training Act (1940), **III:**28
Selling of the President, The, **V:**96
Selma, Alabama, **V:**20–21
Selznick, David, **IV:**96
Semiconductors, **IV:**81
Sennett, Mack, **I:**105
"September 1, 1939" (poem), **III:**104
Serbia, World War I and, **I:**48, 49
Sergeant Pepper's Lonely Hearts Club Band, **V:**90
Serial movies, **I:**105
Service industries, **IV:**65, 66, 74; **VI:**33, 66, 77
Servicemen's Readjustment Act (1944), **IV:**11–12, 17, 64, 65
Sesame Street, **V:**98
Settlement houses, **I:**15
Sevastopol, **III:**48, 55
Seventeenth Amendment, **I:**22
Severinsen, Doc, **V:**99
Sèvres, Treaty of, **II:**51
Sexual Politics, **V:**97
Shackleton, Ernest, **I:**89
Shame, **VI:**103
Shame of the Cities, The, **I:**14, **I:**99
Shangdong province, **II:**53–54
Shantytowns, **III:**14
Shapiro, Karl, **III:**104
Sharecroppers, **I:**20, 75; **II:**21; **IV:**77
Shaw, Artie, **III:**100, 101
Shaw, Bernard, **VI:**92
Shaw, George Bernard, **II:**105, 112; **V:**100
Sheik, The, **II:**100
Shelterbelt Project, **III:**15
Shepard, Alan B., Jr., **IV:**85; **V:**75
Sheppard, Morris, **II:**27
Sherlock Junior, **II:**99
Sherman Antitrust Act (1890), **I:**27, 66, 67, 73
Sherwood, Robert, **III:**98
She's Gotta Have It, **VI:**96, 97
Shining Path movement, **VI:**59
Shirer, William L., **III:**97
Shockley, William, **IV:**81
Show Boat, **II:**96
Showtime, **VI:**92
Shuffle Along, **II:**89
Sicily, **III:**51
Siegel, Jerry, **III:**92
Sierra Club, **I:**116
Sihanouk, Prince Norodom, **VI:**57
Sikorsky, Igor, **III:**84
Silent films, **II:**99
Silent Spring, **IV:**89; **V:**68
Silicon Valley, **VI:**71
Simmons, "Colonel" William J., **II:**32
Simon, Neil, **V:**102
Simon, Paul, **V:**92; **VI:**98
Simon and Schuster, **II:**106
Simpson, O. J., **V:**106, 111, 112
Simpson, Wallis, **III:**36
Sinatra, Frank, **III:**102; **IV:**96, 102
Sinclair, Upton, **I:**14, 27, 97
Singapore, **III:**57; **VI:**56
Singer, Isaac Bashevis, **V:**96
Single European Act (1986), **VI:**47
Singleton, John, **VI:**97
Sinn Fein, **II:**47
Sirhan, Sirhan, **V:**17
Sister Carrie, **I:**97
Six-Day War, **V:**35–37
Sixteenth Amendment, **I:**30
$64,000 Question, The, **IV:**93
Sklowdowska, Marie (Curie), **I:**84
Skylab space station, **V:**79
Skyscrapers, **I:**79, **II:**19
Slaney, Mary Decker, **VI:**108
Slang, **IV:**117
Slaughterhouse-Five, **V:**96
Slayton, Donald K., **IV:**85
Sloan, Alfred P., **II:**69
Sloan, John, **I:**103
Smiles of a Summer Night, **V:**101
Smith, Alfred K., **II:**16; **III:**17
Smith, Bessie, **II:**89
Smith, Kate, **III:**96
Smith, Margaret Chase, **IV:**26
Smith, Michael, **VI:**89
Smith, "Moe," **II:**28–29
Smith, Red, **V:**97
Smith, Roger, **VI:**73
Smith, Samantha, **VI:**30
Smith, Tommie, **V:**17, 116
Smith, Wendell, **IV:**108
Smoking, **V:**83; **VI:**83–84
Snead, "Slammin'" Sammy, **IV:**115
Snow White and the Seven Dwarfs, **III:**94
Soccer, **IV:**113–114; **V:**115
Social Democratic party (West German), **V:**44
Socialism, **II:**43; **IV:**47; **V:**46
Socialist Democratic Labor party (Russian), **II:**41, 44
Socialist party
  German, **I:**47
  Italian, **IV:**49
Socialists, **I:**45
Social Security, **IV:**18, 19; **V:**25; **VI:**28
Social Security Act (1935), **III:**20, 22
Social welfare programs, **VI:**17, 19–20, 24, 35, 65
Social welfare reforms, **I:**45, 47
Socoloff, Harry, **III:**63
Soil Conservation and Domestic Allotment Act (1936), **III:**68
Soil Conservation Service, **III:**15
Solar eclipse, **V:**56
Solidarity trade union, **VI:**30, 44, 45
Solvay Congress, **II:**83
Solzhenitsyn, Aleksandr, **V:**48
Somoza family, **VI:**31
Sonar, **III:**88
Sondheim, Stephen, **III:**98; **IV:**99; **V:**101
Sonny and Cher, **V:**92
Son of the Sheik, The, **II:**100
Sony Corporation, **V:**86; **VI:**94
Sony Walkman, **VI:**98, 116
Soul Experience, **V:**33
Souls of Black Folk, The, **I:**21, **II:**90
Sound and the Fury, The, **II:**93
Sound of Music, The, **IV:**99
"Sounds of Silence, The," **V:**92
Sousa, John Philip, **I:**94; **III:**98
Souter, David, **VI:**27
South
  migration from, **I:**20, 22; **II:**17–19; **IV:**15–16
South Africa, **IV:**56–58; **V:**57; **VI:**54–56, 76, 106, 107
Southeast Asia, **VI:**22, 72
Southern Christian Leadership Conference, **IV:**31
Southern Methodist University, **VI:**113
Southern Tenant Farmers' Union (STFU), **III:**69
South Korea, **VI:**56, 71, 72
South Pacific, **IV:**97, 98
South Pole, **I:**89; **II:**79

Soviet Union, **II**:40–44; **III**:55, 62; **IV**:23–24, 25–26, 38, 47, 49, 113; **V**:26–27, 37, 38, 44, 48–51, 56; **VI**:14, 21, 29, 32, 38, 49, 51, 57, 80, 88, 106–107. *See also* Arms race; Cold War; Gorbachev, Mikhail; Khrushchev, Nikita; Space race; Stalin, Joseph
arms control and, **VI**:21, 29, 32, 39
China and, **IV**:44
collapse of communism in, **VI**:40, 41–44
Cuba and, **IV**:61
economy of, **IV**:37–38
Spanish Civil War and, **III**:39
test ban treaty with, **IV**:22, 34, 80
as U.S. ally, **IV**:37–38
World War II and, **III**:40–41, 44, 47–49, 55
Soyuz 19, **V**:79
Space flight, **V**:*75*, 75–79; **VI**:88–89
Space race, **IV**:19, 23, *79*, 84–86
Spain, **IV**:40; **V**:46; **VI**:47, 49, 81
Spanish-American War, **I**:99
Spanish Civil War, **III**:38–39, 40
Sparrows, **II**:100
Speakeasies, **II**:27–28, 29, 89
Speaker, Tris, **I**:112
Speculation, in stock market, **II**:72–73
Sperry-Rand, **V**:84–85
Spiegel, **I**:61
Spielberg, Steven, **VI**:94, 95
Spillane, Mickey, **IV**:103
Spinks, Michael, **VI**:114, 115
Spirit of St. Louis, **II**:78
Spirit of the Border, The, **I**:96
Spitz, Mark, **V**:116
Spock, Dr. Benjamin, **IV**:14, 88; **V**:16
Spoon River Anthology, **I**:97
Sports, **I**:107–115; **II**:105–106, 107–117; **III**:*107*, 107–114; **IV**:107–116; **V**:105–116; **VI**:92, **VI**:105–116
African-Americans in, **II**:110, 112; **IV**:107–108, 110, 112
professional, **V**:*105*, 105–106; **VI**:106. *See also specific sports*
women and, **I**:108–109, 110; **II**:113, 114, 115, 117; **IV**:111, 112; **V**:106, 108, 109; **VI**:113, 116
SportsChannel, **VI**:106
Sports Illustrated magazine, **IV**:94, 111
Sports journalism, **II**:105–106
Sports shoe market, **VI**:66
Springsteen, Bruce, **VI**:98
Sputnik, **IV**:23, 84
Spy Who Came in from the Cold, The, **V**:96
Sri Lanka, **IV**:52; **VI**:39
Stabler, Ken, **V**:112
Stagflation, **V**:61; **VI**:13
Stalin, Joseph (Joseph Dzugashvili), **II**:43–44; **III**:31, 40–41, 44, 47, 48, 53, 55; **IV**:23, **IV**:38, 39, 41, 42; **V**:48; **VI**:43
Stalingrad, **III**:49
Stalin Revolution, **III**:40–41
Stallone, Sylvester, **VI**:95
Standard Oil Company, **I**:65, 67
Standard Oil of New Jersey, **II**:67
Stand Up and Cheer, **III**:92
Stanley, Sir Frederick Arthur, **I**:115
Stanley, Sir Henry Morton, **I**:38; **V**:97
Stanley, Robert Morris, **III**:87
Stanley Cup, **I**:115; **II**:113
Stanley-Elkins Act (1910), **I**:63
Stanton, Elizabeth Cady, **II**:22
Starr, Ellen, **I**:15
Starr, Ringo, **V**:90
Star Trek, **V**:99
START talks, **VI**:32
Star Wars (defense program), **VI**:30, 32
Star Wars (film), **VI**:94
Status Seekers, The, **IV**:104
Steamboat Willie, **II**:98
Steam engine, **I**:35
Steel, Danielle, **VI**:103
Steel industry, **II**:61; **III**:73; **V**:71; **VI**:15, 70–71
Steeplechase Park, **I**:92
Steffens, Lincoln, **I**:14, 99
Steichen, Edward, **I**:103
Steiger, Rod, **V**:101
Stein, Gertrude, **II**:93; **III**:104
Steinbeck, John, **I**:105; **III**:67, 104
Steinbrenner, George, **VI**:108–109
Steinem, Gloria, **III**:32; **V**:31
Stengel, Charles Dillon "Casey," **IV**:109, 110; **V**:113
Stevenson, Adlai E., **IV**:19, 94
Stewardesses, first, **III**:12
Stewart, Alexander T., **I**:62
Stewart, Jimmy, **III**:95
Stieglitz, Alfred, **I**:103; **II**:103
Sting, **VI**:98
Stock market, **II**:60, 63–64, *72*; **V**:62, 63; **VI**:20, 65, *68*, 69
crash of 1929, **II**:*72*, 73
Great Depression and, **II**:72–73
Stokowski, Leopold, **III**:102
Stone, Harlan Fiske, **III**:22
Stone, I. F., **V**:16
Stone, Oliver, **VI**:95
STOP ERA, **V**:31
Stop Flirting, **II**:95
Stoppard, Tom, **V**:102
Stores, **II**:67
Stout Air Lines, **II**:77
Strassman, Fritz, **III**:78
Strategic Defense Initiative, **VI**:30, 32
Stravinsky, Igor, **I**:101–102
Streep, Meryl, **VI**:95
Streetcar Named Desire, A, **IV**:99
Streptomycin, **III**:85
Strikes, **I**:39, 73; **II**:30, 60; **IV**:17, 72; **VI**:77, 109, 111
in Britain, **II**:46
Student Nonviolent Coordinating Committee (SNCC), **IV**:31; **V**:21, 22
Students Against Drunk Driving (SADD), **VI**:34
Students for a Democratic Society (SDS), **V**:16
Studio system, **III**:93; **IV**:96
Stultz, Wilmer, **III**:86
Styron, William, **V**:96
Submarines, **I**:31, 50–51, 57; **III**:49; **IV**:81
Suburbs, **I**:64; **II**:19, 70; **IV**:12–13, 15–16, 67, 75; **VI**:23
Subways, **I**:79–80
Sudan, **I**:38; **VI**:54
Sudden Unexplained Death Syndrome (SUDS), **VI**:21
Suez Canal, **I**:36; **II**:52; **IV**:55; **V**:35, 37, 38, 39; **VI**:49
Sugar Bowl, **III**:109
Suharto, General, **V**:55
Sukarno, **IV**:51; **V**:55
Sulfa drugs, **III**:84–85
Sulfanilamide, **III**:85
Sullivan, Ed, **IV**:92
Sullivan, John L., **I**:109, 113
Summit meetings, **IV**:23, 34, 42; **VI**:32
Sun Also Rises, The, **II**:93
Sun Belt, **VI**:23, 77
Sun Bowl, **III**:109
Sunday, Billy, **II**:97
Sunshine Boys, The, **V**:102
Sunshine Hour, The, **II**:97
Sun Yixian (Sun Yat-sen), **I**:44, 45; **II**:54; **IV**:42
Super Bowl, **IV**:113; **V**:*112*, 112; **VI**:92, 111
Superconductors, **VI**:87
Superman, **III**:92
Supermarkets, **II**:67
first, **III**:63
Supersonic transport (SST), **V**:47, 81
Supply-side economics, **VI**:17, 19, 64–65
Supreme commander of Allied powers (SCAP), **IV**:50
Supreme Court, U.S., **IV**:28–30, 31, 96; **V**:21, 26, 28, 71; **VI**:18, 26, 27
under Franklin Roosevelt, **III**:22, 23, 26
race relations and, **I**:19
Supremes, **V**:*89*, 92
Surgeon General's Report on Smoking and Health, **V**:83
Surgery, **IV**:83, 88; **V**:81–82
Surveyor spacecraft, **V**:76, **V**:86–87
Susann, Jacqueline, **V**:96
Sutton, William, **I**:83
Swados, Elizabeth, **V**:96
Swanson, Gloria, **II**:100
Sweden, **IV**:47
Swift, Gustavus, **I**:66
Swift and Company, **I**:66
Swimming, **II**:117
Swing Era, **III**:100
Swing Mikado, The, **III**:99
Switzer, Barry, **VI**:113
Sykes-Picot Agreement, **II**:50
Syria, **II**:53; **III**:37; **IV**:55; **V**:36, 38, 39, 60; **VI**:51, 52
Szilard, Leo, **III**:77, 79

Tabloid newspapers, **II**:94
Taft, Robert A., **IV**:17
Taft, William Howard, **I**:29, 30, 57, 67, 111; **III**:32
Taft-Hartley Act (1947), **IV**:17, 18, 72
Tai-Pan, **V**:96
Taiping Rebellion, **I**:43
Taiwan, **I**:44; **IV**:43–44; **VI**:56
Talkies, **II**:99
Talking Heads, **VI**:98
Tan, Amy, **VI**:103
Tanks, **I**:54
Tarbell, Ida, **I**:14, 63, 99
Tariffs, **I**:30, 35
Depression and, **III**:12, 61
Tarkanian, Jerry, **VI**:113
Tarpley, Roy, **VI**:112
Tarzan, **I**:97; **III**:91
Tarzan Escapes, **II**:117
Tarzan of the Apes, **I**:96
Tarzan the Ape Man, **II**:117
Tasaday people, **V**:52
Tax Reduction Act (1964), **V**:14
Taylor, Elizabeth, **III**:94
Taylor, Lawrence, **VI**:112
Taylor, Robert, **III**:95
Teamsters union, **IV**:73; **V**:69
Teapot Dome scandal, **II**:14–15
Technology, **I**:60–61, 77–80; **II**:63, 71; **IV**:65, 66, 72, 76, *79*, 81–84, 86, 100; **V**:50, 79–80, 84–85; **VI**:75, 85–86
Teddy bear, **I**:117
Teenagers, **III**:117; **IV**:97, 99–102, 116; **V**:90
Tektite, **V**:87
Telegraph, **I**:78–79
Telephone, **I**:78
Telephone, The, **IV**:93
Television, **IV**:20, 33, 66, 67–68, 81, 86, 91–95, 103, 109, 113, 116; **V**:97–100, 111, 112, *112*; **VI**:91–94, 99–100, 106
impact on culture, **IV**:94–95
movies and, **IV**:*91*, 96–97
Temperance movement, **II**:24–26
Temple, Shirley, **III**:92, 94
Temple Mount, **II**:53
Temptations, **V**:92
Ten Commandments, The, **II**:100; **IV**:97
Tender Is the Night, **III**:103
Tenements, **I**:13
Tennessee, **II**:84–85
Tennessee Valley Authority (TVA), **III**:21–22
Tennis, **I**:108–109, 115; **II**:113–114; **III**:113, 115; **IV**:112, 115; **V**:112–113; **VI**:113–114
Tenzing Norgay, **IV**:114
Terminal Tower, **II**:19
Terminator, **VI**:95
Terms of Endearment, **VI**:95
Terrorism, **V**:41, 47, 49; **VI**:39, 49, 51, 52
Test ban treaty, **IV**:22, 34, 80
Tet offensive, **V**:16–17
Texas, **I**:64
Texas Air Corporation, **VI**:68
Texas Instruments, **V**:84
Thailand, **VI**:56
Thalberg, Irving, **III**:93
Thatcher, Margaret, **VI**:40, 47–48
"That's All Right, Mama," **IV**:101
Theater, **I**:92–93; **III**:98–100; **IV**:98–99; **V**:101–102; **VI**:101
Their Finest Hour, **III**:47
Thief of Bagdad, The, **II**:100
Thin Man, The, **III**:104
Third World nations, **IV**:42, 70; **VI**:38, 39, 81
38th parallel, **IV**:20, 21, 22
thirtysomething, **VI**:93
This Side of Paradise, **II**:92
Thomas, Clarence, **IV**:23; **VI**:27, 92
Thomas, Lowell, **II**:101
Thomson, J. J., **I**:84
Thorpe, Jim, **I**:110; **II**:111; **IV**:110
Thoughts of Chairman Mao, The, **IV**:44
Thousand Days, A, **V**:96
Three Ages, The, **II**:99
Three Dog Night, **V**:92
Three Mile Island, **VI**:15, 81
Threepenny Opera, **IV**:99
Thriller, **VI**:98
Thurmond, Strom, **IV**:18, 32
Tiananmen Square, **VI**:58
Tilden, William Tatem "Big Bill," **II**:113–114, **IV**:110
Time magazine, **II**:94, 95; **IV**:32
Tin Pan Alley, **I**:93, **III**:102
Titanic, **I**:78; **II**:79; **VI**:85

Tito, Marshall, **VI:**61
To Have and to Hold, **I:**96
Tojo, General Hideki, **III:**56
Tokyo, **II:**53; **III:**57; **VI:**40
  bombing of, **III:**88
Tokyo Express, **III:**58
Tolan, Edward, **III:**110
Toland, John, **III:**30
Toledo, **I:**16–17
Tombaugh, Clyde W., **III:**84
Tommy, **V:**91
Tonight Show, The, **V:**99; **VI:**94
Tonka Toys, **IV:**116
Tony Award winners, **V:**102
Tork, Dave, **IV:**115
Torrey Canyon, **V:**80
Toscanini, Arturo, **III:**96, 102; **IV:**93, 94
Tour de France, **VI:**116
Tournament of Roses parade, **II:**96
Tower, John, **VI:**31
Tower committee, **VI:**31–32
Townshend, Pete, **V:**91
Toys, **I:**117; **IV:**116–117; **V:**117
Tracy, Spencer, **III:**94
Trade, international, **I:**35–36, 54; **II:**46, 56; **IV:**46, 58; **V:**41, 43–44, 50, 53, 62, 63, 70–71; **VI:**15, 38–39, 56, 59, 66, 72, 73, 74, 77
Trade deficit, **VI:**66, 72
Traffic accidents, **I:**70
Traffic and Motor Vehicle Safety Act (1966), **V:**14
Trailers, **III:**115
Tranquilizers, **IV:**88
Transjordan, **II:**53; **III:**36
Transportation, **I:**62–64, 67–71, *77,* **I:**117; **II:**67–70, 77–79. *See also* Aircraft; Automobile industry; Railroads
Transvaal, **I:**40, 41
Trans World Airlines (TWA), **VI:**67, 68
Treaty of Brest-Litovsk, **II:**42, 43
Treaty of Sèvres, **II:**51
Treaty of Versailles, **II:**37, 38, 45, 46, 48; **III:**41
Trench warfare, **I:**50
Triangle Shirtwaist Company fire, **I:**12
Tribune Tower, **II:**19
Triple, **VI:**102
Trivial Pursuit, **VI:**117
Trolleys, **I:**64, 117
Trotsky, Leon, **I:**52; **II:**40, 42, 43
Trudeau, Garry, **IV:**94; **V:**96
Trudeau, Pierre Elliott, **V:**40–41; **VI:**61
True Story magazine, **II:**94
Truffaut, François, **IV:**98
Truman, Harry S., **III:**33, 48, 55, 80; **IV:**16, 17, 18, 20, 26, 59, 66, 72, 80; **V:**14, 27
  Fair Deal of, **IV:**17, 18
  foreign policy of, **IV:**18, 20, 21, 39–40
Truman Doctrine, **IV:**20, 40
Trump, Donald, **IV:**23; **VI:**70
Trump Shuttle airline, **VI:**70
Trusts, **I:**65, 75, 104. *See also* Antitrust laws
Truth in Packaging Act (1966), **V:**14
Truth-in-Securities Act (1933), **III:**20, 69
Truth or Consequences, **IV:**92
T-shirts, **VI:**117
Tubman, Harriet, **I:**19
Tunisia, **VI:**51
Tunnel of Love, **VI:**98
Tunney, Gene, **II:**112–113
Tupper, Earl S., **III:**80
Turkey, **II:**51; **III:**37, 38; **IV:**20, 39, 40; **V:**53. *See* Ottoman Empire
Tuskegee Institute, **I:**21
Tutankhamen's tomb, **II:**81; **V:**50
TV Guide magazine, **IV:**94
Twain, Mark, **I:**105; **V:**97
Twentieth Amendment, **III:**19
20th Century-Fox, **III:**92
Twenty-fifth Amendment, **V:**26
Twenty-first Amendment, **III:**21
Twenty-fourth Amendment, **IV:**33
Twenty-One, **IV:**93–94
Twenty-second Amendment, **IV:**17
Twenty-sixth Amendment, **V:**32
26th of July Movement, **IV:**60
Twin Peaks, **VI:**93
'Twixt Twelve and Twenty, **IV:**103
2001: A Space Odyssey, **V:**100
Tyson, Mike, **V:**113; **VI:**114–115

U2, **VI:**98
U-boats, **III:**49. *See also* Submarines
Uesles, John, **IV:**115
Uganda, **V:**49, 56–57
Ukraine, **II:**42
Ulster, **I:**40
Ulysses, **II:**94
Uncertainty principle, **II:**83
Uncle Sam, **I:**97
Underwood-Simmons Tariff Act (1913), **I:**30
Unemployment, **II:**22; **III:***11,* 24; **IV:**11, 17, *37,* 64; **V:**46, 47, 59, 61, 62, 64, 70; **VI:**15, 19, 20, 63, 64, 65, 69
  during Depression, **III:**14, 17, *17,* 19, 62
  in Germany, **II:***35*
Union Cigar, **II:**73
Union of South Africa, **I:**41
Union of Soviet Socialist Republics (USSR). *See* Russia; Soviet Union
Unions. *See also* Labor movement
  New Deal and, **III:**20, 22–23, 25
  racial discrimination and, **III:**29
Unitas, Johnny, **IV:**112
United Auto Workers (UAW), **III:**72–73; **IV:**73
United Cloth Hat and Capmakers Union, **I:**19
United Farm Workers (UFW), **V:**69
United Federation of Teachers (UFT), **V:**70
United Mine Workers of America (UMWA), **III:**71
United Nations, **IV:**20, 21, 43–44, 52, 53, 56, 57; **V:**39; **VI:**41, 52
United Services Organization (USO), **III:**95
United States Football League (USFL), **VI:**111
U.S. Air Service, **I:**88
U.S. Army, **IV:**27, 33
U.S. Housing Act (1937), **III:**20
U.S. mail, **II:**77
U.S. Steel, **II:**62
U.S. Steel Corporation, **I:**65
U.S. Steel Hour, The, **IV:**92
United Universal Negro Improvement Association (UNIA), **II:**18
UNIVAC computer, **IV:**83
Universal, **III:**92, 93
Unsafe at Any Speed, **V:**67
Untouchables, The, **IV:**92
Updike, John, **IV:**104; **V:**96; **VI:**103
Uranium U-235, **III:**78, 79
Uranus, **VI:**89
Urbanization, **I:**12, 14, *20,* 45; **II:**19–20, *20,* 29, 67–68
Urey, Harold, **III:**77, 79
Uruguay, **VI:**60
USAir, **VI:**75
USA Today, **VI:**100
USSR. *See* Soviet Union
Utopian communities, **V:**33

Vacuum tube, **I:**79
Valentino, Rudolph, **II:**100, 106
Vallee, Rudy, **II:**102
Van Allen Radiation Belts, **IV:**85
Vanderbilt, Alfred G., **III:**116
Vanderbilt, Amy, **IV:**117
Vanderbilt, Cornelius, **I:**12
Van Gogh, Vincent, **VI:**102
Van Peebles, Mario, **VI:**97
Vanzetti, Bartolomeo, **II:**31
Vargas Llosa, Mario, **VI:**103
Vaudeville, **I:**92–93, 103
V-1 buzz bombs, **III:**54, 55, 87, 89
Venezuela, **V:**43; **VI:**59
Venus (planet), **V:**79
Verdi, Giuseppe, **I:**105
Vereeniging, Peace of, **I:**41
Verrazano-Narrows Bridge, **V:**77
Versailles, Treaty of, **II:**37, 45, 46, 48; **III:**41
Veterans, **IV:**11–12, 17, 71; **V:**18; **VI:**28–29
VH-1, **VI:**92
Vice president, U.S., term of, **III:**19; **IV:**17
Victor Emmanuel III, king of Italy, **II:**48; **III:**51
Victoria, queen of England, **I:**39
Victorian Era, **I:**39
Victory gardens, **I:**33
Victory in Europe (VE) day, **III:**55
Victory in Japan (VJ) day, **III:**59
Vidal, Gore, **VI:**103
Videocassette recorders (VCRs), **VI:***91,* 94
"Video Killed the Radio Star," **VI:**92
Viet Cong, **IV:**53; **V:**14, 15, 16
Viet Minh, **III:**36; **IV:**53; **V:**55
Vietnam, **IV:**22, 25, 48, 52–53; **V:**55; **VI:**22, 57
Vietnam Veterans Against the War, **V:**18
Vietnam Veterans Memorial, **VI:**28, 99
Vietnam War, **V:***11,* 13–19, *15,* 25, 41, 60, 98; **VI:**11, 14, 57, 63
  antiwar movement and, **V:**16, 18, 96, 107
Viking Penguin, **VI:**103
Viking probes, **VI:**89
Villa, Francisco "Pancho," **I:**53
Vimy Ridge, Battle of, **I:**50
Vinci, Leonardo da, **I:**101
Virginian, The, **I:**96
Virgin Islands, **I:**49
Visa card, **V:**59
Vitamins, **I:**81; **IV:**89
  discovery of, **III:**84
Vogue magazine, **II:**94
Voice of America, **IV:**39
Volcanic events, **VI:**87
Volkswagen, **VI:**72
Volkswagen Beetle, **III:**40; **IV:**69
Volstead Act (1920), **II:**26
von Braun, Werner, **III:**89
Vonnegut, Kurt, Jr., **V:**96
von Neumann, John, **IV:**82
von Ohain, Hans, **III:**87
Voodoo Macbeth, **III:**99
Vostok 1, **IV:**85
Vote, **IV:**33; **V:**20, 21, 32. *See also* Elections
  African-Americans and, **I:**20, 22; **II:**22; **IV:**30, 32; **V:**13, 14, 20–21, 26
  Native Americans and, **II:**23
  women and, **I:**17–18, 19; **II:**22–24
Voting Rights Act (1965), **V:**13, 14, 21, 26
Voyager probes, **VI:**89
V-2 rocket bombs, **III:**54, 55, 89

Wage and price controls, **V:**62–63
Wages, **I:**12–13, 20, 62, 67, 69, 71; **II:**17, 22, 60, 64, 76, 110; **IV:**15, 18, 19, 73, 74; **V:**14, *23,* 30, 60, 61, 70, 92, 105, 106; **VI:**26, 33, 77, *105,* 106, 109
  during Depression, **III:**63, 68
  minimum, **III:**24; **IV:**18, 19
  during World War II, **III:**75
Wagner, Honus, **I:**111, 112; **III:**109
Wagner Act (1935), **III:**20, 22–23
Waikiki Beach, **VI:**72
Wailing Wall, **II:**53
Waiting for Godot, **IV:**99
Walesa, Lech, **VI:**44
Walker, Alice, **III:**98; **VI:**103
Walker, Herschel, **VI:**111
Wallace, DeWitt, **II:**95
Wallace, George, **IV:**30; **V:**20; **VI:**18
Wallace, Henry Agard, **III:**65
Wallace, Lila, **II:**95
Wallis, Barnes, **III:**88
Wall Street, **VI:**69
Walt Disney, **III:**92
Walt Disney Productions, **II:**98
Wanamaker, John, **I:**62
War Bonds, **III:**31, 75
War Communism, **II:**42–43
War crimes, **IV:**38
Ward, Aaron Montgomery, **I:**61
Warhol, Andy, **VI:**100
War Industries Board (WIB), **I:**33, 74; **II:**59–60
Warner, Malcolm-Jamal, **V:**102
Warner Brothers, **III:**92, 93
War on Drugs, **VI:**34
War on Poverty, **V:**13, 14, 60
Warren, Earl, **IV:**29, 35; **V:**27; **VI:**27
Warren Commission, **IV:**35
War reparations, **II:**12, 36, 37, 45, 48; **IV:**38
Warsaw Pact, **IV:**40; **V:**50, 51
War That Will End War, The, **I:**53
Washington, Booker T., **I:**19, 21, 22
Washington, D.C., **II:**18; **VI:**23, 25
Washington Conference, **II:**39–40
Washkansky, Louis, **V:**82
Waste disposal, **VI:**80, 81
Waste Land, The, **II:**94
Waste Makers, The, **IV:**68
Watergate scandal, **V:**27–29, 63; **VI:**113
Water Quality Act (1965), **V:**14
Watson, James D., **IV:**86, 87; **V:**86
Watson, Tom, **VI:**116
Watson-Watt, Sir Robert, **III:**88
Watt, James, **I:**35

Watts riot, **V:**17, 22–23
Wayne, John, **VI:**100
WEAF, **II:**80
Weapons, during World War II, **III:**86–89
Weapons, in World War I, **I:**53–55
Weary Blues, The, **II:**91
Weaver, Robert Clifton, **V:**13
Webber, Andrew Lloyd, **VI:**101
Weeks, Sinclair, **IV:**64
"We Hold These Truths," **III:**97
Weill, Kurt, **IV:**99
Weimar Republic, **II:**48
Weiss, Ehrich (Harry Houdini), **I:**109; **II:**100
Weissmuller, Johnny, **I:**109; **II:**117; **III:**91, 110; **VI:**113
Weizmann, Dr. Chaim, **II:**50–51, 52
Welch, Joseph, **IV:**27
Welfare state, **III:**24; **IV:**47–48; **VI:**16
Welles, Orson, **III:**94, 95, 97, 99; **VI:**100
Wells, H. G., **I:**53
West, Mae, **III:**92, 117
Westinghouse, George, **I:**60, 77, 78
Westinghouse Electric Company, **I:**60; **II:**79
Westmoreland, General William, **V:**16–17
West Point, **V:**31; **VI:**26
West Side Story, **IV:**99, 105; **V:**94, 101, 102
Wharton, Edith, **II:**93
What's My Line? **IV:**92
Wheat prices, **III:***68*
Wheeler, Harvey, **IV:**103
White, Edward, II, **V:**76, 77
White, G. H., **II:**31–33
White, George, **III:**99
"White Christmas," **III:**95
"White City, The," **II:**91
White-collar workers, **II:**19–20, 60; **IV:***15, 74;* **V:**70; **VI:**19
Whiteman, Paul, **II:**102
"White Man's Burden, The," **I:**37
White Rose Industrial Association, **I:**15
White Russians, **II:**42
White Terror, **IV:**43
Whitney, Casper W., **II:**111
Whittle, Frank, **III:**87
Who, The, **V:**89, 91, 93
Wholesome Meat Act (1967), **V:**67
Who's Afraid of Virginia Woolf? **IV:**99; **V:**102
Why Are We in Vietnam? **V:**96
Why Not Use the 'L'? **III:**105
Whyte, William H., **IV:**71, 104
Wiggin, Kate Douglas, **I:**96
Wild Bunch, The, **V:**100
Wilder, Douglas, **VI:**25
Wilder, Thornton, **III:**98
Wilderness Preservation Act (1965), **V:**14
Wilkes, Charles, **I:**89
Wilkins, Maurice, **IV:**87
Willard, Jess, **I:**114; **II:**112
William I, king of Prussia and emperor of Germany, **I:**46
William II, king of Prussia and emperor of Germany, **I:**38, 46–47
Williams, Ted, **III:**108, 109, 115
Williams, Tennessee, **III:**100; **IV:**99; **VI:**100
Willkie, Wendell, **III:**28
Wills, Helen, **II:**113, 114
Wilson, Charles, **IV:**68, 70
Wilson, Harold, **V:**47
Wilson, Samuel, **I:**97
Wilson, Woodrow, **I:**18, 22, 24, 29, 30–31, 33, 50, 53, 67, 74, 111; **II:**23, 32
  economy and, **II:**59
  foreign policy of, **I:**31
  Fourteen Points of, **II:**35–36
  New Freedom program of, **I:**30–31
  Paris Peace Conference and, **II:**11–12, 35, 36
  Treaty of Versailles and, **II:**37, 38
  World War I and, **I:**31, 33
WIN: Whip Inflation Now, **V:**29, 64
Windsor, Edward David (Edward VIII), **III:**36
Winfrey, Oprah, **VI:**93
Wings, **II:**99–100
Winter Light, **V:**101
Winterset, **III:**98
Wister, Owen, **I:**96
Witt, Katarina, **VI:**108
Wobblies, **I:**73
Wohlstetter, Roberta, **III:**30
Wojtyla, Karol (Pope John Paul II), **VI:**46
Wolfe, Tom, **V:**90, **VI:**33
Wolverines, **II:**89
Woman Rebel, **I:**82
Woman's Day magazine, **IV:**66; **VI:**101
Women, **II:**29; **V:**31, 97; **VI:**18, 26, 27
  automobiles and, **I:**70–71
  during Depression, **III:**25–26, 70
  education of, **I:**19, *19*
  employment of, **I:**18–19; **II:**22–23, 62; **III:**25, 32, 70, 74; **IV:**14–15, 65; **V:**30, 31, 70; **VI:**24, 26, 28, 75
  labor movement and, **I:**18–19
  leisure and, **I:**116
  in military, **VI:**26
  in politics, **I:**16; **II:**24; **V:**30, 31; **VI:**18
  as reformers, **I:**15–16
  roles of, **I:**18–19
  in sports, **II:**113, 114, 115, 117; **IV:**111, 112; **V:**106, 108, 109; **VI:**113, 116
  sports and, **I:**108–109, 110
  suffrage and, **I:**17–18, 19; **II:**22–24
  World War I and, **I:**74; **II:**22–23
  during World War II, **III:**32, 74
Women's Army Corps (WACs), **III:**32
Women's Campaign Fund, **V:**31
Women's Christian Temperance Union, **II:**25
Women's movement, **II:**22–24; **V:**30–31
Wonder, Stevie, **IV:**102; **V:**92
Wonder Years, **VI:**93
Wood, Grant, **II:**102; **III:**105
Woodbury's Facial Soap, **II:**66
Wooden, John, **V:**114
Woodstock Music and Art Fair, **V:**33, 93
Woodward, Bob, **V:**28
Woodward, Ellen Sullivan, **III:**70
Woolworth, **II:**67
Woolworth, Frank Winfield, **I:**61
Woolworth Building, **I:**79
Work. *See* Employment
Works Progress Administration (WPA), **III:**21, 64, 66, 98, 99, 100–102, 105
Workweek, **I:**12; **II:**76; **III:**14, 24
World, The, **I:**99
World Court, **II:**38
World Health Organization (WHO), **IV:**53; **VI:**82
World League of American Football (WLAF), **VI:**111
World Series, **I:**111; **II:**107, 109; **III:**108, 109, 115; **IV:**109, 110; **V:**108; **VI:**92, 108, 109
World's Fairs, **I:**109; **III:**115, 116–117; **V:**40, 103
World War I, **I:**49–57
  Africa and, **II:**55
  aircraft in, **I:**55, 57, 88
  casualties in, **I:***35,* 57
  economy and, **II:**59, 64
  employment and, **I:**18, 74
  end of, **I:**33, 51
  Europe after, **I:***56,* 57; **II:**44–49
  Europe before, **I:***56*
  events leading to, **I:**31, 43, 45–49
  farming and, **I:**74–75
  important dates of, **I:***51*
  Middle East and, **II:**49–53, *50*
  Paris Peace Conference and, **II:**11–12, 35, 36–37, 51–52
  propaganda and, **I:**55
  Russian revolutions and, **I:**51, 52
  at sea, **I:**50–51, 57
  start of, **I:**49–50
  technology and, **I:**79
  Treaty of Versailles and, **II:**37, 45, 46, 48
  trench warfare in, **I:**50
  U.S. involvement in, **I:**32–33, 51
  weapons of, **I:**53–55
  women and, **II:**22–23
  women and minorities and, **I:**74
World War II, **III:**59, 115; **IV:**28, 37
  casualties in, **III:***35*
  concentration camps and, **III:**50–51, 52
  economy during, **III:**73–75
  entertainment during, **III:**95, 99–100
  in Europe, **III:**43–45, 47, 51, *51,* 53–55
  events leading to, **III:**38–43
  home front and, **III:**31
  military strength in, **III:***43*
  in North Africa, **III:**49–50
  in Pacific, **III:**56–59, *57*
  radio reporting of, **III:**97
  in Soviet Union, **III:**47–49
  U.S. entry into, **III:**27–28, 29–31
  weapons during, **III:**86–89
  women during, **III:**32, 74
  Yalta Conference and, **III:**55
World Zionist Congress, **II:**50
Worthy, James, **VI:**113
Wouk, Herman, **IV:**103
Wounded Knee, South Dakota, **V:**18
Wright, Frank Lloyd, **I:**100; **II:**103; **III:**105
Wright, Orville, **I:**87–88
Wright, Richard, **III:**104, 112
Wright, Wilbur, **I:**87–88
Wynne, Arthur, **I:**117

X-ray, **I:**83–84

Yachting, **VI:**116
Yalta Conference, **III:**48, 55; **IV:**20, 38, 39
Yamamoto, Admiral Isoroku, **III:**56
Yankee Doodle Dandy, **III:**95
Yeager, Charles, **IV:**86
Yellow Cab Company, **II:**70
Yellow Drive-It-Yourself System, Inc., **II:**70
Yellow fever, **I:**79
Yellow journalism, **I:**99
Yellow Kid, The, **I:**98
Yeltsin, Boris, **VI:**43, 44
Yemen, **III:**36
Yom Kippur War, **V:**38, 60, 64
Young, Cy, **I:**112; **IV:**110
Young, John, **V:**76
Young Turks, **I:**48
You Only Live Twice, **V:**96
Your Show of Shows, **IV:**92
Ypres, Battle of, **I:**54
Ypres, Second Battle of, **I:**50
Yuan Shih-k'ai, **I:**45
Yugoslavia, **II:**37; **III:**38; **VI:**39, 45
Yuppies, **VI:**19, 23, 33, 34

Zaharias, George, **III:**114
Zaharias, Mildred "Babe" Didrikson, **III:**110, 114, 115; **IV:**110
Zaire, **I:**36; **V:**56
Zambia, **V:**57
Zangwill, Israel, **I:**23
Zen Buddhism, **VI:**33
Zeppelin, Graf Ferdinand von, **I:**55
Zeppelins, **I:**55, 57; **III:**83–84
Zhivkov, Todor, **VI:**45
Zia al-Haq, General Mohammed, **VI:**49
Ziegfeld, Florenz, **I:**93; **III:**98, 99
Ziegfeld *Follies,* **I:**93; **II:**95–96; **III:**99
Zimbabwe, **V:**57
Zimmermann telegram, **I:**31–32
Zionism, **II:**50; **II:**52; **IV:**53, 54
Zola, Emile, **I:**46
Zuckerman Unbound, **VI:**103